# THE INDIA COOKBOOK

# *The* INDIA COOKBOOK

### FROM THE TABLES OF MY FRIENDS

*Selected and edited by*

# SUNITA KOHLI

**ALEPH**

**ALEPH**

ALEPH BOOK COMPANY
An independent publishing firm
promoted by **Rupa Publications India**

First published in India in 2023
by Aleph Book Company
7/16 Ansari Road, Daryaganj
New Delhi 110 002

ISBN: 978-93-90652-44-0

1 3 5 7 9 10 8 6 4 2

Printed in India.

To Rome, with Love
The Long-distance Runner


&
Mama & Doc
Loving and True

# Contents

## SOUTH

## EAST

# Introduction

Cuisine is an integral part of our intangible cultural heritage. This book is a personal culinary journey that celebrates the friendships and goodwill of well-wishers across India. Compiled here is a repository of recipes that are associated with warm memories. Many recipes from the homes of these friends and family members have been handed down through the generations, but they invite further culinary inventiveness. Such is the magic of cuisine. *The India Cookbook* is not a panoramic overview of food in the Indian subcontinent; rather, it is about the pluralism of Indian food and the variety in home-style cooking. It is about artisanal food, cooked and served in the homes of one's many friends throughout the length and breadth of India. I am fortunate in my friends!

India is a vast country, a subcontinent that is one-third the size of Europe with perhaps a greater diversity of people. In this nation of multiple ethnicities and multiple perspectives on food, the range of cuisine is also extraordinarily extensive. Today UNESCO recognizes culinary traditions from around the world as an important part of food cultures—like Mexican cuisine, the Armenian lavash, Singaporean street food, Georgian Qvevri wines, Japan's Washoku and North African couscous. By UNESCO'S definition, many varieties of regional cuisine that are cooked and served throughout India would meet all its criteria for inclusion.

Good designers and architects have the gift of an inner eye which helps them visualize projects to the last detail. Similarly, good cooks also have a visual sense of food in their head and can almost intuit the possibilities of culinary creativity. My mother was an excellent cook as was her mother. This is an inherited trait. Whilst reading a recipe and as each ingredient is added, one can imagine its changing colour and zaika, particularly with north Indian food. I love the zaika of other people's home-cooked food. Eating is always an adventure and I am very partial to cuisine from different parts of the world. I am one of those travellers who does not miss Indian food whilst out of the country. Occasionally I may think of gol guppas and miss eating a paan after dinner.

Nita Khanna, a good friend who has also contributed to this book and is in the midst of writing her own book, has opined that 'Food in India is a religion, an identity, a cultural and social signifier beyond the pale of our quest for unity in diversity.... The often-used phrase, 'fasting and feasting' routinely surfaces as a popular ordering principle for a vast and seemingly disparate panoply of taste preferences and food choices. Most communal fasts, of all major religions in India, are followed by a festive feast. Dietary taboos have defined different religions and food has played an important part in it.

Hindus celebrate myriad festivals throughout the year for which various and particular savouries and sweetmeats are prepared. Similarly, Muslim homes and kitchens have, over the centuries, perfected an aromatic variety of dishes which break the rigorous sunrise to sunset fast during the holy month of Ramzan.

Food is an important part of culture and sharing. Food and recipes are about personal histories and collective memories. They are a part of social history. This cookbook is an account of how culture most intimately expresses itself—there are dishes for all occasions and for all seasons. There are recipes that can be used for dinner parties with friends as well as recipes for relaxed family meals.

~

From an early age, our parents had taken us around India and exposed us to many different places and their different cuisines and architectural wonders. I remember a visit to Srinagar where a colleague of my father's had invited us home for a wazwan—a traditional Kashmiri meal comprising of several courses. It was a magnificent and impressive repast of great epicurean heights. The satisfaction after a great meal is almost sensual.

Similarly, wonderful meals were had with my parents' friends in Madras, Colombo, Calcutta, Bombay, Hyderabad, and in many small cities in UP. At the time of Partition, my father and mother had left their homes in Lahore and Quetta, respectively, and settled in Lucknow. My father worked hard and eventually became the largest representative in North India for Philips of Holland. He would often visit his dealers, particularly in UP, and took us with him on some of these visits. To host my father and his family, the most delectable food, often the speciality of that town, would be prepared, like the famous samosas of Jaunpur and the mixed vegetable pakoras of Sitapur. Even today, those particular savouries still evoke memories of great khatirdari (hospitality).

As one grew older and started working in Delhi and travelling around the country, one's circle of friends widened to many parts of India. One was fortunate that in some cities one had friends and friends of those friends also became part of the friends circle. Through their generosity one would be served food made from recipes that had been passed down through generations of their families, like the Chettinad cuisine in the homes of Visalakshi Ramaswamy and her sister Meenakshi Meyyappan (of The Bangala fame) and Nalini and P. Chidambaram. Many of these recipes have been shared with me and I have tried to recreate them in our own home. Every time I do so, I think of the friend who first introduced me to that particular dish.

A prime example of a recipe being passed down five generations is the malpua. This is considered India's oldest dessert. Malpua are small deep-fried pancakes that are soaked in honey. Interestingly, this dessert is first mentioned in the Rig Veda, the oldest of the four Vedas, where it is called apupa and its recipe is also included. My maternal grandmother who hailed from Multan made the best malpua that I've ever tasted. My mother, Chand Sur, learnt it from her. An indelible memory of one's childhood is of long summer holidays in Mussoorie with my maternal grandmother and many cousins. My grandmother would sit on a low stool in front of an angithi, surrounded by her various grandchildren and fry these delicious malpua in an iron kadhai and remove them with a brass pauni (ladle with holes). This pauni travelled with my grandmother from her maternal home in Multan to my grandfather's home in Quetta where she gave it to my mother when she got married and left Quetta to settle in Lahore, my father's home. After Partition, my mother brought this pauni with her to Lucknow via Delhi and Rajpur in Dehradun. And now it is with me. Vessels and cooking implements have lifespans beyond our own. In this book this pauni is a leitmotif as it evokes many memories and the thoughts of why this simple kitchen implement was so important to my mother that she carried it with her when they left Lahore as refugees. It now sits on my desk in my study and is often used as a paper weight.

~

This book collates recipes by the region they originated from—north, south, east, west, and central India. And while Partition amputated India, I have included some subcontinental recipes from friends across the border because our syncretic culture cannot be contained within recently created political boundaries. And as one has had wonderful opportunities to sample the delicious cuisine of various countries in the homes of their respective envoys, some international-Delhi recipes have been included in the first section.

This collection has thrown up the many similarities and differences in the cuisines of different regions of India. Every region has its own cooking methods. And their own particularly designed utensils, the shapes of which have evolved over generations.

The manner in which Indians dine also varied from region to region. In the North, people dined on dastarkhans (a tablecloth that is spread on the floor). These could be luxurious like the jamawar dastarkhans of Kashmir and in the various courts of Awadh and Hyderabad or they would be simple hand-spun and hand-woven mejposhes, laid on the floor or on a wooden takht (bench). The use of dining tables and dining chairs came in with British influence. Otherwise, food was laid out in thaals that were placed on low baajots (tables) and one ate sitting cross-legged on the ground.

In South India, to date, food is traditionally served on banana leaves that symbolize hospitality and abundance. This is a wholly sustainable and hygienic way of eating, as is the use of kullads for serving drinks and sikoras for serving desserts. Sustainability may be a new buzz word in the West, but it is inherent in our subcontinental culture, whether in our cuisine or in our vernacular architecture.

Ingredients also vary across the country. The staple food of India is based on rice and wheat. Rice in its many avatars is eaten across India such as pulavs, biryanis, bhaats, khichdis, khichdas and even the British version of a curried rice, kedgeree. It is interesting to note that every region seems to have a version of khichdi—a comfort food. From the grand Shahjahani khichdi to the khichda of Shia Muslims to a Gujarati khichdi to a Marathi one.

Similarly flat breads. Most Indians eat unleavened bread, unlike the double roti that was introduced by the British and which influenced traditional delicacies like the Maharashtrian puran poli (a sweet stuffed bread). Across India are varieties of parathas, phulkas, bakarkhanis, shirmals, rumali rotis, naans, kulchas, bhaturas, puris, bhakris, theplas, dosas, aapams and kadumbuttus. The list is endless as every region in India has its own specific speciality.

There are a variety of cooking mediums in India. Traditionally desi ghee (clarified butter) or vanaspati ghee is used together with various vegetable oils such as groundnut, sesame, coconut, and mustard. Much of Bengali cooking uses mustard oil. South of the Vindhyas, coconut milk and coconut oil are favoured.

The variety of masalas and flavouring is also legion. The equivalent of bouquet garni in Lucknow is the potli, the flavourful lazzat-e-taam which comprises thirty spices. Similarly, Bengal has its panch phoron which comprises five spices, North India its garam masalas, South India has its sambar and rasam powders and other podis—and every region its own variation. These masalas and tadkas enhance the sense of taste.

Indian cuisine contains all five basic tastes—sweet, sour, salty, bitter, and umami. Many souring agents are used, like tamarind in the north and kokum in the west. A version of balsamic vinegar, kachampuli, was invented by the Coorgis. Kaveri Ponnapa's delicious family recipes, such as pandi curry, use this ingredient.

There is also a huge variety of baghaars and tadkas that add to the gorgeous foodscapes of India. Everybody's baghaar is different. I always add a pinch of hing (asafoetida) in the tadkas of some dals, in the tradition of my mother-in-law, who lived much of her married life in Dehradun which is considered the hing capital of India. The recipes in this book have many different baghaars.

It is interesting to see how dishes change when non-vegetarians become vegetarian, or vice versa. The delicious vegetarian Avakkai Biryani that I ate at the home of Preetha Reddy whose mother is a legendry cook is a case in point.

'A recipe is a culinary word painting', Lawrence Durrell famously said in his Preface to Marcel Rouff's *The Passionate Epicure*. '…cookery is the art of taste, as painting is the art of sight and music that of hearing'. Durrell continues '…food is a universal language, a therapeutic language of love and an expression of it'. *The Passionate Epicure* was the first culinary novel, a treasury of almost aphrodisiacal inventiveness.[*]

Ishita Banerjee-Dube in *Cooking Cultures* refers to cuisine as 'the defining characteristic of a culture' and says that people and cultures relate to food and cuisine, and that 'such bonding has shaped cartographies of belonging and identities' and that 'food is produced by means of a delicate blend of emotions and creativity, nostalgia and affect, and cultural exchange'.[**] Memories of a place are as much about the cuisine of that place as it is about great archaeological sites and museums one may have seen there. Equally well-remembered is the cuisine of that region.

Films about food and cuisine have become hugely popular such as *Lunch Box*, *Cheeni Kum*, and *The Wedding Banquet*. Perhaps the greatest

---

[*]Marcel Rouff, *The Passionate Epicure: La Vie et la Passion de Dodin-Bouffant*, Gourmet, Modern Library, 2002.

[**]Ishita Banerjee-Dube, *Cooking Cultures: Convergent Histories of Food and Feeling*, CUP, 2016.

classic among food films are *Babette's Feast* and *Like Water for Chocolate*, the latter of which is essentially about a love affair and the seductive power of food.

*Babette's Feast* reminds me of my Danish friend Wera Hildebrand, wife of a previous US ambassador to India, Robert Blackwill and, more importantly, the author of *Icelandic Sagas*, a subject she taught for several years at Harvard University. She became a good friend with whom I had some remarkable experiences including a trek to Chomolhari in Bhutan which had been organized for her by the previous King of Bhutan. Throughout this ten-day trek, one had freshly cooked Bhutanese Ema Datshi (a chilli and cheese dish). The recipe of this national dish has been included in this book by Kusum Haider whose husband served as the Indian ambassador to Bhutan.

Wera told me that 'Danish food is so devoid of any spice that if you add pepper, they find it hot'. I have never forgotten this and, therefore, can fully understand what this great gourmet meal that Babette cooked did to the psyche of the inhabitants of that dour Danish village.

'Delectable cuisine must please the eye as well as excite the palate', says Salma Husain, the author of the superb *The Emperor's Table: The Art of Mughal Cuisine*. She observes that the Mughals who had come from Central Asia revolutionized the culinary arts, which they took to its zenith. Indian cuisine enriched other cuisines whilst itself getting enriched with foreign influences of food and ideas that travelled through the Silk Routes and the Spice Routes.[*]

Lucknow's own delicate refinement is seen in items like malai paan, made with pressed layers of cream filled with sweet nuts and spices and rolled like a betel leaf. Awadhi food was about refined tastes. Lucknow had a vibrant syncretic culture that combined elements of North Indian Hindu and Muslim music, dance, clothing, painting and cuisine. Lucknawi cuisine was disseminated to the courts in Hyderabad which further went on to carve a distinct culinary tradition of its own.

Cuisine is a cultural manifestation. It is an important cultural artifact which is an expression of place and personality. The many

---

[*]Salma Husain, *The Emperor's Table: The Art of Mughal Cuisine*, Lustre, 2009.

friends who have contributed recipes to this book are all epicurean gastronomes. Many of the recipes are culinary word-paintings.

This collection of recipes straddles different narratives. Each recipe is a small microcosm of a much larger macrocosmic world of that particular cuisine and region. The sense of pride is palpable in each of these recipes.

It is India's magnificent geography that has created India's histories that have created its many distinct cuisines. Probably the most beautifully articulated lines written on the geological beginnings of India are by the late Abraham Eraly in *Gem in the Lotus*.

> In the beginning there was no India. All the landmass of the earth then lay huddled together in protocontinents in the lap of the idling primeval sea. Around 170 million years ago this cluster of continents began to break up and drift apart.... In the process, some 100 million years ago, a huge and roughly triangular chunk of land broke off from the eastern flank of Africa above Madagascar, and, pivoting slighting anticlockwise, began a millennially slow, 4000-odd-kilometre-long slide north-north-eastward across the ancient Tethys Sea, baring a stark, crystalline massif like a granite sail. Eventually, after about a forty-million-year-long ocean journey, it docked into the soft underbelly of the sprawling Asian landmass, to become the land that would be known many aeons later as India.

'The underthrust of that impact' caused the Himalayas, which left along the entire length of the mountain an 'immense marshy trough'. Gradually, over millions of years, this lagoon got filled with alluvium from the mountains and built up, layer by layer, the Indo-Gangetic Plain, 'a gift of the Himalayas.... The Indian plate continues to push and grate against Asia. The Himalayas are still rising.'[*]

The Indo-Gangetic Plain is the deepest alluvial plain in the world and is splendidly suitable for agriculture. The greatest and richest empires of India were established here. It was a land of milk and honey, and food always reflects the produce of the land, as is the case in

---

[*]Abraham Eraly, Gem in the Lotus: The Seeding of Indian Civilisation, Penguin India, 2000.

Awadhi cuisine. In shirmal, a bread that Lucknow claims as its unique invention, the dough is made without any water, only ghee and milk are used.

North Indian cuisine is a culinary treasure trove that reflects the rich heritage of the region. It has been influenced by history and has evolved over centuries. It blends indigenous ingredients and cooking techniques with Persian, Mughal and Central Asian influences. This culinary heritage has a unique depth and complexity and is also visually appealing. North India is renowned for its tandoori (clay oven) cooking methods and its slow cooking processes. The range of North Indian cuisine ranges from succulent kebabs to aromatic biryanis and pulavs, to delectable curries and to an extensive range of vegetarian dishes.

South Indian cuisine is unique. Its distinctive flavours are from rice, lentils, coconuts and an array of spices that tantalize the taste buds. Each state within South India has its own distinctive culinary traditions using a variety of spices that grow in this region…from the fiery curries of Andhra Pradesh to the subtlety of Kerala's coastal delicacies. Coconut is a key ingredient. The Malabar coast of Kerala offers a delectable variety of fish and shrimp curries that are infused with aromatic spices and coconut milk, whereas the Chettenad cuisine of Tamil Nadu has a range of spicy and flavourful meat dishes. The concept of Sadhya that is a grand feast served during festivals and special occasions is illustrative of the community nature of South Indian dining.

In Central India, cuisine is not only about food but is also about the dining experience. The region is famous for its baithak that is traditional seating areas where people gather to enjoy a meal. The baithak culture promotes a sense of community, togetherness, and conviviality, all enjoyed over good food.

Western India's diverse geographical features that range from fertile plains to coastal regions to arid deserts has greatly influenced the local cuisines.

Over the last couple of decades, Indians have been discovering their own regional cuisines. Today idli, dosa and sambar are popular throughout North India as chhola bhatura and butter chicken and naan have become popular in South India. Classic dishes, particularly if they are regional street food, become a part of a city's collective consciousness.

We have all become more adventurous, rather than just ordering tandoori chicken, butter chicken, kadhai paneer and tandoori roti in the north and dosas and idlis in the south. Today friends around India are also cooking regional and international cuisine in their homes—be it Japanese, Mexican, Thai, Chinese, Sri Lankan, Italian and Middle Eastern mezzes, Spanish paellas, Burmese khow suey, Moroccan akuri and Turkish shakshuka. There is experimenting with many different spices such as harissa and the delicious Turkish sumac.

Through food there is an integral bonding between friends and the keeping of friendships. It is wonderful when friends gather together at a table to share a delicious meal and exchange views and recipes. Good food ignites conversational combustion. When I look back, many of my friendships are integrally linked to the memory of meals that one has had at the various tables of my epicurean friends.

~

# North

~

# SURKH MURG

DILSHAD SHEIKH                                              KASHMIR

SERVES: 4                                          PREPARATION TIME: 40 MINUTES

INGREDIENTS

| | |
|---|---|
| Chicken | 750 gms |
| Red tomatoes | 6, ground to paste |
| Raw onion rings | to garnish |
| Red chilli powder | 1 tsp |
| Turmeric powder | ½ tsp |
| Green chillies | 4–5, vertically sliced |
| Coriander leaves | a bunch |
| Salt | to taste |

METHOD

Generously salt the chicken and set aside.

Heat oil in a heavy-bottomed pan and deep fry the chicken until it is half-cooked; remove the chicken. Turn down the heat and add the tomato paste, red chilli powder, turmeric powder, and salt. Cook until the tomato paste dries up.

Add the chicken back to the pan and cover with a lid; let the chicken cook in its juices. After about 15 minutes, take the lid off.

Add the green chillies and cook till all the liquid has dried up, then take off heat.

Garnish with coriander leaves and onion rings. This is best served with finger chips dressed with boiled peas.

# TABAK MAAZ

ROHIT KHATTAR                                                      KASHMIR

SERVES: 5–6                                        PREPARATION TIME: 1 HOUR

INGREDIENTS

| | |
|---|---|
| Mutton spareribs (good quality lamb ribs with fat) | 1 kg (5–6 pieces) |
| Milk | 100 ml |
| Oil | 25 ml |
| Green cardamom | 5 gms |
| Asafoetida | 10 ml, diluted in water |
| Salt | to taste |
| Ginger garlic paste | 25 gms |
| Dried ginger powder | 5 gms |
| Fennel seeds powder | 20 gms |
| Cinnamon powder | 5 gms |
| Nutmeg powder | 5 gms |
| Black cardamom pods | 5 gms |
| Cloves | 5 gms |
| Bay leaves | 3 gms |
| Turmeric powder | 5 gms |

METHOD

In a deep pot arrange the mutton ribs and add all spices with water, except milk. Allow to boil till the meat is tender. Add a little oil so that the ribs don't stick to each other.

Once the ribs are tender, remove the pieces and allow to cool for some time. Cut into pieces.

Strain the stock from the pot. Add this back to the pot, add milk, and bring to a boil. Check the seasoning of the lamb pieces and if required add some more seasoning to the stock.

Boil the cut rib pieces in the stock for 2 minutes. Remove them and keep aside.

Grill the lamb pieces on a hot plate or shallow fry in a pan till the outside is evenly browned. Serve hot with pulao or steamed rice.

# KHUBANI CHAAWAL

(APRICOT RICE)

ROHIT KHATTAR                                                    KASHMIR

SERVES: 8                                        PREPARATION TIME: 1 HOUR

INGREDIENTS

| | | |
|---|---|---|
| Dry apricots | 500 gms, washed |
| Basmati rice | 600 gms |
| Desi ghee | 30 gms |
| Black cumin | 2 gms |
| Black cardamom pods | 4–5 |
| Cinnamon sticks | 1–2 |
| Turmeric powder | 10 gms |
| Salt | to taste |
| Garam masala | 5 gms |

METHOD

Wash and soak rice for half an hour. Drain and set aside.

Heat ghee in pan. Fry cumin seeds, black cardamom, and cinnamon sticks in the ghee until the cumin crackles.

Add turmeric powder, garam masala, and salt. Stir well. Add the soaked rice and sauté for a few minutes until the rice is lightly toasted. Add a litre of water and bring to a boil.

When the rice is almost cooked, add in the washed apricots.

Cover the pan tightly with a lid and place it on a pre-heated tawa. Cook till the rice is cooked through and the water has been absorbed.

Serve hot.

# NADROO YAKHNI

ROHIT KHATTAR

KASHMIR

SERVES: 8

PREPARATION TIME: 1 HOUR

## INGREDIENTS

| | |
|---|---|
| Lotus stem (nadroo) | 1 kg |
| Yoghurt | 1.2 kg |
| Salt | to taste |
| Fennel seed powder | 25 gms |
| Dried ginger powder | 10 gms |
| Asafoetida | 5 ml, dissolved in water |
| Refined oil | 100 ml |
| Corn flour | 20 gms |
| Green cardamom | 5 gms |
| Cinnamon stick | 5 gms |

## METHOD

Wash, peel, and cut the lotus stems into thin slices.

Heat oil in a pan. Fry the lotus stems and then boil in water till tender. Keep aside.

Whisk yoghurt with the remaining ingredients and cook on a slow flame while stirring continuously, so it doesn't curdle. Cook till the yoghurt's sourness is reduced.

Now add the fried lotus stems and simmer for about 15 minutes.

In a separate pan, heat 2 tablespoons oil and add all the spices. Once the spices give off their aroma, add this temper to the nadroo yakhni and stir well.

Taste and adjust seasoning and serve hot with rice or naan.

*The India Cookbook*

# KHATTEY SEB BAINGAN

## (AUBERGINE AND APPLE)

ROHIT KHATTAR                                                    KASHMIR

SERVES: 5–6                              PREPARATION TIME: 40 MINUTES

INGREDIENTS

| | |
|---|---|
| Pink Kashmiri aubergines | 1 kg |
| Green cooking apples | 500 gms |
| Refined oil | 100 ml (plus more for frying) |
| Cloves | 7 |
| Kashmiri red chilli powder | 10 gms |
| Ginger powder | 5 gms |
| Fennel seed powder | 15 gms |
| Salt | to taste |
| Garam masala | 10 gms |

METHOD

Wash the aubergines and apples. Cut them into wedges with the skin.

Fry both separately in hot oil and keep aside. Do not mix the apples and aubergines.

Heat oil in a medium kadhai. Add cloves and Kashmiri red chilli powder and fry till the cloves splutter. Add 1 cup of water and stir.

Add ginger powder, fennel powder, and salt. Keep stirring so that the masala is mixed well.

Add 3 cups of water to this and bring to a boil. Add in the fried apples and cook for 10–15 minutes.

Add fried aubergines. Stir gently so that they do not fall apart.

Add garam masala. Mix well. Serve hot.

# RISHTA

SHIBAN GANJU                                            JAMMU & KASHMIR

SERVES: 6                                        PREPARATION TIME: 1 HOUR

INGREDIENTS

| | |
|---|---|
| Mutton | 750 gms minced |
| Meat stock | 1 cup |
| Ghee | 4 tbsp |
| Oil | 2 tbsp preferred |
| Onion paste | 3 tbsp |
| Red chillies | 2 tsp, ground |
| Black cardamoms | 3, dry roasted and powdered |
| Ginger powder | 1 tsp |
| Green cardamoms | 4 |
| Turmeric | ½ tbsp |
| Cloves | 3 |
| Cinnamon stick | ½-inch piece |
| Aniseed | ½ tsp |
| Saffron | 6 strands, soaked in water |
| Salt | to taste |

METHOD

Clean the minced mutton. Then pound it on a smooth stone with a wooden mallet.

To the minced mutton, add brown cardamom powder, one teaspoon ginger powder and a little salt. After mixing well, grease your hand with some oil and make the koftas (small round meat balls).

Boil 2 cups of water in a pan and add the meat balls. Cook for 10 minutes, till the mince balls rise to the surface of the water. Turn off the flame and keep aside.

In a pan, heat the oil, then add the ghee and gradually add the spices—turmeric, chilli paste, cloves, cinnamon stick, green cardamom, and onion paste and cook till light brown. Next, add the saffron water along with the meat balls and meat stock. Add salt to taste. Cover the lid and let it cook for 10 minutes until the gravy thickens. Heat

1 tablespoon ghee in a separate pan and add to the kofta curry. Cover for 2 minutes.

Garnish with aniseeds and serve hot.

# GOSHTABA WITH MOOLI KI CHUTNEY

RUPIN PAHWA                                                    KASHMIR

SERVES: 4–6                          PREPARATION TIME: 1 HOUR 30 MINUTES

INGREDIENTS
For the mutton balls

| | | |
|---|---|---|
| Lamb | 1 kg, very finely minced (800 gms boneless meat and 200 gms meat fat) |
| Salt | 1½ tsp |
| Mustard oil | 1 tsp |
| Ghee | 1 tbsp |
| Full cream yoghurt | 1 tbsp |
| Black cardamom seeds | 1 tbsp, crushed |
| Fennel seeds | 1 tbsp, freshly ground |

For the bouquet garni

| | |
|---|---|
| Fennel seeds | 1 tbsp |
| Cumin powder | 1 tbsp |
| Cinnamon powder | 1 tbsp |
| Dried ginger powder | 1 tbsp |
| Green cardamom seeds | 2, crushed |
| Cloves | 6, crushed |
| Bay leaves | 2 |
| Fine cotton cloth | 1 piece |

For the sauce

| | |
|---|---|
| Onions | 3 medium-sized, chopped |
| Ghee | 3 tbsp |
| Caraway seeds | ½ tsp |
| Yoghurt | 1½ cup, whipped |
| Full fat milk | 1½ cup |
| Salt | to taste |

| | |
|---|---|
| Rose petals | to garnish |

For the chutney

| | |
|---|---|
| Medium-sized white radishes | 4, grated |
| Walnuts | 40, chopped very finely |
| Hung curd | 8 tbsp |
| Green chillies | 4, deseeded and ground to paste |
| Ground coriander leaves | 4 tsp |
| Salt | to taste |

METHOD

Add all the ingredients for the mutton balls to a bowl and mix well. Make medium-sized mutton balls (about 30 grams each or 2–3 inches in diameter).

Make a bouquet garni of the dried herbs using the muslin cloth and make a knot in such a way that all the herbs remain inside. Put a litre of water in a big pan and heat the pan on a full flame. Soak the bouquet garni in the water.

Once the water has boiled, simmer it on low heat for about 5 minutes and then gently immerse the mutton balls in the boiling water. They will expand a little bit.

Cover and cook on low heat for about half an hour, till most of the broth has evaporated. Take out one meatball to check that it is cooked through. If the meat seems underdone, add some more hot water to the pan and cook the balls till they are done. Do not discard the remaining water.

Once the pot has cooled, remove the bouquet garni and squeeze it out into the pot.

Add a tablespoon of the ghee to a frying pan on high heat. Fry the caraway seeds and remove from the pan.

Heat the remaining ghee in the pan and fry the onions in this until they are brown. Grind the onions in a blender and set aside.

Heat a large pan. Add the onions, then the caraway seeds, then the whipped curd, stirring constantly to prevent curdling, then the milk and salt. Taste and adjust the seasoning if required.

Add the meat balls along with the remaining water and let them warm through on a low flame for about 5 minutes. If preparing the dish in advance, do this just before serving.

Garnish with rose petals, if you have them.

For the white radish chutney, squeeze out some but not all the water from the grated radish by pressing between your hands. The radish should still be wet to the touch. Mix all the ingredients and serve.

**Note:** If you find yourself missing a couple of the spices listed, feel free to follow the recipe without them. You can also change up the amounts of herbs and spices you use: if you prefer a stronger fennel flavour, add more fennel, or add one or two dry whole red chillies along with the shahi jeera if you wish to make the dish spicier. You can also replace the lamb with minced chicken.

# AMBAL

KOMAL SHARMA                                                       JAMMU

SERVES: 4                                        PREPARATION TIME: 30 MINUTES

INGREDIENTS

| | |
|---|---|
| Pumpkin | ½ kg |
| Fenugreek seeds | 1 tsp, heaped |
| Cumin seeds | ½ tsp |
| Red chilli powder | 1 tsp |
| Turmeric powder | 1 tsp |
| Tamarind | 100 gms |
| Jaggery | 100 gms |
| Clove | 2–3 |
| Bay leaves | 3–4 |
| Garam masala | 1 tsp |
| Mustard oil | 3 tbsp |
| Green chillies | 2–3, sliced lengthwise |
| Salt | ¾ tsp, or to taste |

METHOD

Cut pumpkin into medium-sized cubes.

Heat the mustard oil in a pan. Add fenugreek seeds and sauté till brown. Add cumin and pumpkin pieces and sauté slightly. Now add salt, red chilli powder, turmeric, cloves, bay leaves, and garam masala and sauté until well combined.

Add tamarind and jaggery pieces and stir.

Add enough water to cover the pumpkin and simmer. The water will halve in quantity and the pumpkin will soften. Continue simmering till the tamarind and jaggery have blended and the gravy has become slightly thickened.

Throw in the green chillies, sprinkle the garam masala, and immediately cover. Take off the heat and serve hot.

# QEEMA MATAR

VISHWAJIT SINGH AND VIJAY THAKUR SINGH

SITAPUR,
UTTAR PRADESH

SERVES: 6–8

PREPARATION TIME: 1 HOUR
(PLUS 1 HOUR MARINATION TIME)

INGREDIENTS

| | |
|---|---|
| Mutton | 1 kg, minced |
| Green peas | 1 kg, shelled |
| Red chilli powder | ½ tsp |
| Garlic cloves | 20–25, ground |
| Ginger piece | 2 inch, ground |
| Yoghurt | 250 gms (2 cups) |
| Desi ghee | 250 gms (1¼ cups) |
| Onions | 250 gms (2 medium), sliced |
| Coriander powder | 2 tbsp |
| Green chillies | 2, chopped |
| Salt | 2 tsp |
| Turmeric powder | 1 tsp |
| Garam masala | 1 tsp |
| Cinnamon stick | 1 |
| Bay leaves | 2 |

METHOD

Wash mutton mince properly. Mix salt, turmeric, red chilli, garlic, ginger, and yoghurt with mince. Marinate for one hour.

Heat the ghee in a pan. Then add cloves, cinnamon, and bay leaves. Once the leaves change colour, remove them and the cinnamon stick. Add in onions and fry till golden brown. Drain and keep aside.

Add minced meat to the remaining ghee in the pan.

Crumble the fried onions into the minced meat. Stir to mix well and cook till well-browned. Pour in 1 litre of water, cover and cook for 30 minutes.

Add peas and cook till the mince is dry. Stir in the coriander powder, garam masala, salt, and green chillies.

Serve qeema matar with chapattis or plain parathas.

# DUM ALOO

DEVI CHERIAN                                          HIMACHAL PRADESH

SERVES: 6–8                                        PREPARATION TIME: 1 HOUR

INGREDIENTS

| | |
|---|---|
| Baby potatoes | 1 kg (medium sized) |
| Mustard oil | as needed |
| Yoghurt | ½ kg, whisked |
| Fennel seed powder | 4 tbsp |
| Ginger powder | 2 tbsp |
| Cumin powder | 3 tbsp |
| Asafoetida | a pinch |
| Turmeric powder | ½ tsp or to taste |
| Red chilli powder | ½ tsp or to taste |
| Salt | to taste |
| Cardamom and cinnamon powder | ¼ tsp each |

METHOD

Boil potatoes in a pressure cooker for one whistle. Turn off the heat and leave them in the hot water to soften. Once the water has cooled, peel potatoes with a fork or toothpick.

Heat mustard oil in a pan till it smokes. Fry the softened potatoes in this till they are crispy and dark brown in colour. Remove potatoes on to a plate.

Take 4 tablespoons of the mustard oil (which has been used for frying) in a kadhai. Add asafoetida, beaten yoghurt, and all the ground spices. Keep stirring to avoid the yoghurt from curdling. Add salt, haldi, and red chilli powder. Then add 3 cups of warm water and bring to a boil. Add the fried potatoes and simmer till the desired consistency is obtained.

Sprinkle cardamom and cinnamon powder. Mix and serve hot.

# GRILLED LAMB CHOPS

GUNMALA SINGH AND DARSHAN SINGH          DELHI/DEHRADUN

SERVES: 6–8                    PREPARATION TIME: 20 MINUTES
                              (PLUS OVERNIGHT MARINATION)

INGREDIENTS

| | | |
|---:|:---|:---|
| Lamp chops | 1 kg, doubled-cut, pounded |
| Mint leaves | 2 bunches |
| Olive oil | 15 tbsp |
| Soy sauce | 7 tbsp |
| Garlic paste | 1 tsp |
| Mustard (whole grain) | 1 tsp |
| Tabasco hot sauce | ½ tsp |
| Hot and sweet ketchup | 1 tbsp |
| Peppercorns | 10—12, crushed |
| Salt | 1 tsp |
| Small lemons | 3–4, juiced |

METHOD

Mix the olive oil, soya sauce, garlic paste, mustard, tobacco, ketchup, peppercorn, salt, and lemon juice to make a marinade. Carefully rub the above marinade on the lamb chops.

Place the chops in a dish and lay mint leaves between the lamb chops. Cover and refrigerate, preferably overnight for best results.

Cook the marinated lamb chops on the grill until they are cooked through but still tender, approximately 4 minutes on each side.

# HARE CHANE KI SABZI

## (HARA CHHOLIYA)

O. P. JAIN

SERVES: 6

PREPARATION TIME: 30 MINUTES

INGREDIENTS

| | |
|---|---|
| Green Bengal gram | 3, cups fresh and shelled |
| Onion | 1 large, chopped |
| Oil | 3 tbsp |
| Garlic paste | ½ tbsp |
| Ginger paste | 1 tbsp |
| Yoghurt | 1 ½ cup |
| Green chillies | 3 |
| Asafoetida | ¼ tsp |
| Cumin seeds | ½ tsp |
| Turmeric powder | ¼ tsp |
| Coriander powder | ½ tbsp |
| Cumin powder | 1 tsp |
| Red chilli powder | 1 tsp |
| Garam masala | 1 tsp |
| Water | ¼ cup |
| Salt | to taste |
| Fresh coriander | a small bunch |

METHOD

In 3 cups water add salt and cook Bengal gram for 20 to 25 minutes. Remove the excess water. Then in a deep non-stick pan heat the oil and add asafoetida and cumin seeds. Once the cumin seeds brown, add the chopped onions and sauté for 1 minute. Add chopped green chillies, garlic and ginger paste and brown for 1 minute. Then add turmeric, coriander, cumin, and red chilli powders and mix well. To this add the yoghurt and drained Bengal gram with salt. Add ¼ cup of water and garam masala and cook for a few minutes.

Garnish with a few sprigs of fresh coriander and serve hot.

# MOONG DAL KE PAKORE WITH TAMARIND CHUTNEY AND MINT CHUTNEY

ALKA PANDE                                                    PUNJAB

SERVES: 4                                  PREPARATION TIME: 45 MINUTES
                                           (PLUS 4 HOURS FOR SOAKING)

INGREDIENTS

For the pakore

| | |
|---|---|
| Yellow moong dal, split | 150 gms |
| Full cream yoghurt | 500 gms |
| Cold milk | 1 cup |
| Mustard oil for frying | 500 ml |
| Tamarind | 75 gms |
| Jaggery | 150 gms |
| Rock salt | 1 tsp |
| Dried ginger powder | 1 tsp |
| Cumin powder | 1 tsp |
| Deggi mirch/red chilli powder | 2 tsp |

For the chutneys

| | |
|---|---|
| Dried tamarind | 75 gms |
| Jaggery | 150 gms |
| Rock salt | ¼ tsp |
| Dried ginger powder | 1 tsp |
| Chilli powder | ½ tsp, heaped |
| Cumin powder | ½ tsp |
| Raw mango | 1 |
| Coriander leaves/mint | 1 bunch |
| Salt | to taste |
| Green chillies | 4–5 |

For the garnish

Deggi mirch
Roasted ground cumin seed powder
Rock salt
Fresh coriander
Green chillies and ginger, finely chopped
Pomegranate seeds

METHOD

Prepare the tamarind chutney: soak the dried tamarind in 250 millilitres of water. Boil the tamarind water till it starts thickening. Add the jaggery and keep on the heat till it melts. When the tamarind–jaggery liquid starts thickening, add the salt, red chilli/deggi mirch powder, dried ginger powder, rock salt, and up to a teaspoon of salt, and cook till the chutney achieves a thick pouring consistency.

Prepare the mint chutney: grind the mint or coriander leaves, raw mango (can be replaced with 2 tablespoons raw mango powder/amchur), green chillies, and salt into a thick paste.

To begin preparing the pakoras, soak 150 gms of moong dal for 4 hours and then grind on a stone slab into a thick paste. You may also use a mixer-grinder.

Whip the paste, preferably with your hand, in long strokes so that the air is incorporated into it and the paste becomes light and airy.

In a kadhai, heat the mustard oil. To the hot oil, add small amounts of the dal batter so that they are formed into small balls approximately 1 inch in diameter.

Fry the pakoras till they are light golden colour on a medium flame. They should rise to the top of the oil once they are cooked through.

Place the hot pakoras in a large deep bowl half full of room temperature water. Let them sit in the water for 5 minutes.

In the meantime, whip the yoghurt into a thick milky consistency by adding a cup of chilled milk little by little. Add salt to taste.

Gently squeeze the moong pakoras and place four to six on each platter.

Add two tablespoons of yoghurt to each serving. The pakoras should be completely soaked in the yoghurt. Add more whipped yoghurt if required.

Drizzle some tamarind sauce on top and add a few dollops of green mint chutney.

Sprinkle table salt and rock salt to taste.

Garnish with finely chopped coriander, two or three slices of finely chopped ginger, a few pomegranate seeds, roasted cumin powder, red chilli powder, and chopped green chillies, as per individual taste.

# MUTTON CURRY

ARUN KAPUR                                                    PUNJAB

SERVES: 4–6                                PREPARATION TIME: 1½ HOURS

INGREDIENTS

| | |
|---|---|
| Mutton | 1 kg |
| Ghee | 3 tbsp |
| Green chillies | 4–5, finely chopped |
| Garlic | 1 tbsp, finely chopped |
| Ginger | ½ tbsp, grated |
| Onions | 3–4, finely sliced |
| Tomatoes | 3–4, roughly chopped |
| Red chilli powder | ½ tsp |
| Turmeric powder | 1 tsp |
| Coriander powder | 1 tsp |
| Garam masala | ½ tsp |
| Salt | to taste |
| Coriander leaves | few sprigs |

METHOD

Fry the green chillies, garlic, and ginger in ghee.

Next add the onions. Once onions are brown, add the meat and fry on high heat for 5–7 minutes.

Turn down the heat and add the dry spices and salt. Cover and cook the meat on low for 20 minutes.

Add the tomatoes and cook for 15–20 minutes more, until the tomatoes dry out a little.

Garnish with ghee and fresh coriander leaves and serve hot with roti or rice.

# STUFFED PANEER

KUSUM ANSAL                                                    PUNJAB

SERVES: 4                                      PREPARATION TIME: 1 HOUR

## INGREDIENTS

| | |
|---|---|
| Paneer | 500 gms |
| Almonds | 6, chopped |
| Cashew nuts | 4, chopped |
| Raisins | 8, chopped |
| Boiled potatoes | 2, medium-sized |
| Red chilli powder (deggi variety) | 1 tsp |
| Salt | to taste |

### For coating batter

| | |
|---|---|
| Besan | 4 tbsp |
| Neutral oil | 2 tbsp |
| Yoghurt | 1 cup |
| Red chilli powder (deggi) | 1 tsp |
| Dried fenugreek leaves | 1 tsp |
| Carom seeds | 1 tsp |
| Lemon juice | 1 tbsp |
| Salt | a pinch |

### For the garnish

| | |
|---|---|
| Green, yellow, and red bell peppers and onion | 1 each |
| Coriander leaves | Few sprigs |

## METHOD

Cut the paneer into two-inch cubes. Scoop out the centre of each cube using a knife to create a hollow for the filling.

For the filling, mix the chopped dry fruits with the mashed potatoes, add salt and chilli powder to taste. Fill this mix into the hollow of the paneer cubes. Set aside.

For the coating, heat 2 tablespoons of oil in a saucepan. Add besan and stir till it has browned. Let the paste cool for about twenty minutes. Add yoghurt, chilli powder, methi, ajwain, and lemon juice to this and mix well.

Heat a non–stick pan. Dip the paneer pieces gently into the besan batter and place them one by one on the pan to cook. If the pieces start to stick to the pan, add a little oil. Keep turning the pieces till they are equally browned on all sides. Arrange them in the centre of a serving dish.

Cut the bell peppers and onion into strips. Sauté them in a pan with the leftover besan and yoghurt batter. Cook till they soften, then remove from heat.

Place the cooked vegetables around the paneer on the serving dish. Garnish with some coriander leaves and serve hot.

# OKRA GOSHT

MINU BAKSHI                                                    PUNJAB

SERVES: 6                                    PREPARATION TIME: 1 HOUR

INGREDIENTS

| | |
|---|---|
| Desi ghee/refined oil | 150 ml |
| Black cardamom pods | 4 |
| Green cardamom pods | 5 |
| Cumin seeds | 1 tsp |
| Cinnamon stick | 1, up to 2 inches long |
| Cloves | 6–7 |
| Black peppercorns | 10 |
| Onions | 300 gms, thinly sliced |
| Ginger paste | 1 tsp |
| Garlic paste | 1 tsp |
| Tomatoes | 300 gms, chopped |
| Cumin powder | 1 tsp |
| Coriander powder | 1 tsp |
| Turmeric powder | 1½ tsp |
| Kashmiri red chilli powder (deggi) | 1 tsp |
| Mutton (or lamb) | 1 kg |
| Okra | 500 gms |
| Garam masala | 1 tsp |

| | |
|---|---|
| Salt | 1 tsp, or to taste |
| Whole green chillies | 2 |
| Fresh coriander leaves | 2 tsp |

METHOD

Heat a pressure cooker. Add the ghee (or refined oil) and wait for it to heat up, then add the green and black cardamom, bay leaves, cloves, peppers, and cinnamon stick. Fry the spices for 2–3 minutes till they become aromatic and then add the whole cumin seeds. As soon as the cumin seeds start to crackle, add the sliced onions. Cook till onions turn golden brown, then add the ginger and garlic pastes. Add about 2–3 teaspoons of water to avoid burning the pastes. Sauté for 40–45 seconds and then add the chopped tomatoes. The tomatoes should soften in about 2 minutes. Once the tomatoes have softened add the cumin powder, coriander powder, turmeric powder, and chilli powder.

Sauté for 12–15 seconds, again adding 2–3 teaspoons of water so that the spices do not burn. Add the mutton and stir on a medium flame, then cover the cooker. Stir the mutton every 2–3 minutes, always remembering to cover in the intervening periods. Do this for 30 minutes at least to allow the spices to soak in, sprinkling in water as and when needed.

Now add half a litre of water to the pressure cooker and seal the lid tightly, allowing the cooker to pressurize for 15 minutes on medium heat or until the first whistle. Once all the pressure is released, open and remove the lid. The mutton should be cooked by this time. Turn the heat to low.

Remove the tops of the okra, then cut into pieces, approximately 2 inches in length.

Heat 2–3 tablespoons of oil in a pan and sauté the okra pieces for 3–4 minutes on medium–high heat to remove their stickiness. Towel-dry the okra and add to the cooked mutton. Add the garam masala and cook for 5–7 minutes while stirring lightly. Your dish is now ready.

Garnish the okra ghosht with the green chilli and coriander leaves and serve.

**Note:** This dish is best eaten with naan or tandoori roti.

# CHICKEN CURRY

NEELAM KHANNA AND ASHOK KHANNA                              PUNJAB

SERVES: 4–6                              PREPARATION TIME: 1 HOUR 30 MINUTES

                                         (PLUS MARINATION TIME OF 2 HOURS)

INGREDIENTS

| | | |
|---|---|---|
| Chicken pieces | 800 gms |
| Vegetable oil | 100 ml |
| Tomato sauce | ¾ cup |
| Spring onions | 2 |
| Potatoes | 2, boiled, halved, and deep fried |

For the marinade

| | | |
|---|---|---|
| Ginger garlic paste | 2 tbsp |
| Ground black pepper | 1 pinch |
| Worcestershire sauce | 2 tbsp |
| Hot sauce, such as Tabasco | 1 tsp |
| Sour yoghurt | 2 tbsp |
| Onion | 1 large, sliced into rings |
| White vinegar | 1 tbsp |
| Salt | to taste |

METHOD

Make the marinade and leave the chicken to rest in this for at least 2 hours.

Heat the oil in a pan. Remove the chicken pieces from the marinade, making sure to wipe off the excess as you do so. Fry the chicken pieces in the hot oil until browned; remove and set aside.

Remove the onion from the marinade and fry in the same pan until golden brown.

Add the remaining marinade to the onions and mash this mixture while cooking till the oil separates.

To this, add the chicken, tomato sauce, and water, and cook on a low flame till the chicken is cooked and the oil separates from the gravy.

Add the whole spring onions and the deep fried potatoes and simmer on low heat for about 10 minutes. Serve hot with buttered rice or pasta.

# SAAG GOSHT

RAJESH AND NISHI MEHRA                                    PUNJAB

SERVES: 8                                     PREPARATION TIME: 2 HOURS

## INGREDIENTS

| | |
|---|---|
| Desi ghee | ½ kg |
| Onions | 5–6, grated |
| Coriander powder | 4 tsp |
| Spinach | 250 gms, washed and chopped |
| Dried fenugreek leaves | 250 gms |
| Mutton | 2 kg |
| Fresh dill | 200 gms |
| Coriander leaves | 100 gms |
| Green chillies | 6–7, cut lengthwise |
| Ginger | 2 inches, cut into thin and long strips |
| Ginger garlic paste | 1 tbsp |
| Tomatoes | 5–6, grated |
| Cinnamon sticks | 2 |
| Cloves | 5 |
| Bay leaves | 2 |
| Green cardamom | 4 |
| Black cardamom pods | 6 (seeds only) |
| Black peppercorns | 12 |
| Red chilli powder | 2½ tsp |
| Garam masala | 2½ tsp |
| Salt | to taste |

## METHOD

In a heavy bottom pan, heat approximately two-thirds of the desi ghee. Add the grated onion and dhania powder to this. Fry till golden brown.

Add ginger garlic paste and then mutton. Stir well, then cover with lid. Keep stirring and replacing the cover every few minutes, until the mutton is tender and has lost some of its moisture.

In a separate kadhai heat the remaining ghee. Add tomatoes. Add 1 teaspoon of the red chilli powder. Let simmer till the oil separates.

Now add the spinach and methi to the mutton. Add salt to taste. Keep on the flame till both greens and the mutton are cooked through.

Add the ginger strips, dill, coriander leaves, black cardamom seeds, green cardamom, cinnamon, cloves, bay leaves, and green chilli. Cover and let it simmer on low heat. You can place a thin tava under the patila to keep the temperature low. Add the fried tomatoes to this.

Add the garam masala. Cover the dish. If the gravy looks too thick, you may add a little water. Let it simmer on low heat for 10 minutes; serve hot.

# DILLI KA PURDAH PULAO

RENUKA AND RANA TALWAR                                    DELHI

SERVES: 4                              PREPARATION TIME: 2 HOURS

INGREDIENTS

| | |
|---|---|
| Basmati rice | ½ kg |
| Bay leaves | 2–3 |
| Black cardamom pods | 2–3 |
| Salt | 2 tsp |
| Saffron | few strands |
| Milk | 2 tbsp |
| Chicken | 1 kg |
| Onion rings | 1¼ kg, deep fried |
| Ghee | 2 tbsp |

To make purdah (quantities will
differ based on size of cooking utensil)
All-purpose flour
Salt
Neutral oil

METHOD

Boil enough water in a pot to cook the rice. Add the bay leaves to this, and then add the rice. Cook until the rice is done three-quarters of the way, then drain the water and continue to cook the rice in the same pot. Once the rice is ready, add the ghee and fried onions and mix.

In a separate bowl, mix saffron and milk and keep aside. Preheat oven to 180°C.

For the purdah, knead maida, salt, oil, and water in a bowl and roll out the dough as required to cover the inside and the top of a round aluminium pot. Take a sheet of aluminium foil and cover the bottom and sides of the inside of the pot. Layer the dough over this in such a manner that the pot is entirely covered, leaving some dough to cover the top.

Next, begin layering the pulao ingredients as follows: one-third of the rice, then some of the saffron–milk mixture, then half of the chicken. Repeat this sequence again, and then put the remaining rice and saffron–milk on top. Cover the top of the pot with the remaining dough and then the aluminium foil, making sure there is no leakage of air.

Cook for 1 hour 15 minutes in an oven at 180°C. Keep reheating the pot every 15 minutes in the oven until it is time to serve.

# METHI CHICKEN

SUNIL MEHRA                                                              PUNJAB

SERVES: 4                          PREPARATION TIME: 1 HOUR (PLUS 1 HOUR
                                                          MARINATION TIME)

INGREDIENTS

| | |
|---|---|
| Chicken | 250 gms |
| Fenugreek leaves | 1 small bunch, washed and chopped |
| Onion | 1, large, sliced |
| Tomatoes | 2 medium-sized, chopped |
| Green chillies | 2 chopped |
| Thick yoghurt | 1 tbsp |
| Ginger garlic paste | 1 tbsp |
| Mustard oil | 2 tbsp |
| Kashmiri red chilli powder | 1¾ tsp |

| | |
|---|---|
| Turmeric powder | ½ tsp |
| Black pepper powder | ¼ tsp |
| Coriander powder | 1 tsp |
| Cumin powder | ¾ tsp |
| Garam masala | ⅓ tsp |
| Cashews | 8–10, ground into paste |
| Dried fenugreek leaves | ¼ tsp |
| Salt | to taste |

## METHOD

Marinate chicken with ½ teaspoon salt, 1 teaspoon kashmiri red chilli powder, the black pepper powder, and ¼ teaspoon turmeric powder. Cover and keep in the refrigerator for an hour.

Heat 1 tablespoon oil in a pan, fry the sliced onion until translucent, then take out. In the same oil, fry the fenugreek leaves till it crisps up slightly, take out and keep aside.

Grind the fried onion, tomatoes, curd, and green chilli together into a fine paste.

In the same pan, add the remaining oil, and put in ginger garlic paste. Cook till the raw smell goes away. Add the prepared paste, the remaining red chilli and turmeric powder, and the coriander powder, cumin powder, and dried fenugreek leaves. Cook till the oil separates from the masala.

Add the marinated chicken, cook on high flame for 2–3 minutes, stirring continuously so the masala nicely coats the chicken.

Lower the flame, add garam masala, mix and cook on low flame till oil separates (around 10 minutes). Add cashew paste and fried fenugreek leaves, mix and cook on low flame till oil separates.

Add a cup of water, mix, cover and cook for 15 minutes, or till the chicken is cooked through. Serve with khameeri roti, tandoori roti, or paratha.

# PAKORA KARHI

GURSHARAN KAUR                                          PUNJAB

SERVES: 8                        PREPARATION TIME: 1 HOUR 30 MINUTES

INGREDIENTS
For the pakoras

| | |
|---|---|
| Coarse besan | 1½ cup |
| Onion | 1 medium-sized, roughly chopped |
| Green chilli | 1, chopped |
| Ginger | 1 inch, finely chopped |
| Neutral oil | enough for frying |
| Coriander leaves | few sprigs, chopped |
| Salt | to taste |

For the karhi

| | |
|---|---|
| Yoghurt | 2 cups |
| Besan | 4 tbsp |
| Cumin seeds | ½ tsp |
| Fenugreek seeds | ½ tsp |
| Garam masala | ½ tsp |
| Turmeric powder | up to ½ tsp |
| Onion | 1 medium-sized, chopped roughly |
| Ginger | 1 tsp, chopped or minced |
| Green chilli | 1, chopped |
| Oil | 2 tbsp |
| Salt and red chilli powder | to taste |

METHOD

Make the pakora batter by combining the besan, chopped onion, ginger, green chilli, and coriander leaves, and salt with a little water; mix well. Add more water to make a smooth medium-thick batter which is not too runny.

Heat enough oil in a kadhai (wok) for frying the pakoras. Using a medium-sized spoon put spoonfuls of the batter into the hot oil and fry till they turn golden. Make sure the pakoras are soft and not too big (approx. 2 inches in diameter). Set aside.

Next, prepare the karhi. Make a lassi by mixing the yoghurt and 4 cups of water. Take out a half cup of this lassi and add the besan to this. Mix well so that there are no lumps and then combine this mixture with the rest of the lassi.

In a pan, heat the cooking oil. When it is a little hot, add the jeera and methi seeds and wait till they turn golden. Add the onions, ginger, and green chillies to this, and sauté them for a while. Add the turmeric, red pepper, and salt, and cook for 1–2 minutes. Then add the lassi mixture. Stirring every now and then, cook on high heat until the mixture starts boiling. When it starts boiling turn the heat down; simmer for about 15–20 minutes until a little oil appears on the surface of the karhi. Now add the pakoras and boil for 2–3 minutes. The karhi should be ready.

**Note:** If you like you can use vegetables, such as potatoes, green beans, cauliflower, cabbage, and spinach, instead of pakoras. Cut the vegetables the way you like but the vegetables will have to be added earlier to the karhi so that they are well cooked. This karhi is much simpler and healthier and I personally like it better. This should be served with steamed basmati rice.

## AMRITSARI ALOO PARATHA

SUNIL AND MUKTA MUNJAL                    AMRITSAR, PUNJAB

SERVES: 4                           PREPARATION TIME: 30 MINUTES

INGREDIENTS

For the special Amritsari masala

| | | |
|---|---|---|
| Coriander seeds | 1 tbsp |
| Cumin seeds | 1 tbsp |
| Black peppercorn | 1 tbsp |
| Melon seeds | 1 tbsp |

For the parathas

| | |
|---|---|
| Whole wheat flour | 4 cups |
| Salt | ½ tsp, or to taste |
| Ghee | 1 tbsp |
| Large green chilli | 1, deseeded and finely chopped (optional) |

## For dusting and frying

| | |
|---|---|
| Whole wheat flour | 1 cup |
| Desi ghee | 4 tbsp |

## For the stuffing

| | |
|---|---|
| Potatoes | 4 medium-sized |
| Chilli powder | ¾ or ½ tbsp |
| Coriander powder | 1 tbsp |
| Salt | 1 tbsp |
| Carom seeds | ¼ tbsp |
| Dried fenugreek leaves | 1 tbsp |
| Fennel powder | ½ tbsp |
| Coriander leaves | 2 tbsp, finely chopped |
| Amritsari masala | 1 tbsp |

## METHOD

Prepare the Amritsari masala. Except for the melon seeds, dry roast the other ingredients. Let them cool down and then coarsely grind along with the melon seeds.

Wash and rinse well the potatoes, then boil them. If using a pressure cooker for boiling then use 4 cups of water and place the potatoes in it. Put the pressure cooker on medium heat for 4–5 whistles.

Peel the boiled potatoes. Then, mash or grate them to a smooth texture and ensure no hard lumps remain. Add the spices and salt and mix well.

To prepare the dough, take 2 cups of whole wheat flour and half a teaspoon of salt, one tablespoon of ghee or oil and half a cup of lukewarm water in a large mixing bowl. Mix everything and continuously knead, adding small amounts of water, as and when required, to form a soft and fluffy non-sticky dough.

Divide the dough into six balls. Make into small flat discs. Take a small amount of the potato mixture and put inside each disc. Close the disc and seal it on top.

With a rolling pin, flatten the discs of dough into circular shapes with equal thickness on all sides.

Heat a flat frying pan or tawa and add one tablespoon of ghee or refined oil. Fry the flattened paratha till golden brown. Then flip and cook the other side till golden brown. Remove from the pan. Sprinkle the Amritsari masala on top. Similarly cook all six parathas, one by one.

Serve the aloo parathas hot with yoghurt, pickle, and/or green chutney.

# CHICKEN BIRYANI

ROMI CHOPRA                                                    DELHI

SERVES: 8                           PREPARATION TIME: 1 HOUR 10 MINUTES

INGREDIENTS:

| | |
|---|---|
| Chicken | 1 kg, cut into medium sized boneless pieces |
| Long grain rice | 400 gms |
| Caraway seeds | ½ tsp |
| Bay leaves | 2 |
| Lime juice | 1 tbsp |
| Onions | 2 medium, sliced |
| Tomatoes | 2, chopped |
| Ginger paste | 1½ tsp |
| Garlic paste | 1 ½ tsp |
| Turmeric powder | 1/3 tsp |
| Red chilli powder | 1 ½ tsp |
| Garam masala | 1 tsp |
| Milk | ½ cup |
| Butter | 1 tbsp |
| Cream | 1 tbsp |
| Oil | ½ cup |
| Salt | to taste |

METHOD:

Wash the chicken pieces and drain them in a colander.

Wash the rice and soak for 30 minutes. Drain the water. Boil 1½ litres of water along with bay leaves, caraway seeds, lime juice, and salt. When the water starts boiling, add the rice and cook for 7 to 8 minutes until it is two-thirds done. Drain out the water and put the rice in a flat pan.

To cook the chicken, heat the oil and fry the onions till golden brown. Add the ginger and garlic paste. After about 20 seconds add salt, turmeric, red chilli powder, and ½ tsp garam masala. Then sprinkle half cup of water and add the chopped tomatoes. Cook for 2 to 3 minutes. Then add the chicken pieces and fry for about 5 minutes. Add a little water and cook the chicken for 7 to 8 minutes till it is half done. Cover the chicken and cook till it is tender and there is about ½ cup of gravy left.

Take a heavy bottomed pan and grease it with oil (make sure it is a pan with a tight-fitting lid). Then spread two thirds of the par-boiled rice in the pan and place the chicken and gravy over it. Spread the rest of the rice on top. Sprinkle milk with the ½ tsp garam masala. On this place blobs of butter and fresh cream and cover with the lid. Cook for almost 2 minutes over medium to high flame to heat the dish. Then on a low flame, for about 15 to 20 minutes cook till the rice is steaming hot. Serve hot.

# RABRI

NIDHI CHOUDHARY                                                    DELHI

SERVES: 3–4                              PREPARATION TIME: 1 HOUR 15 MINUTES

INGREDIENTS

| | |
|---|---|
| Full cream milk | 1½ litres |
| Sugar | 2½ tbsp |
| Green cardamom powder | ¼ tsp |
| Slivered almonds and pistachios | for decoration |

METHOD

Put the milk in a pan and bring to a boil, stirring continuously. Continue stirring till only a litre of milk remains and a thick cream starts forming. Remove this thick cream and set aside in a bowl. This cream should be removed periodically and added to the bowl.

When only 250 millilitres of the milk remains, add the sugar and the cardamom powder. Keep stirring and let the sugar dissolve. Remove from heat and let the rabri cool down completely.

Add all the cream from your bowl into the cooled milk and mix. Pour this into a dish and serve. You may decorate the platter with almonds and pistachios if you choose.

# RAMPURI TAAR GOSHT

SYEDA HAMEED                                                    DELHI

SERVES: 6–8                          REPARATION TIME: 1 HOUR 30 MINUTES

INGREDIENTS

| | |
|---|---|
| Ghee/refined oil/mustard oil | 1 cup |
| Onion | 2 large, finely diced |
| Green cardamom pods | 10 |
| Cloves | 7–8 |
| Bay leaves | 6–7 |
| Mutton | 1 kg |
| Onion paste | 3–4 tbsp |
| Garlic paste | 2 tbsp |
| Ginger paste | 1 tbsp |
| Yoghurt | 1 cup |
| Red chilli powder | 2–3 tsp (or as per taste) |
| Turmeric powder | 2 tsp |
| Coriander powder | 5 tsp |
| Green cardamom powder | 2 tsp |
| Garam masala | 1 tsp |
| Melon seed powder | 2 tbsp (optional) |
| Milk | ½ cup |
| Kewra water | 4–5 drops (optional) |
| Salt | to taste |

METHOD

Heat the ghee in a large saucepan or a round cooking pot. Fry the diced onions till golden then strain and place them on a large plate. Let them cool, then dry grind them and set aside.

In the hot ghee, add the cardamom pods, cloves, and bay leaves.

Immediately add the meat, onion paste, ginger and garlic pastes, yoghurt, and drops of kewra water, if using. Stir well and cook over medium heat for 5 minutes.

Mix turmeric, red chilli, and coriander powders with salt and enough water to make a paste. Put this blend into the cooking pot and stir. Bring to a boil on high heat and let the meat cook for 10 minutes, stirring frequently.

Reduce to medium heat and add 2–3 cups of water. Cover and cook till the meat is tender or about 30 minutes. You may use a pressure cooker for cooking the mutton, but slow-cooked meat tastes better. If using a pressure cooker, only use a cup of water.

Check the meat; it should be tender. Add the melon seed powder and the milk and keep stirring. If the meat is still tough or the gravy looks too thick, add more water and cook until the meat tenderizes.

When most of the liquid has evaporated, add the fried onion paste. Sauté on medium heat. You may add a teaspoon of water in case the curry begins sticking to the bottom of the pot.

When the oil separates from the masala, add hot water to achieve the desired consistency of the gravy. Bring to a boil. Stir and switch off the flame. Serve hot with tandoori roti.

# SAT SAAG

CHINNA AND VINOD DUA                                    DELHI

SERVES: 4                                    PREPARATION TIME: 1 HOUR

INGREDIENTS

| | |
|---|---|
| Kulfa leaves | ½ kg |
| Cauliflower stalks | 4, finely chopped |
| Tomatoes | 100 gms, chopped into large pieces |
| Regular or small aubergine | 50 gms, sliced or chopped into large pieces |
| Okra | 2, halved |

| | |
|---|---|
| Ridge gourd | 50 gms, cut into 1½ inch sizes |
| Bottle gourd | 125 gms, cut into 1½ inch sizes |
| Apple gourd | 50 gms, quartered |
| Colocasia | 50 gms, quartered |
| Potato | 50 gms, quartered |
| Lotus stem | 75 gms, cut into ½-inch-thick rounds |
| White radish | 50 gms, cut into 1½ inch pieces |
| | (leaves to be finely chopped) |
| Slim green chillies | 4, finely chopped |
| Ginger | 25 gms, peeled and finely chopped |
| Whole black peppercorns | ¾ tsp |
| Asafoetida | ¼ tsp |
| Dried seeds of pomegranate | 1½ tsp |
| (or anardana powder) | |
| Whole coriander seeds | 1 tbsp |
| Deggi mirch powder | ½ tsp (optional) |
| Coarse red chilli powder | 1 tsp (optional) |
| Ghee | 1 tbsp |
| Salt | to taste |

METHOD

Wash all the vegetables very well. Drain the water. Cut off a slice of the lotus stem at both ends and wash in running water to clean it completely. Prepare all the ingredients as listed.

Place the greens at the bottom of your cooking pan, followed by the tomatoes and the rest of the veggies. The tomato and the greens will release water on being heated and settle at the bottom, thereby preventing the kulfa from burning and sticking to the base. Add all the spices and herbs. Cook on high heat for 10 minutes till the water is released by the vegetables.

Thereafter cover and cook on low heat for about 30 to 45 minutes.

Check if the tougher vegetables like potato and colocasia are cooked through. Once that happens, uncover the pan and increase the heat. Cook until most of the water has dried out. The end result should be a semi dry dish.

Add the salt now. Mix and taste; adjust seasoning if needed.

To serve, drizzle a tablespoon of ghee on top. One can also heat the ghee, add deggi mirch powder and red chilli powder, and then drizzle on top. Serve piping hot with puri/chapatti/steamed rice.

**Note:** It is best to make this dish with seasonal ingredients. In case of unavailability of one vegetable, it may be replaced with an equal quantity of another. For example, any of the three gourds can replace another. The key ingredient is the kulfa saag, which is available for a very short while in March–April. It is slightly sour and when I make this dish, I omit the tomatoes and cut down on the pomegranate seeds. Spinach is the substitute for the rest of the year.

# GUCCHI AUR SAFED MUSHROOM KI GALOUTI

JYOTSNA SURI                                                      DELHI

SERVES: 4                                    PREPARATION TIME: 1 HOUR

INGREDIENTS

| | |
|---|---|
| Fresh mushroom | 250 gms |
| Dry morel | 5 gms |
| Desi ghee | 30 gms |
| Deggi mirch powder | 4 gms |
| Brown onion paste | 50 gms |
| Brown cashew nut paste | 20 gms |
| Salt | 10 gms, or to taste |
| Yellow chilli powder | 2 gms |
| Green cardamom powder | 2 gms |
| Cardamom water | 5 ml |
| Roasted gram flour | 10 gms |
| Garam masala | 3 gms |
| Saffron | $1/8$ gms diluted in 5 ml water |
| Rose water | 5 ml |
| Turmeric powder | 3 gms |
| Betel root | 1 gm |
| Rose petal powder | 1 gm |
| Sugar | 5 gms |
| Mashed potato | 45 gms |
| Cloves | 2 gms |

METHOD

Wash and blanch mushrooms.

Soak the dry morels in warm water for 10–15 minutes. Then wash under running water to cleanse them of dirt/sand particles.

Finely grind the mushrooms and morels into pastes separately in a blender.

Heat two-thirds of the ghee in a pan and sauté both the mixtures together till all the moisture evaporates.

Add salt and turmeric powder and cook for 5 minutes. Take off heat and let it cool down.

Add to this the mashed potato, roasted gram flour, brown cashew nut paste, brown onion paste, green cardamom powder, yellow chilli powder, garam masala, betel root, rose petal powder, sugar, saffron water, rose water, and kewra water. Mix well with the sautéed mixture to make a smooth paste.

Place this mixture in a bowl. Place a small bowl in the centre of the mixture with small pieces of live charcoal and cloves. Put a couple of drops of melted ghee on the charcoal and tightly cover the larger bowl quickly with silver foil. Leave undisturbed for 8–10 minutes.

Uncover and remove the small bowl. Divide this mixture into patties each weighing 35–40 grams.

Cook these patties on both sides on a hot plate at medium heat greased with a few drops of desi ghee. When the patties are golden brown, take off the heat.

Place the cooked patties on top of sheermal bread and serve with mint sauce, lemon slices, and green chillies.

# BUTTER CHICKEN

SURINA NARULA                                                    DELHI

SERVES: 4                       PREPARATION TIME: 2 HOURS (PLUS 30 MINUTES
                                                       FOR MARINATION)

## INGREDIENTS

|              |                                                    |
| -----------: | -------------------------------------------------- |
| Chicken      | 1 kg, cut into medium size pieces with bones       |

### For the marinade

|                     |              |
| ------------------: | ------------ |
| Full fat yoghurt    | 2 tbsp       |
| Ginger garlic paste | 1 tbsp       |
| Cumin seeds         | 1 tsp        |
| Coriander seeds     | 1 tsp        |
| Red chilli powder   | 1 tsp        |
| Olive oil           | 1 tbsp       |
| Lemon               | half, juiced |
| Salt                | to taste     |

### For the gravy

|                            |                           |
| -------------------------: | ------------------------- |
| Tomatoes                   | 1 kg, roughly chopped     |
| Onion                      | 1 large, roughly chopped  |
| Unsalted butter or olive oil | 50 gms or 1 tbsp        |
| Ginger garlic paste        | 1 tbsp                    |
| Ground cumin seeds         | 1 tsp                     |
| Coriander seeds            | 1 tsp                     |
| Black cardamom pods        | 3, large                  |
| Cinnamon sticks            | 3–4                       |
| Turmeric powder            | ½ tsp                     |
| Red Kashmiri chilli powder | 1 tsp                     |
| Dried fenugreek leaves     | 1 tsp                     |
| Sugar                      | 1 tbsp                    |
| Lemon                      | ½, juiced                 |
| Yoghurt or cream           | 2 tbsp                    |

## METHOD

Mix the marinade ingredients together and massage mixture into the chicken. Leave the chicken covered in the fridge for 30 minutes to marinate.

Remove the marinated chicken from the fridge. Heat the oven to 176°C and grill the chicken pieces until they are cooked through.

Sauté the chopped onion in 50 grams of butter or a tablespoon of olive oil. Add the garlic and ginger paste. Add turmeric and black cardamom and cinnamon sticks.

Add the roughly chopped tomatoes and the red chilli powder and sauté. Add half a cup of water and simmer.

Add the sugar and cumin and coriander powders.

Once it is blanched and cooked let it cool and then put it through a sieve. Put the purée back into the pan.

Add the lemon juice, chicken, and fenugreek leaves and let simmer for 5 minutes. Remove from heat and add the yoghurt or cream. The dish is ready to serve with bread or naan.

## SINDHI KADHI

SHIRIN AND PRIYA PAUL                    DELHI AND SINDH

SERVES: 10–12                    PREPARATION TIME: 1 HOUR

INGREDIENTS

| | |
|---|---|
| Besan | 1½ cups, sieved |
| Fenugreek seeds | 2 tsp |
| Cumin seeds | 3 tsp |
| Asafoetida | ¾ tsp |
| Salt | 4 tsp, or to taste |
| Red chilli powder | 2 tsp |
| Turmeric powder | 1½ tsp |
| Ginger | 1 large piece, grated or finely chopped |
| Kokum flowers | 10–12, soaked in hot water |
| Jaggery or sugar | 1 tbsp |
| Oil | ¾ cup |
| String beans | 8–10, chopped into equal lengths |
| Potatoes | 2–3, diced |
| Drumsticks | 2–3 |
| Okra | 10–15 |
| Carrots | 4 |
| Tamarind water | 2 tbsp |

## METHOD

Heat oil in a large pan and add the asafoetida. When it splutters, add the besan and keep stirring continuously on medium flame for about 10 minutes until the flour is lightly toasted.

Add fenugreek and cumin seeds and fry till light brown (5–6 minutes). Add turmeric, ginger, and red chilli and fry for a minute.

Add 16 cups of water and kokum and leave to boil on high heat. When mixture comes to a boil, add the carrots, potatoes, and drumsticks and let them boil on medium flame (for about ½ hour).

Add okra and beans and cook for 5 minutes. Add salt and jaggery or sugar and a little tamarind water, as per taste.

**Note:** If kokum flowers are unavailable, replace entirely with a lemon-sized ball of tamarind pulp soaked in hot water.

## SAI BHAJI

SHIRIN AND PRIYA PAUL                    DELHI AND SINDH

SERVES: 4                    PREPARATION TIME: 40 MINUTES

(PLUS 30 MINUTES SOAKING TIME)

## INGREDIENTS

| | |
|---|---|
| Split Bengal gram | 2½ tbsp |
| Spinach | 1 bunch |
| Sorrel leaves | 1 bunch |
| Onion | 1, medium size |
| Potato | 1, medium size |
| Tomato | 1, medium size |
| Elephant foot yam and aubergine | few pieces (optional) |
| Dill and fenugreek leaves | handful each |
| Garlic cloves | 12 |
| Ginger | 1 inch piece |
| Turmeric powder | ½ tsp |
| Salt | 1¼ tsp |
| Green chillies | 4 |
| Oil | 2 tbsp |

METHOD

Soak dal in water. Wash all the leafy vegetables and then chop roughly. Chop garlic and ginger finely.

Heat a tablespoon of oil in the pressure cooker and fry half the garlic in this. Add all the vegetables, dal, masalas, and 2 cups water. Close lid of pressure cooker and leave on high heat.

When the cooker whistles, reduce flame and leave the cooker on the heat for 15 minutes. Then, take off the heat.

Once the cooker has cooled down, open and thoroughly mix the bhaji.

Fry the remaining garlic in the remaining oil in a small pan and add on top before serving. If you want to take the easy way out, fry all the garlic initially and proceed in the same fashion.


# FRESH FIGS POACHED IN RED WINE

MANJARI AND LALIT NIRULA                                    DELHI

SERVES: 4                              PREPARATION TIME: 30 MINUTES

INGREDIENTS

| | | |
|---|---|---|
| Fresh figs | 8 |
| Red wine | ½ litre (2 cups) |
| Sugar | 50 gms (4 tbsp) |
| Lemon | 1, rind only |
| Vanilla extract | 1 tbsp |

METHOD

Wash the figs and cut off the stem, but not entirely. Cut them into quarters, but not all the way through so the quarters stay together. Arrange them in a saucepan in which they fit snugly. Add the sugar, lemon rind, and red wine. The figs should be barely covered with the red wine. They may float a little.

Bring to a boil. Turn off the heat as soon as the wine boils. Then allow the figs to cool off in the hot wine. This will poach the figs. Take the figs out of the wine as soon as they have cooled off. Sieve the wine into another pan. Bring the wine to a boil to burn off the remaining alcohol and concentrate the flavour into a sauce.

Serve the figs with this sauce.

# PANAUCHA

ADVAITA KALA                                                    DELHI

SERVES: 4                          PREPARATION TIME: 1 HOUR 15 MINUTES
                                      (PLUS 30 MINUTES SOAKING TIME)

INGREDIENTS

| | |
|---|---|
| Yellow moong dal | 500 gms |
| Whole coriander seeds | 4 tbsp |
| Asafoetida | ¼ tsp |
| Black cardamom seeds | 4 |
| Cloves | 8 |
| Cinnamon stick | 2, 2 inches long |
| Black pepper | 2 tsp |
| Bay leaves | 6 |
| Oil | enough for cooking |
| Red chilli powder | to taste |
| Salt | to taste |

METHOD

Soak the dal in water for at least 30 minutes.

Roughly grind the dal leaving the texture granular.

Grind all the masalas and add to the dal.

Heat cooking oil in a pan and cook the dal over a low flame till the consistency is dry and it becomes dough-like and binds with itself.

Spread the dal out on a flat baking tray and leave to cool.

Heat oil in a deep pan. Cut the cooled dal into rectangular or circular shapes and deep fry.

Add the pieces to any gravy of your choice. Please keep in mind that the panaucha absorbs a lot of gravy so make an adequate quantity of gravy.

# DRIED FRUIT IN ORANGE SAUCE WITH CUSTARD

RATI AND DHRUV SAWHNEY                                    DELHI

SERVES: 4–6                    PREPARATION TIME: 1 HOUR (PLUS OVERNIGHT
                                                 SOAKING TIME)

INGREDIENTS

| | |
|---|---|
| Dried figs | 12 |
| Dried apricots | 12 |
| Munakka | 20 |
| Raisins | ¼ cup |
| Orange juice | 1½ litres |

METHOD

Soak all the dried fruits in orange juice and leave in the fridge overnight. Remove the fruit and set aside.

Take the soaking liquid and place in a saucepan on medium-heat. Let this reduce until the liquid has achieved a sauce-like consistency.

To serve, spoon the cinnamon custard* in serving glasses. Top with some of the dried fruit and then drizzle the orange sauce on top.

## *HOMEMADE CUSTARD BY CHAND SUR

INGREDIENTS

| | |
|---|---|
| Full-fat milk | ½ litres |
| Vanilla extract | ½ tsp |
| Egg yolks | 5, room temperature |
| Golden caster sugar | 1 cup |
| Cinnamon powder | 1 tsp |

METHOD

Pour full-fat milk into a heavy-based saucepan. Just before it reaches boiling point, remove from the flame. Set aside. Put egg yolks into a large bowl with the caster sugar. Whisk by hand until thick and pale. Pour the vanilla-infused milk over the whisked egg yolk and sugar mixture, stirring constantly. Return the pan to a low heat and let it cook slowly, stirring continuously with a wooden spoon, until the custard is thick enough to coat the back of the spoon, for about 8-10 minutes.

Mix in the cinnamon powder. Custard is ready.

Let it cool, then refrigerate. Serve cold.

# DHANSAKH WITH BROWN RICE AND KACHUMBER

FRENNY BILLIMORIA                                                    DELHI

SERVES: 6–8                              PREPARATION TIME: 2 HOURS

INGREDIENTS

For the dhansakh

| | |
|---|---|
| Mutton leg or shoulder | 960 gms |
| or | |
| Chicken (not broiler) | 1½ kg jointed, cut into 2 inch pieces on the bone |

For boiling

| | |
|---|---|
| Pigeon peas | 210 gms |
| Red lentils | 60 gms |
| Black grams | 30 gms |
| Bengal gram | 30 gms |
| Red pumpkin | 200 gms, cubed |
| Aubergine | 1 small, cubed |
| Potatoes | 2 medium, cubed |
| Onion | 1 medium, chopped |
| Ginger paste | 1 tbsp |
| Garlic paste | 1 tbsp |
| Green chillies | 4, de-seeded |
| Fenugreek leaves | 1, small bunch |
| Turmeric powder | 1 tsp |
| Chilli powder | 1 tsp |

| | |
|---|---|
| Cumin powder | 1 tsp |
| Coriander powder | 1 tbsp |
| Dhansakh masala powder | 1 tbsp |
| Green cardamom pods | 2, crushed |
| Cinnamon | 1 inch stick |

## For frying

| | |
|---|---|
| Ghee | 3 tbsp |
| Onion | 2 large, sliced |
| Ginger paste | 1 tsp |
| Garlic paste | 1tsp |
| Turmeric powder | 1 tsp |
| Green chillies | 2, de-seeded and finely chopped |
| Dhansakh masala powder | 2 tbsp |
| Chilli powder | 1 tsp |
| Black pepper powder | ½ tsp |
| Clove powder | ¼tsp |
| Cinnamon powder | ½ tsp |
| Cardamom powder | ½ tsp |
| Cumin powder | 1 tsp |
| Tomatoes | 2 medium-sized, chopped |
| Jaggery | 2 tbsp walnut-sized, crumbled |
| Salt | to taste |

## For brown rice

| | |
|---|---|
| Rice (Basmati) | 750 gms |
| Ghee | 2 tbsp |
| Onions | 2, finely sliced |
| Cloves | 6 |
| Cinnamon | 1 inch stick |
| Black cardamom pods | 2, split |
| Green cardamom pods | 3, split |
| Whole peppercorns | 6 |
| Bay leaves | 2 |
| Sugar | 1 tsp |

## For garnish

| | |
|---|---|
| Onions | ½ cup, sliced and fried |
| Raisins | 1 tbsp, fried |

| | |
|---|---|
| Almonds/cashew nuts | 1 tbsp, fried |

For kachumber

| | |
|---|---|
| Onions | 4, chopped |
| Tomatoes | 4, chopped (same size as onions) |
| Green chillies | 3, deseeded and chopped |
| Coriander leaves | 1½ tbsp, chopped |
| Vinegar | 1½ tbsp |
| Sugar | to taste |
| Salt | to taste |
| Raw mango (if in season) | 1, chopped finely |

METHOD

First, begin preparing the dhansakh. Wash the meat and dals thoroughly.

Place the meat in a pot with enough water to cover. To this, add all the ingredients listed under 'for boiling'; bring this pot to a boil. Cook until the meat is tender.

While the meat cooks, wash the rice and soak in water for half an hour. Strain and leave to drain for 15 minutes.

Remove the meat and reserve. Pass the boiling liquid with the dal through a strainer so the dal becomes almost paste-like. Set aside and discard residue.

Heat ghee in a wok. Add onions to this and fry till golden blown. Add ginger and garlic paste and fry for a minute.

Add all the other ingredients under 'for frying' and fry on a low flame till the ghee floats to the top. Add jaggery and taste for salt. Add this to the dal. Put the meat back into the dal and bring to a boil, then take off the heat.

For the brown rice, heat ghee in a large pan and add the sliced onions and fry them till golden brown.

Add cloves, cinnamon, cardamom pods, peppercorns, and bay leaves and fry for a minute on low heat.

Add sugar and let it caramelize until it turns a rich brown colour. Then add four cups of hot water and bring to a boil.

Add rice and cook covered over low heat till the rice is done and all the water has been absorbed.

While the rice cooks, prepare the kachumber by mixing all the listed ingredients together.

Serve the rice in a flat dish and sprinkle with fried onions and dried fruits alongside the dhansakh (reheat if needed) and kachumber.

# CHICKEN KEBABS

CHARU GUPTA ABRAHAM                                                    DELHI

SERVES: 4                              PREPARATION TIME: 1 HOUR 10 MINUTES
                                                       (PLUS SOAKING TIME)

INGREDIENTS

| | |
|---|---|
| Split chickpea lentils | 1 cup |
| Refined oil | 2–3 tsp |
| Cumin seeds | 1 tsp |
| Cloves | 7–8 |
| Black peppercorns | 7–8 |
| Cinnamon | 2 sticks |
| Coriander seeds | 2 tsp |
| Caraway seeds | 1 tsp |
| Whole red chillies | 3 |
| Chilli flakes | ½ tsp |
| Boneless chicken thighs | 500 gms (or 250 gms boneless chicken + 300 gms chicken thigh pieces) |
| Salt | 1 tsp |
| Ginger | 2 tsp, finely chopped |
| Green chillies | 2 |
| Onion | 1 medium sized, finely chopped |
| Garlic | 3 tsp, finely chopped |
| Coriander leaves | ½ cup, chopped |
| Mint leaves | ¼ cup, chopped |
| Eggs | 2, small (or 1 large) |
| Lemon juice | around 2–3 tsp |

METHOD

Wash the dal thoroughly and soak in water for approximately 1 hour, or at least 30 minutes. The soaking water will be also used to cook the dal.

In a pressure cooker heat oil and add cumin seeds, cloves, black peppercorns, cinnamon, coriander seeds, caraway seeds, whole red chillies, and chilli flakes. Sauté for 1–2 minutes.

Now add the soaked lentils with the water in which it was soaked and mix thoroughly.

Add the chicken pieces and salt. Bring to a simmer, adding a cup of water or enough to just cover the chicken pieces. Too much water might make the kebabs very mushy.

Pressure cook for two or three whistles. Let the pressure drop and open the cooker. Remove the chicken pieces (remove the meat from the bones if using chicken with bones and discard the bones) and set aside. Cook the dal in the cooker until all the water from the cooker has evaporated.

Let this cool for some time and then grind all the ingredients (from the cooker and the chicken pieces) to a thick paste.

To this paste add ginger, green chilli, garlic, coriander leaves, finely chopped onion, lemon juice, and mint leaves. Mix all the ingredients to combine well.

Now add the eggs and mix thoroughly. This will help in holding the kebab shape and also add to the taste.

Using your palm make the kebabs into the desired shape and size. Generally they are made into flat roundels.

Refrigerate the kebabs for at least for half an hour. This helps the kebabs hold their shape and prevents them from breaking while shallow frying. At this stage, the kebabs can also be frozen for two–three weeks for use later; they will simply need to be thawed before frying.

When it is time to serve, shallow fry the kebabs in a pan on both sides until they are golden brown. Serve hot with green coriander and mint chutney.

**Note:**
You may adjust the salt and chilli powder amount as per your taste. The caraway seeds can be omitted if not available.

The mint leaves should not be very bitter. There are many varieties available, so please taste them to check the bitterness level.

The ground paste should not be very moist or wet.

If you don't want your kebabs to taste eggy, only use egg white.


# PEANUT ROAST

AARYAMAN BHATI                                                    JODHPUR

SERVES: 4–6                          PREPARATION TIME: 1 HOUR 15 MINUTES

INGREDIENTS

| | | |
|---|---|---|
| Whole unsalted peanuts | 240 gms, shelled | |
| Onions | 2, medium size | |
| Tomatoes | 4 large | |
| Dessert apples | 2 small | |
| Cashew nuts | 1 tbsp | |
| Neutral oil | 4 tbsp, plus extra for greasing | |
| Oats (rolled or quick cook) | 30 gms | |
| Fresh sage or thyme | 4 tsp, chopped | |
| Salt and pepper | to taste | |
| Egg | 1 | |
| Milk | 2 tbsp or as needed | |

METHOD

Preheat oven to 180°C. Grease a 1-pound loaf tin generously with oil.

Finely chop, mince, or grind the peanuts and cashew nuts, separately. Chop the onions and skin, deseed, and chop the tomatoes. Peel, core, and dice the apples.

Heat the oil in a pan, add the onions, fresh tomatoes, and apples and fry until softened.

Add the peanuts, cashew nuts, oats, tomatoes, sage, or thyme, and salt and pepper to taste.

Add the egg and just enough milk to bind all the ingredients. The final product should have a moist consistency but shouldn't be wet.

Press into the loaf tin so the roast is the same thickness throughout.

Bake in the preheated oven for 45 minutes or until the top is evenly browned. Insert a wooden skewer or toothpick in the centre; if it comes out clean, then the roast is ready.

Serve hot with a stew/soup of your choice or at room temperature with a green salad.


# MALPUA

CHAND SUR                    MULTAN, QUETTA, LAHORE, AND LUCKNOW

SERVES: 4                              PREPARATION TIME: 1 HOUR 10 MINUTES

INGREDIENTS

| | |
|---|---|
| All-purpose flour | 1 cup |
| Khoya | 1 cup, grated |
| Ghee | 6 tbsp |
| Cardamom powder | $1/3$ tsp |
| Fresh yoghurt | 3 tbsp |
| Sugar syrup | 4 cups |
| Pistachios | 10, blanched and thinly sliced |
| Almonds | 8, blanched and thinly sliced |
| Saffron | few strands |

METHOD

Warm 1½ cups of water to approximately 60–70°C. Mix with the flour to form a smooth batter.

Mix the khoya and flour batter together to form a smooth, thick batter.

Mix in the yoghurt and let it rest for 30 to 40 minutes.

Melt ghee in a pan. Cook on low heat for a a few minutes.

Add a tablespoon of batter in a circular motion in the centre of the hot ghee. Put some more spoonfuls around the centre.

When one side of the malpuas are set, turn them over, one at a time, so that the other side gets cooked. Cook for while till the edges start turning red.

Remove from the ghee and dip the malpuas in the sugar syrup.

Take them out after about 10 minutes, and layer them on a plate.
Garnish with almonds, pistachios, and saffron.

**Note:** Sugar syrup is made with combining equal parts of sugar with water. Let it simmer and cook on a low to medium flame until the sugar has dissolved. Till it is used, keep the pan of sugar syrup in a larger pan filled with hot water so that it does not congeal.


# SUNEHRE BAINGAN

MADHAVI KUCKREJA AND
ASKARI NAQVI

LUCKNOW, UTTAR PRADESH

SERVES: 4–6

PREPARATION TIME: 30 MINUTES

## INGREDIENTS

| | |
|---|---|
| Aubergine | 500 gms, medium size long variety, quartered |
| Oil | 100 ml |
| Tamarind pulp | 50 gms |
| Roasted poppy seeds | 20 gms |
| Roasted white sesame seeds | 20 gms |
| Roasted peanuts | 25 gms |
| Roasted coconut powder | 25 gms |
| Turmeric powder | ½ tsp |
| Red chilli powder | ½ tsp |
| Garlic paste | 2 tbsp |
| Curry leaves | 10–11 |
| Whole dried red chilli | 1 |
| Salt | to taste |

## METHOD

Heat oil in a pan. Add curry leaves, whole red chilli, garlic paste, turmeric powder, red chilli powder. Fry for 2 minutes on a low flame, then take off heat.

Heat a heavy-bottomed pan or wok, and add the masala powders to it. Add the chopped aubergine and salt and stir. Cook for 2 minutes on medium heat.

Add tamarind pulp and cook for 5 minutes more, or until the aubergine is cooked through. Taste and adjust seasoning if needed.

Serve hot with steamed rice.

# PEARLY LUCKNOW FIRNI

NASIMA AZIZ                                          LUCKNOW, UTTAR PRADESH

SERVES: 4–6                                          PREPARATION TIME: 1 HOUR

INGREDIENTS

| | |
|---|---|
| Basmati rice | ¼ cup |
| Whole milk | 6 cups (1½ litres) |
| Sugar | 1 cup |
| Green cardamom | 2–3 |
| Green pistachios | 6–8 |
| Silver leaf | 3–4 sheets |
| Shallow earthenware saucers | 15–20 |

METHOD

Soak the saucers in cold water for an hour, wash lightly; allow to drain and dry—this removes any dust and dirt. If earthenware saucers are not available, use any small dessert bowls.

Soak the rice in water for 10 minutes; drain; spread on a tea towel for 20 minutes to dry out. Grind in a clean coffee grinder till it looks like a powder but feels grainy.

Powder the cardamom seeds. Have everything measured out and ready because you will be stirring non-stop.

Put the milk in a large pan and bring to a boil; reduce to low boil—even while stirring constantly, the surface of the milk should be bubbling gently. Take a spoon of ground rice and scatter it over the surface of the milk, stirring constantly; repeat till all the ground rice has been added. Stir on low boil about 12 minutes. At this point the powdered rice should look like translucent and swollen dots.

Add the sugar and continue to cook. The mixture thins slightly as the sugar dissolves, and then thickens even more than earlier; the rice dots swell up even more. By the end of 10 minutes, the rice dots will be evenly spread through the liquid and it will look like a loose paste. It will bubble hard in the centre but it should not leave the sides of the pan—that would be over-cooking it. Remember that it will thicken further while cooling. Remove the pan from the stove and stir in the cardamom powder.

Continue stirring till cool. Don't go away. This is a crucial stage. As you are stirring you have to (a) judge if you have allowed it to become too thick—correct this mistake by stirring in a tablespoon or two of milk; (b) judge the right stage to pour it into the earthenware saucers—if the mixture has cooled and thickened too much, it will not set with a smooth top and it will look lumpy.

Garnish with pistachio and silver leaf before it sets so that the garnish sticks. After several hours, when it is fully set and cold, even if you turn it upside down the firni will not fall!

# KALI GAJAR KA HALWA

NASIMA AZIZ                                    LUCKNOW, UTTAR PRADESH

SERVES: 3                                    PREPARATION TIME: 45 MINUTES

INGREDIENTS

| | |
|---|---|
| Grated black carrots | 250 gms, (weigh after grating) |
| Whole milk | ½ litre |
| Ghee | 1 tbsp, heaped |
| Green cardamom pods | 2 |
| Sugar | ¾ cup |
| Silver leaf | 1 sheet |
| Cream | to serve |

Place the grated carrots in a non-stick pan on low heat. Let some excess water evaporate, then add the milk and cook on high heat without the lid for a few minutes. Cover and cook on medium heat till the carrots are completely soft. Remove the lid, stir and mash to a purée with the back of the spoon, while the milk reduces.

When the milk has been completely absorbed, make a space in the middle, add the ghee and cardamom pods and let them sizzle. Stir the mixture till the ghee shows at the sides. Add the sugar for a Lucknow-standard sweetness, or remove one-eighth of a cup. Stir just till the sugar melts and gets absorbed.

Transfer to a serving dish and garnish with silver leaf (chandi ka warq). Serve warm or at room temperature, with cream.

**Note:** To make a large quantity use 2 kg carrots before grating, 2 litres milk, 1½ kg sugar, and 200 gms ghee.


# CHANEY KI DAL KA HALWA

NASIMA AZIZ                                      LUCKNOW, UTTAR PRADESH

SERVES: 4                      PREPARATION TIME: 2 HOURS (PLUS 1 HOUR
                                                          SOAKING TIME)


INGREDIENTS

First stage

| | | |
|---|---|---|
| Split Bengal gram | 1⅓ cups | |
| Whole milk | 2⅓ cups | |

Second stage

| | |
|---|---|
| Melted ghee | 1 cup |
| Green cardamom pods | 4 |
| Pureéd dal | from the first stage |
| Sugar (fine) | 2 cups |
| Saffron | 1 pinch, dissolved in 1 tbsp milk |
| Almonds | 2 tbsp, finely slivered |
| Silver leaf | 2 sheets |

METHOD

Wash the dal well, cover with cold water and let it soak for one hour so that it starts to swell. Drain thoroughly.

Put the dal and milk in a wide, shallow pan on medium-high heat, stirring till it is very well heated all the way through and almost comes to a boil; then lower the heat and simmer. After about fifteen minutes, check a grain of dal—it should be tender enough to squash almost completely when you press it. When most of the milk has been absorbed, use the ladle to push the dal back and forth, and help the rest of the milk to get absorbed/evaporated; do not let your attention wander. When the dal looks as though it is coated lightly with a white paste, take the pan off the heat. If you are planning on grinding the dal the traditional way by using a grinding stone, you can let all the liquid evaporate from the mixture. Otherwise, there should be about a tablespoon of thickened milk visible.

Purée the cooked dal in a blender/food processor. If your grinder blades won't move due to the dal's dry texture, add a little milk, the minimum amount possible. Don't aim for a completely smooth texture at this stage; any small lumps will disappear later.

In the same pan (that has been washed and dried), warm the ghee gently. Add the cardamom pods and let them sizzle for a few seconds.

Add the dal purée to the pan. Cook on medium heat, stirring constantly. To start with, the mixture will be very soft. But it will thicken gradually, making it harder and harder to stir, till all you are doing is pushing it back and forth in the pan. The colour will deepen as well. After 10–15 minutes of stirring, you will be able to see a few bubbles of ghee at the edges. Don't stop stirring until the ghee bubbles ring the mixture and glaze the surface. By now the mixture should be drastically reduced in volume. When it begins looking golden and shiny and starts giving off a toasted smell, mix in the sugar and continue cooking for approximately another 15–20 minutes with non-stop stirring. At first the mixture will become looser as the sugar releases its water, but it will soon thicken again and the colour will deepen further. Large bubbles will pop on its smooth and glossy surface.

Add the saffron soaked in milk at any point (the timing is not critical). There are a few ways to tell if the halwa is ready: when you make a line using a spoon on the surface of halwa, it does not immediately disappear; the mixture comes away from the sides; there is a kind of mesh formation that appears briefly as you turn the mixture. You may drop a pellet of the mixture in a cup of water to cool it, then try to roll it into a ball shape. You have to stop cooking when the mesh formation appears and the pellet feels as though it will retain its shape.

Turn the halwa onto a thali or baking tray that has been well greased with ghee, and press to form a layer, about an inch thick. Smooth the surface with the greased base of a steel katori, or the greased flat of a knife. Scatter the finely slivered almonds over the surface and pat them in gently so that they stick. Allow to cool. Garnish with silver leaf; then cut into neat squares with a sharp knife. The surface of the halwa should be firm and the inside should be mealy with a mellow flavour. If you took it off the heat too soon, it will be too soft to cut, and you will have to eat it with a spoon—but it will taste just as fabulous! The amount of ghee used in this recipe almost eliminates the danger of it turning rock hard with overcooking.

# KALI KANJI

VANDANA AND YOGESH NARAIN — LUCKNOW, UTTAR PRADESH

SERVES: 6 — PREPARATION TIME: 1 WEEK

INGREDIENTS

| | |
|---|---|
| Black carrots | 1 kg |
| Water | 4 cups |
| White salt | 2 tsp |
| Black salt | 2 tsp |
| Kashmiri red chilli powder | 1 tsp |
| Small mustard seeds | 150 gms, powdered |

METHOD

Scrape the carrots cut into 3-inch pieces lengthwise Boil the water, add the cut carrots and half boil. Let it cool completely. Now add white salt, black salt, Kashmiri chilli powder and mustard powder. Mix and keep in sun for about a week covered with a muslin cloth. Kanji is ready to drink

## DAHI WALA KUKKAR

VEENA OLDENEBERG                              LUCKNOW, UTTAR PRADESH

SERVES: 4–6                          PREPARATION TIME: 1 HOUR 15 MINUTES

INGREDIENTS

| | |
|---|---|
| Free-range chicken | 1 kg, plucked and skinned, cut into 8 pieces |
| Onions | 1 kg, cut into thin rings |
| Ginger | 1 inch piece, chopped finely |
| Red chilli powder (deggi mirch) | 1 tbsp |
| Green cardamom | 6, ground to powder |
| Black pepper | 2 tsp, freshly ground |
| Full cream yoghurt | 1 cup, beaten in with 3 tbsp water (like a thick lassi) |
| Pure ghee | 1 cup |
| Salt | to taste |

METHOD

Heat the ghee in a large wok. Take half of the onions and fry them until crisp and brown. Remove the fried onions and set aside on newspapers or paper towels. Repeat this with the remaining onions.

Add the ginger and the chicken to the wok and brown them together till the flesh of the chicken is no longer pink. Check the drumsticks and the breast pieces with a fork to make sure that they are cooked through.

Add the black pepper, red chilli powder, and cardamom powder to the chicken and mix thoroughly. Sautée some more till the chicken is browned. The dish should smell strongly of cardamom and pepper. If this is not the case, add more of the spices.

Now stir in the yoghurt lassi. Cover and cook for about twenty minutes to half an hour until the chicken is perfectly tender.

Crumble the fried onions on the cooked chicken and mix. Serve in a silver serving dish with a lid.

# BHUNE PASANDE

RITA LAL MATHUR

LUCKNOW, UTTAR PRADESH

SERVES: 4

PREPARATION TIME: 1 HOUR (PLUS 1 HOUR<br>MARINATION TIME)

## INGREDIENTS

| | |
|---|---|
| Pasande (thin strips of pounded prime mutton) | 500 gms |
| Raw papaya paste | 1 tbsp |
| Oil or ghee | ½ cup |
| Onions | 3 medium, finely sliced |
| Onions | 3 large, finely chopped |
| Garlic paste | 1 tbsp |
| Ginger paste | 1 tbsp |
| Green cardamom powder | a pinch |
| Coriander powder | 2 tsp |
| Kashmiri red chilli powder | ½ tsp |
| Dry roasted cumin powder | big pinch |
| Garam masala powder | ¼ tsp |
| Salt | to taste |
| Yoghurt | 1 cup, well beaten |
| Cashew nut paste | 2 tbsp |
| Mint leaves | 2 tbsp, chopped almonds and chopped blanched and slivered, coriander leaves for garnishing |

### For the sabut garam masala

| | |
|---|---|
| Cloves | 4 |
| Black cardamom pods | 2 |
| Bay leaves | 2 |
| Green cardamom pods | 3 |
| Peppercorns | 5 |

METHOD

Wash and pat dry the pasande and marinate in papaya paste and ½ teaspoon salt for an hour.

Heat oil in a pressure cooker or heavy bottom pan. When the oil is hot, add the sabut garam masalas and the sliced onions. Briskly fry for 6–7 minutes till golden brown then add the marinated pasande, stirring the bottom and sides of the pan, so masala doesn't stick, for a few minutes.

Lower the heat and cover for 10 minutes, but keep stirring every 2 minutes. Now add the chopped onions, garlic and ginger pastes and fry for 7–8 minutes. Keep sprinkling a little water if the masala starts sticking.

Add coriander, roasted jeera, red chilli, and cardamom powders. For a few minutes then add the chopped mint leaves. Stir well.

Gradually add yoghurt and cashew paste and stir well for 4–5 minutes. Add 4–5 tablespoons water and garam masala powder and salt to taste. Put heat on low, put lid on, and cook for 8–9 minutes. Switch off heat and let the meat rest for 10 minutes.

Garnish with slivered almonds and chopped coriander leaves and serve.

**Note:** All spice measurements can be tweaked a bit as per one's liking.

# PETHA KHEER

INDIRA BAPTISTA GUPTA                    LUCKNOW, UTTAR PRADESH

SERVES: 6                                      PREPARATION TIME: 1 HOUR

INGREDIENTS

| | |
|---|---|
| Full cream milk | 1½ litres |
| Meetha petha | ½ kg, grated |
| Paneer (see Kalakand recipe for steps if required) | made from ½ litre milk |
| Green cardamom powder | ½ tsp |
| Saffron | few threads |
| Any dry fruits (almonds, cashews, walnuts, pistachios, or raisins) | a fistful, fried in desi ghee and chopped |

METHOD

Boil milk with saffron and cardamom powder until it thickens and is a quarter of its original quantity. Allow to cool slightly.

Add petha and boil for a few minutes. Don't add petha to boiling milk—this will cause the milk to curdle. Take the milk off the flame and let cool slightly, add the petha, and then boil again.

Take off the heat and add the saffron and dry fruits while the milk is still hot.

Stir well and serve.

# HIMALAYAN TERAI PASANDA

MEERA AND MUZAFFAR ALI          FOOTHILLS OF THE HIMALAYAS,
                                                    UTTAR PRADESH

SERVES: 4–6          PREPARATION TIME: 2 HOURS (PLUS MARINATION TIME)

INGREDIENTS

| | |
|---|---|
| Mutton leg (raan) | 1 kg, sliced |
| Ghee or equivalent neutral cooking oil | 250 gms |
| Yoghurt | 200 gms |
| Roasted chickpeas | 150 gms, ground to a dry powder |
| Onions | 1 kg, chopped |
| Ginger garlic paste | 150 gms |
| Whole red chillies | 4–5 medium size |
| Garam masala | 1½ tsp |
| Coriander seeds | 1½ tsp |
| Cloves | 2 |
| Kewra water | 10–12 drops |
| Salt | to taste |

For the marinade

| | |
|---|---|
| Raw papaya | 100 gms, minced |
| Salt | ½ tsp |

To smoke the meat

| | |
|---|---|
| Cooking coal | as needed |
| Banana leaf/onion skin | as needed |
| Ghee | 1 tsp |

For the garnish

| | | |
|---|---|---|
| Mint | 5–6 sprigs |
| Onion | 1 medium size, sliced into rings |

METHOD

Make the marinade by adding ½ teaspoon salt to the minced raw papaya. Cover the mutton with this paste and set aside to marinate in the refrigerator for at least an hour in the summers and 3 hours in winter.

Dry roast the red chillies and coriander seeds in a frying pan. Then grind them and set aside.

Heat cooking oil in a pan. Fry the chopped onions in the pan until they are golden brown. Add the meat and fry for 20 minutes. Then add salt, yoghurt, chickpea powder, garam masala, ginger garlic paste, and the dry roasted red chilli and coriander mixture.

Keep frying on very low heat for at least an hour or till the meat is tender. Add kewra water. Taste and adjust seasoning.

Right before serving, take a small steel bowl and place burning coal in it along with two cloves. Place this bowl on a washed banana leaf or the skin of an onion in the cauldron containing the meat dish.

Drop 1 tsp of ghee on this burning coal. As it begins to smoke, cover the pan with a lid. Keep the dish covered for 15 minutes.

Garnish with raw onion rings and fresh green mint leaves just before serving.

# BAKED EGG HALWA

NISHAT SIDDIQUI                                         LUCKNOW, UTTAR PRADESH

SERVES: 4–6                                               PREPARATION TIME: 1 HOUR

INGREDIENTS

| | |
|---|---|
| Eggs | 250 gms |
| Khoya | 250 gms |
| Sugar | 225 gms |
| Ghee | 125 gms |
| Cardamom powder | ½-1 tsp |

## METHOD

For the halwa, heat ghee with cardamom powder and set aside to cool. Grease a baking dish generously with ghee or butter. Preheat oven to 180°C.

Beat the eggs until slightly fluffy, then add in khoya and sugar. Mix well to combine.

Add the cardamom-ghee to this and mix. Pour in greased dish and bake in preheated oven for 30–35 minutes or until the top of the halwa appears set and a wooden skewer inserted into the halwa comes out clean.


# SEMOLINA HALVAH

## (TURKISH SUJI KA HALWA)

SERAN AND RAVI TREHAN

LUCKNOW, UTTAR PRADESH

SERVES: 6

PREPARATION TIME: 30 MINUTES

### INGREDIENTS

| | |
|---|---|
| Semolina (suji) | ½ kg |
| Pine nuts | 2 tbsp |
| Sugar | 600 gms |
| Butter | 100 gms |
| Milk | 4 glasses |
| Orange rind | ¼ |
| Lemon rind | ½ |
| Cinnamon sticks | 2 small, powdered |

### METHOD

Roast pine nuts in 2 tablespoons of melted butter. Melt the rest of the butter, add the semolina and stir with a wooden spoon. Boil milk separately. When semolina is roasted, add rind of lemon and orange. Stir and add the boiled milk. When semolina absorbs the milk, add sugar and stir. Cook over low heat. When the sugar is also absorbed, stir and place on a serving plate. Sprinkle powdered cinnamon and serve hot.

# RAS KI KHEER/RASAWAAL

JIMMY JAHANGIRABAD

LUCKNOW, UTTAR PRADESH

SERVES: 4–6

PREPARATION TIME: 1 HOUR

INGREDIENTS

| | |
|---|---|
| Fresh sugarcane juice | 3 litres |
| Jeera Samba or Basmati rice | 250 gms (soaked for 15 minutes and drained) |
| Raw peanuts | ¾ cup, freshly roasted |
| Mixed pine nuts, almonds, and raisins | ¾ cup, slivered |
| Desiccated coconut | 2 tbsp |

METHOD

Put the previously well-sieved cane juice in a heavy bottomed pan and bring to a boil on a medium flame. After a while, a foam shall start forming on the top. Keep removing this froth by bringing to a boil two or three times, or till no foam forms. This will give clarity and a better colour to the kheer.

When the juice has relative clarity, add the rice and cook on a low flame till it is tender.

Then blend the rice and juice properly with a wooden spoon, still on a low flame. Finally take off the heat and add in the peanuts. This is what is used traditionally. You may choose to add slivered pine nuts, almonds, and raisins, topped with 2 tablespoons of desiccated coconut before serving.

# QEEMA LAL MIRCH

SHEEBA IQBAL JAIRAJPURI

LUCKNOW, UTTAR PRADESH

SERVES: 4–6

PREPARATION TIME: 1 HOUR 15 MINUTES

## INGREDIENTS

| | |
|---|---|
| Hand-pounded mutton mince | 1 kg |
| Red mini sweet peppers | ½ kg |
| Onions | 150 gms |
| Cumin seeds | 1 tsp |
| Dry red chillies | 5 |
| Ginger paste | 2 tsp |
| Black pepper powder | ½ tsp |
| Amchur powder | 1 tsp |
| Oil | 150 ml |
| Garam masala powder | 1 tsp |
| Salt | to taste |

## METHOD

Heat oil in a pressure cooker. Add cumin seeds, onions, and dry red chillies.

Take the onions and red chillies out and crush them with a rolling pin. Set aside.

In the leftover oil in the pressure cooker, add the mince and salt. Sauté it for a few minutes, then add ginger paste, the crushed onions and chillies, and black pepper powder. Cover and cook it for three whistles.

Open the lid and roast the mince until browned. Add the amchur powder and garam masala and mix. Take off heat and cool.

Slit the red peppers and stuff them with the cooked qeema once it cools.

There will be leftover mince. Arrange the stuffed peppers on top of the qeema and cook uncovered for a few minutes, until the peppers are hot.

Serve in an open dish.

# GALAWAT KE KEBAB

SHEEBA IQBAL JAIRAJPURI                    LUCKNOW, UTTAR PRADESH

SERVES: 4                                  PREPARATION TIME: 1 HOUR 15 MINUTES
                                           (PLUS 1 HOUR MARINATION TIME)

INGREDIENTS

| | |
|---|---|
| Mutton (mince) | 125 gms |
| Raw papaya | 50 gms |
| Ghee or oil | 25 gms |
| Coriander seeds | 10 gms |
| Cumin seeds | 5 gms |
| Green cardamom pods | 3 |
| Black cardamom pods | 1 |
| Red chilli whole | 7 |
| Cinnamon | 5 gms |
| Roasted gram flour | 75 gms |
| Mace | 3 gms |
| Cloves | 5 |
| Nutmeg | 1½ |
| Charcoal pieces | 2 |
| Salt | to taste |

METHOD

Grind raw papaya into a fine paste.

Sauté coriander and cumin seeds, green and black cardamom pods, red chillies, cinnamon, mace, nutmeg, and three cloves in a pan on low flame and then finely grind.

Mix mince mutton, salt, and raw papaya paste. Keep it aside to marinate for 1 hour.

Mix all ingredients except charcoal, a couple of cloves, and ghee.

Place the mixture in a large pan. Now put a small steel bowl with burning charcoal, two cloves, and a teaspoon of ghee in the centre of the pan. Cover the pan with the lid.

Divide the mixture into eight equal balls and press each between the palms of your hands to flatten.

Heat a pan on low flame and add ghee. Shallow fry patties for 4 minutes on each side.

Serve hot with paratha and onion rings.

# DAHI CHICKEN

ZOHRAVAR SINGH BHATI

LUCKNOW, UTTAR PRADESH

SERVES: 8

PREPARATION TIME: 1 HOUR
(PLUS 6 HOURS MARINATION TIME)

INGREDIENTS

| | |
|---|---|
| Chicken | 1 kg, cut into 12 pieces |
| Yoghurt | 1 kg |
| Onions | 1 kg, grated |
| Ginger | 2-inch piece, finely julienned |
| All-purpose flour | 1 tbsp |
| Cloves | 4 |
| Whole black peppercorns | 8 |
| Whole dried red chilli | 6 |
| Black cardamom pods | 2 |
| Cinnamon | 2 sticks, each broken in half |
| Kashmiri red chilli powder | 2 tbsp |
| Ghee | 4 tbsp |
| Salt | 1 tsp or to taste |

METHOD

Beat the yoghurt and mix it in with the chicken. Sprinkle the flour over this mixture. Mix well and let it marinate in the fridge for 6 hours.

Heat the ghee and sauté the grated onions and the ginger but do not allow them to brown. Then add all the whole masalas. Cook for 5 minutes.

Remove from the fire and add the Kashmiri chilli. The mixture should become pink in colour. Add the chicken mixture, then the salt and allow it to cook on a low flame, stirring continuously, until it comes to a boil. If this process is not followed the yoghurt will curdle.

Cook the chicken (with the mixture of onions) until it is tender and the yoghurt sticks to it. Serve hot with methi ki roti.

# MEVA KI BARFI

ANADYA BHADARYA BHATI                                    DELHI

SERVES: 10                    PREPARATION TIME: 30 MINUTES (PLUS 1 HOUR
                                              REFRIGERATION TIME)

INGREDIENTS

| | |
|---|---|
| Mawa/khoya | 500 gms |
| Sugar | 150 gms |
| Desi ghee | 2 tbsp |
| Melon seeds, cashew nuts, almonds, fox nuts | 2 cups |

METHOD

Fry in ghee or dry roast the almonds, cashew nuts, and fox nuts separately and keep them aside. Dry roast melon seeds; set aside.

Heat ghee in a non-stick pan. Add mawa and cook till it is light golden in colour.

Add sugar and mix well for a minute, then take off the heat.

Add nuts and lotus seeds.

Grease a flat dish. Pour the mixture into this and flatten with a spatula to the same thickness throughout.

Decorate with more nuts and seeds and refrigerate for 1 hour.

Cut into pieces and serve.


# PAYE KI NIHARI

(TROTTER STEW)

ZAKIA ZAHEER                              LUCKNOW, UTTAR PRADESH

SERVES: 4                          PREPARATION TIME: 4–6 HOURS

INGREDIENTS

| | |
|---|---|
| Sheep's trotters | 4 |
| Onions | 3 medium |

| | |
|---|---|
| Garlic cloves | 25 |
| Coriander seeds | 3 tsp |
| Whole dried red chillies | 2 |
| Salt | 1 tsp, or to taste |
| Turmeric powder | ½ tsp |
| Ghee | ¾ cup |
| Yoghurt | 1½ cups, whipped |
| Green chillies | 2–3, sliced lengthwise |
| Coriander leaves | 2 tbsp, finely chopped |
| Cloves | 6 |
| Garam masala | 1 tsp |

METHOD

Clean the trotters thoroughly in boiling water then cut into pieces. You may ask your butcher to help you with this.

Grind onions, garlic, coriander seeds, chillies, turmeric, and salt together to make a paste. Heat two-thirds of the ghee in a large pan and fry this paste for a couple of minutes.

Add the trotter pieces to the pan and enough water to cover. Cover and cook on low heat for 4–6 hours. Keep checking the water level while cooking; you may add more when needed. Take out the trotters once they begin appearing gelatinous.

Using a marrow spoon or a metal skewer, take out all the marrow and add to the pressure cooker. Discard bones.

Stir and the cook nihari for 5–10 minutes longer. Take off the heat.

Mix in yoghurt, green chillies, and fresh coriander. Heat the remaining ghee in a small pan. Fry cloves and garam masala in this and add to the nihari.

# GREEN MANGO CHUTNEY

GAURI KEELING                                                    DELHI

SERVES: 6                              PREPARATION TIME: 15 MINUTES

INGREDIENTS

|  |  |
|---|---|
| Green mangoes | ½ cup, peeled and chopped (kairi) |
| Fresh coriander leaves | 3 cups, tightly filled |
| Mint leaves | 1 cup, tightly filled |
| Green chillies | 2 tsp, chopped |
| Ginger | 2-inch piece, chopped |
| Garlic cloves | 2, peeled |
| Asafoetida | ¼ tsp |
| Cumin seeds | 1 tsp |
| Lime juice | ½ tbsp |
| Salt | ½ tsp or to taste |

METHOD

Add the raw mangoes, coriander leaves, mint, ginger, garlic, green chillies, salt, asafoetida, and cumin seeds to a blender along with ¼ cup of chilled water. Blend until coarsely smooth. Then mix in the lime juice. Chutney should be served at room temperature and is delicious with most Indian food.

# DHUAN GOSHT

## (SMOKED MUTTON)

NAGHAT ABEDI                              RAMPUR, UTTAR PRADESH

SERVES: 6                              PREPARATION TIME: 2 HOURS

INGREDIENTS

|  |  |
|---|---|
| Mutton | 1 kg |
| Oil | ½ cup + 2 tsp |
| Black cardamom pods | 2 |
| Cinnamon sticks | 2 |

| | |
|---|---|
| Cloves | 4 |
| Green cardamom pods | 3 |
| Whole black peppercorns | 4 |
| Bay leaves | 3 |
| Ginger paste | 1 tbsp |
| Garlic paste | 1 tbsp |
| Onions | 1 large, chopped and fried |
| Onion | 1 medium, chopped |
| Yoghurt | 150 gms |
| Coriander powder | 1 tsp |
| Red chilli powder | 1 tsp |
| Turmeric powder | ½ tsp |
| Salt | 1 tsp or to taste |
| Tomatoes | 2 large, puréed |
| Charcoal | 1 piece |
| Precooked roti | 1 |
| Onion rings and fresh coriander | to garnish |

METHOD

In a wok, heat the oil and add the two types of cardamom, cinnamon, cloves, peppercorns, and bay leaves. Then add the ginger and garlic pastes and fry for a minute.

Add the meat and stir. Add the fried onions and the chopped raw onion together, and stir again.

Now, add the coriander, red chilli, and turmeric powders and mix. Let the meat roast very well at this stage.

Once the masala looks completely dry, add the tomato purée.

When the gravy begins to bubble, add the yoghurt. Cook until the meat is tender; lower heat.

Heat the charcoal for 30 minutes until it is fire red. Once the meat is ready, place the roti on the meat and then put the hot charcoal on top.

Add 2 teaspoons of oil and immediately put a lid on the wok so no smoke escapes. Keep the lid shut for 20 minutes.

Garnish with onions rings and chopped coriander. Serve with naan.

# RAMPURI MACHLI ANDA

NAGHAT ABEDI                                    RAMPUR, UTTAR PRADESH

SERVES: 5                                       PREPARATION TIME: 1 HOUR

INGREDIENTS

| | |
|---|---|
| Eggs | 10 |
| Oil | 2 tbsp |
| Fenugreek seeds | ½ tsp |
| Onions | 2 large, ground into paste |
| Garlic paste | 1 tbsp |
| Ginger paste | 1 tbsp |
| Coriander powder | 1 tsp |
| Turmeric powder | ½ tsp |
| Red chilli powder | ½ tsp |
| Salt | ½ tsp or to taste |
| Yoghurt | 100 gms |
| Coriander leaves | few sprigs |

METHOD

In a round flat pan heat oil and add the fenugreek seeds. When the seeds are slightly browned, add the raw onion and ginger and garlic pastes and stir until the mixture is somewhat reduced. To this add the coriander powder, turmeric powder, red chilli powder, and salt to taste. Cook until oil begins to separate from this mixture.

Add the yoghurt and water and cook until the mixture is golden brown. Turn down the heat.

Crack the eggs and slowly drop them into the flat pan and cover the dish with a lid. The yolks should not break. The eggs will cook in the mixture on low heat.

Once the eggs are ready and yolks look set, carefully take them out and lay them flat in a dish. Garnish with coriander leaves before serving.

# KHUBANI KA MEETHA

NAGHAT ABEDI                           RAMPUR, UTTAR PRADESH

SERVES: 8–10                           PREPARATION TIME: 45 MINUTES
                                       (PLUS OVERNIGHT SOAKING TIME)

INGREDIENTS

| | |
|---|---|
| Dried apricots | 2 kg |
| Almonds | 400 gms, blanched and finely chopped |
| Fresh cream | 250 ml |
| Sugar syrup | 200 ml |

METHOD

Soak the apricots overnight and then boil in water until they soften. Keep aside to cool.

Deseed the apricots. To the cleaned apricots add the sugar syrup and mash well using a fork; the texture should not be too fine and paste-like.

Add the fresh cream along with most of the chopped almonds. Mix well.

Serve in a bowl and garnish with the remaining almonds. Refrigerate for 30 minutes to set.

# MUTTON PICKLE

ROME KOHLI                                        DELHI

SERVES: 12-16                          PREPARATION TIME: 1 HOUR

INGREDIENTS

| | |
|---|---|
| Boneless mutton | 500 gms, cut into small pieces |
| Groundnut oil | 4 tbsp + 4 cups for deep-frying |
| Ginger | 2 inch, sliced |
| Mustard seeds | 2 tsp |
| Dried red chillies | 3 |
| Young curry leaves | 20 |
| Cloves | 6 |

| Cumin powder | 1 tbsp |
| Turmeric powder | ½ tsp |
| Mustard powder | 1 tbsp |
| Red chilli powder | 1 tbsp + 2 tsp |
| Vinegar | ¼ cup |
| Lemon | 1, juiced |
| Salt | to taste |

## METHOD

Pressure cook the mutton with water and salt. Heat oil in a kadhai. Deep-fry the mutton pieces in hot oil till crisp.

Heat 4 tbsp oil in a non-stick pan. Roughly chop dried red chillies. Add mustard seeds, curry leaves, cloves, and ginger to the pan and mix well. Then add red chillies and mix well, add turmeric powder and mix again. Switch off the heat, let the mixture cool to room temperature. Add cumin powder, mustard powder, salt and 1 tbsp red chilli powder and mix well.

Drain and add the mutton pieces to the pan and mix well. Adjust salt and add remaining red chilli powder and mix well.

Take out 2-3 ladles of hot oil from the kadhai and add to the pan and mix well. Cool down the mixture to room temperature. Add lemon juice and vinegar and mix well.

Transfer the mutton pickle into a large sterilized glass jar and pour 2 more ladles of hot oil from the kadhai on top. Screw on the lid and store.

# DOODH-PITHI KHEER

SHASHANK SINGH                                              VARANASI

SERVES: 4                                          PREPARATION TIME: 1 HOUR

## INGREDIENTS

| Whole wheat flour | ½ cup |
| Ghee | 5 tbsp |
| Sugar | ¼ cup or to taste |
| Milk | 1 litre, plus extra for dough |

METHOD

Knead the flour with some milk into a soft dough.

Dust another plate with some flour. Use a little ghee to moisten your fingers. Use the kneaded dough to create small pellets (pithi) by rolling bits of the dough between the thumb and index finger; try to make them all uniform in size. Place these pellets on the dusted plate.

Optional: if possible, dry these pellets in the sun for a few hours before moving on to the next step.

Heat the ghee in a pan and shallow fry the pithi until they are golden brown.

In a separate heavy-bottomed vessel, boil the milk. To this add the fried pithi, and simmer on a low flame, stirring regularly.

Add the sugar and bring to a boil. Keep stirring until the sugar dissolves, take off the heat, and serve.

**Note:** This kheer is best enjoyed hot in the winters, and cold in the summers.


# RIKWACH VEGETABLE WITH MUSTARD

SHASHANK SINGH                                                    VARANASI

SERVES: 4                                        PREPARATION TIME: 1 HOUR


INGREDIENTS

| | |
|---|---|
| Soft colocasia leaves | 24 |
| Gram flour | 2 cups |
| Turmeric powder | ½ tsp |
| Any sabzi masala powder | 2 tsp |
| Mustard oil | 2 tbsp, plus enough for deep frying |
| Dry fenugreek leaves | 1½ tsp |
| Whole red chillies | 2 |
| Yellow mustard paste | 1 tbsp |
| Salt | to taste |
| Fresh lime juice | 2 tsp or to taste |


METHOD

Make a thick paste of the gram flour with turmeric and sabzi masala powder using a little water. Apply this paste over the colocasia leaves and fold them into squares.

Heat mustard oil in a wok. Deep fry these folded squares till they are golden brown on both sides.

Heat some mustard oil in a pan. To this add the dry fenugreek leaves and red chillies. Next add the mustard paste, turmeric powder, salt, and a teaspoon of water. Simmer till you see oil leaving the masala, then add ½ cup of water and fresh lime juice to it. Bring to a boil.

Add the fried colocasia leaf squares and cook on high heat for a couple of minutes. Remove from heat and serve.

## MUTTON KI KARHI

SUVIDHA AND ASEEM CHOUDHARI                                    DELHI

SERVES: 4–6                                      PREPARATION TIME: 1 HOUR

INGREDIENTS

| | | |
|---:|---|---|
| Mutton | 1 kg | |
| Yoghurt | 1 kg | |
| Gram flour | 200 gms | |
| Onions | 1 large, chopped | |
| Garlic cloves | 3–4, chopped | |
| Curry leaves | 1 sprig | |
| Whole red dried chillies | 4–5 | |
| Dried fenugreek leaves | 1 tsp | |
| Mustard seeds | 1 tsp | |
| Cumin seeds | 1 tsp | |
| Turmeric | 1 tsp | |
| Coarse red chilli powder | 1 tsp | |
| Fenugreek seeds | ½ tsp | |
| Oil | 4 tbsp | |
| Salt | to taste | |

METHOD

Heat 3 tablespoons oil in a pressure cooker. Add the mustard, cumin, and fenugreek seeds, fenugreek leaves, and chopped onion and garlic. Fry until the onions are browned.

Add the red chilli powder and curry leaves, then the mutton. Fry on medium heat for 5–7 minutes, then cover and let cook for 5–6 whistles. The fat on the mutton should melt.

Separately, make a mixture of the yoghurt, gram flour, turmeric powder, and salt in a blender. Add this to the cooked mutton and cook uncovered on high heat for 5–7 minutes. The gravy should thicken.

Heat the remaining oil in a small pan and temper the dried chillies. Top the mutton with the chillies and serve.

# DAHI GHIYA

SUVIDHA AND ASEEM CHOUDHARI                      DELHI

SERVES: 4–6                      PREPARATION TIME: 30 MINUTES

INGREDIENTS

| | |
|---|---|
| Bottle gourd | 1 kg, diced |
| Hung curd | ½ kg |
| Coriander leaves | 2 tbsp, finely chopped |
| Cumin seeds | 1 tsp |
| Turmeric powder | ½ tsp |
| Oil | 3 tbsp |
| Salt | to taste |
| Green chillies | 3–4, finely chopped |

METHOD

Heat oil in a wok. Add cumin seeds. Once they splutter add the bottle gourd, salt, and turmeric powder. Cover and cook for 7–8 minutes, stirring occasionally. Once the bottle gourd looks cooked through and soft, set aside to cool. To the cooked bottle gourd add the hung curd with the green chillies and coriander leaves and gently stir to combine.

With a masher, slightly mash the cooked bottle gourd pieces in the wok. Serve cold or at room temperature.

# ARHAR DAL

SHEILA DIKSHIT COURTESY LATIKA DIKSHIT                    NEW DELHI

SERVES: 4                                        PREPARATION TIME: 30 MINUTES

INGREDIENTS

| | |
|---|---|
| Yellow pigeon pea lentils | 2 cups |
| Cumins seeds | 2 tsp |
| Whole dried red chillies | 3–4 |
| Ghee | 3 tbsp for tempering |
| Red chilli powder | to taste |
| Asafoetida | a pinch |
| Turmeric powder | 2 tsp |
| Salt | to taste |

METHOD

Wash the lentils well and soak for 15 minutes in enough water to cover.

Add the lentils with their soaking water to a pressure cooker. Add salt and turmeric powder and cook on high heat for one whistle. Take the lid off the cooker immediately and reduce the heat to low. Let the lentils cook uncovered until they look mushy, about 10 minutes. Lightly stir occasionally. Take off the heat and set aside until time to serve.

Before serving, temper the chillies and cumin seeds in the ghee and mix into the dal. Top with red chilli powder and asafoetida.


# COCADA

BEATRICE DO LAGO                                      DELHI-BRAZIL

SERVES: 6                                          PREPARATION TIME: 1 HOUR

INGREDIENTS

| | |
|---|---|
| Sugar | 200 gms |
| Fresh Grated Coconut | 500 gms |
| Condensed Milk | 1 can |

## METHOD

Place a pot on the stove on low heat and make a syrup with the sugar and 150 millilitres water. Add grated fresh coconut and condensed milk. Cook while stirring until your desired consistency is achieved.

In a greased tray, pour the still warm mixture. Flatten to your desired thickness and let cool.

Use a sharp knife to make small squares and enjoy.

**Note:** To make another version of this dish (doce de leite), make a caramel with the sugar and water. After adding the coconut and condensed milk, cook until the mixture is browned like caramel. You may add a little water after this to achieve the right consistency.


# COCONUT QUINOTTO

JEAN CLAUDE KUGENER                    DELHI-LUXEMBOURG

SERVES: 6                              PREPARATION TIME: 45 MINUTES


## INGREDIENTS

| | |
|---|---|
| Zucchinis | 2, diced |
| Tomatoes | 4 |
| Red pepper | 1, diced |
| Yellow pepper | 1, diced |
| Green pepper | 1 |
| Coconut milk | 1 can |
| Quinoa | 2 cups, tricoloured |
| Olive oil | 2 tbsp |
| Salt | to taste |
| Pepper | to taste |
| Shrimp | 250 gms, medium sized |
| Dry coconut flakes | 2 tbsp |


## METHOD

Boil the quinoa with 4 cups of water until the water evaporates. Set aside. Boil the tomatoes in water and blend them to make a sauce. Add 2 tablespoons of coconut milk, salt, and pepper.

Just before serving, take some olive oil in a pan, heat the diced zucchini and pepper cubes together with salt and pepper. Reheat the quinoa with half the can of coconut milk, salt, and pepper. Add in the vegetables and stir.

At the same time, in a separate pan, brown the shrimps in a bit of olive oil and some dry coconut flakes with salt and pepper.

Warm the tomato sauce.

Dress each plate with a pastry circle, the quinotto, surrounded by the tomato sauce and sprinkle with the shrimps and flakes.

# PAELLA

BIRGITTA KNUDSEN BJÖRK                                    DELHI-SPAIN

SERVES: 6                                    PREPARATION TIME: 1 HOUR

INGREDIENTS

| | |
|---|---|
| Rice | 400 gms, short grain |
| Chicken | 1 small, cut into pieces |
| Carrot | 1, halved |
| Onion | 1, halved |
| Prawns | 6 |
| Clams | 200 gms |
| Mussels | 250 gms |
| Monkfish | 200 gms |
| Green capsicum | 1 |
| Green beans | 200 gms, cut into 2-cm slices |
| Onion | 1 tbsp, chopped |
| Tomato | 1, skin removed and cut into pieces |
| Olive oil | 10 tbsp |
| Garlic | 1 clove, mashed |
| Lemon juice | 1 tbsp |
| Saffron | a pinch |
| Pepper | to taste |
| Salt | to taste |
| Parsley | to taste |

METHOD

Clean the chicken. Cook the chicken with a carrot and an onion until tender. Remove the chicken and set aside. Remove the vegetables and reserve the broth.

Clean the mussels well and place in cold water in a pot. Bring to boil for a minute. Remove from the water. Remove the shells of one of the mussels and keep aside. Reserve the water.

Clean the prawns and clams and set aside.

In a frying pan add half the oil. Then add the onion and fry until it turns golden. Then add the tomato pieces and the beans. Add the fish. Cover and cook for 6–7 minutes. Now add the chicken and stir a bit more, a minute or so.

In a paellera (or a large shallow skillet), add the rest of the oil. Once hot add the rice. Stir until it becomes golden and sounds like sand. Add in the vegetables and fish.

Prepare the consommé with the water used for cooking the mussels, add the mixture of salt, saffron, parsley, and mashed garlic. Add some water if needed to make it two cups.

Add the consommé to the skillet and immediately bring to a boil. When it is boiling add a few drops of lemon juice. Let it boil for 5 minutes, then add the prawns and mussels. Cook for 15 minutes, then take off the heat and let it stand for 5 minutes.

Uncover and let it rest for 5 minutes before serving.


# SWEET AND SOUR SPARE PORK RIBS

CHRISTINE WISNER                              DELHI-USA

SERVES: 4                         PREPARATION TIME: 1½ HOURS


INGREDIENTS

| | |
|---|---|
| Pork spare ribs | 1½ kg, cut into 1-inch pieces |
| Star anise | 1 |
| Ginger | 1-inch piece (optional) |
| Pineapple chunks | 1 cup with juice |
| Green peppers | 2, medium cut into ½-inch pieces |

| | |
|---|---|
| Onion | 1, cut into ½-inch pieces |
| Soy sauce | 1 tbsp |
| Rice vinegar | ¼ cup |
| Ketchup | ½ cup |
| Garlic | 1 clove, minced |
| Brown sugar | ½ cup |
| Cornstarch | 2 tbsp |

METHOD

Place the spareribs in boiling water for about an hour, then strain, discard fat and lay them in an oven–safe dish (about 10 x 7 x 1½ inches).

Combine all the other ingredients and pour evenly over the ribs. Bake in a preheated oven for about 30 minutes at 175°C.

# QUINOA AND LENTIL SALAD

NAVINA HAIDER AND PIA HAYKEL                    DELHI-USA

SERVES: 4-6                              PREPARATION TIME: 1 HOUR

INGREDIENTS

| | |
|---|---|
| Red, plain, or multicoloured quinoa | 1 cup |
| Black or green lentils | ½ cup |
| Slivered almonds | 3 tbsp |
| Onion | ½, finely chopped |
| Tomato | 1, finely chopped |
| Garlic | 2 cloves, finely chopped |
| Cumin seeds | 1/3 tsp |
| Parsley | a small bunch, chopped |
| Coriander leaves | a small bunch, chopped |
| Lemon | 1 |
| Sea salt | to taste |
| Olive oil | 1 tbsp |

METHOD

Boil the quinoa until it is cooked but firm (al dente). Drain and dry and set aside.

Boil the lentils until soft but not mushy and drain.

In a pan, heat some of the olive oil. Add the cumin seeds. When they sizzle, add the onions and garlic.

Once the onions have browned, add the chopped tomato. After it has softened a little, add the drained lentils and mix. Take off the heat.

When quinoa and lentils have cooled combine in a bowl. Add the chopped parsley and coriander leaves. Add salt to taste and squeeze lemon over. Mix and fluff with fork.

Toast the almonds in the remaining olive oil and add salt to them. Top the entire dish generously with toasted almonds and serve.

**Note:** You can use couscous, bulgar wheat, freekeh, or semolina instead of quinoa.

## TIGER PRAWNS

WILLIAM DALRYMPLE                                              DELHI

SERVES: 4                                   PREPARATION TIME: 10 MINUTES

INGREDIENTS

| | |
|---|---|
| Tiger prawns | 500 gms |
| Olive oil | 1 tbsp |
| Red chillies | 2 medium, seeded and chopped |
| Garlic | 2 cloves |
| Paprika, turmeric, ground ginger and cumin | 2 tsp each |
| Onion | 1 medium, sliced |
| Mango | small, half, diced |
| Fresh pomegranate | seeds from half a fruit |
| Fresh lime | half, juiced |
| Fresh coriander leaves | 2 tbsp |

METHOD

For the salad, mix one chilli, the onion, mango, and pomegranate seeds, and dress with some of the lime juice and 1 tablespoon chopped coriander.

Fry the garlic and the other chilli in very hot olive oil for a few seconds. Add the prawns, paprika, turmeric, ginger, and cumin. Sprinkle the rest of the coriander leaves and lime juice over the prawns and serve with the salad and/or plain boiled rice.

# FESENJAN

DAVID HOUSEGO                                                      DELHI-IRAN

SERVES: 6–8                                          PREPARATION TIME: 2 HOURS

### INGREDIENTS

| | | |
|---|---|---|
| Onions | 1½, chopped |
| Butter | 2 tbsp |
| Olive oil | 3 tbsp |
| Concentrated pomegranate juice (molasses) | 5 tbsp |
| Walnuts | 400 gms, finely crushed |
| Chicken | 1 large, cut into pieces with bones |
| Chicken stock | 2 cups |
| Saffron | a pinch dissolved in 2 tbsp water |
| Sugar | 2 tbsp |
| Turmeric powder | ½ tsp |
| Cinnamon | ¼ tsp |
| Nutmeg | ¼ tsp, ground |
| Black pepper | ¼ tsp, ground |
| Lime juice | 1 tsp |
| Salt | to taste |
| For Iranian rice | |
| Long-grain rice | as needed |
| Ground nut oil | as needed |
| Egg yolk | 1 |
| Sumac | 1 tbsp |
| Butter | as desired |

### METHOD

In a large wok, brown the chicken on all sides in butter and olive oil. The bones give the dish extra flavour though they need to be removed before serving.

Set aside the chicken and cook the onions in the wok until translucent. A little more oil and butter may be added here if needed.

Return the chicken to the wok with the onions. Add the walnuts, concentrated pomegranate juice, pinch of saffron, sugar, and spices.

Add the chicken stock, simmer slowly and stir for an hour or until the chicken is cooked and the sauce has thickened. Add salt, pepper, and lime juice. Taste to check the balance of sweetness; you should get a slight sharpness from the pomegranate and lime juice.

Remove the chicken bones using your fingers. It's a messy business but worth it.

Serve with slices of raw onion and Iranian rice. Iranians use long grain rice.

If making the rice, boil the rice of your choice in water for 10 minutes and drain. Pour into a separate cooking pot with a thin layer of oil (ground nut oil is best). Cover this with the semi-cooked rice. Seal the lid and allow to simmer slowly for 30–40 minutes until a crust forms on the bottom. Spoon the rice into a serving dish, leaving the crust behind in the pot. Add a thick slice of butter, the egg yolk and sumac and mix. The rice needs to be hot to absorb the butter and egg yolk. Finally scoop out the crust of the rice and put this on the top.

## HINTERLAND BOUILLABAISSE

### (SEAFOOD STEW)

AMITA AND KHALID BAIG                    DELHI-FRANCE

SERVES: 8–10                    PREPARATION TIME: 1 HOUR 30 MINUTES

INGREDIENTS

| | |
|---|---|
| Mixed fish (Sole or Bhetki fillets, medium and large prawns, and squid) | 1½ kg |
| Tomatoes | 225 gms (or equivalent of a can of Italian tomatoes) |
| Saffron | a pinch soaked in a little water |
| Olive oil | 90 ml |

| | |
|---|---|
| Onion | 1, sliced |
| Leek | 1, sliced |
| Fennel | 1, sliced |
| Garlic cloves | 2 or 3, crushed |
| Bouquet garni or just thyme | 1, or a handful |
| Orange rind | 1 strip |
| Tomato purée | 15 ml (10 ml purée and 5 ml tomato paste) |
| White wine | 1 glass |
| Salt and fresh ground black pepper | to taste |
| Parsley | a bunch, chopped |

METHOD

Clean the fish, and use all the trimmings to make a strong fish stock amounting to 1½ litres.

Heat the oil in a large pan and add finely sliced onions, leek, and fennel and sauté gently until softened. Add garlic, orange rind, and chopped tomatoes and then stir in the saffron with its soaking liquid and the reserved fish stock. Simmer for about 30 minutes adjusting the flavours. I add three to four cleaned prawn heads to augment the flavour at this point.

Separately fry the fish to seal it and also the prawns and finally the squid. The squid has to be fried very lightly to prevent it from becoming rubbery. Then add all to the soup.

Add the white wine and allow the oil to emulsify with the broth and add tomato purée.

Remove prawn heads before serving.

**Note:** I serve the stew in a large Crueset pot with chunks of French bread and aioli served separately.

# South

~

# ALAGAR KOVIL DOSAI

ANITA RATNAM

CHENNAI, TAMIL NADU

SERVES: 12

PREPARATION TIME: 1 HOUR
(PLUS 2 HOURS RESTING TIME)

## INGREDIENTS

| | |
|---|---|
| Samba rice | 3 cups, washed and soaked for 2 hrs |
| Split black gram dal with skin | 1¼ cup, washed and soaked for 4 hrs |
| Salt | 3 tsp, or to taste |
| Dried ginger | 2 inch piece, coarsely pounded |
| Black pepper | 2 tsp, broken very coarsely |
| Whole black peppercorns | 2 tsp |
| Cumin seeds | 1 tbsp |
| Curry leaves | 2–3 |
| Asafoetida | 2 tsp |
| Ghee mixed with oil | 1½ cup + 1½ cup |

## METHOD

Drain the rice and pound finely.

Drain the dal and grind without water to make a smooth batter.

Add the pounded rice to batter and beat well to a thick consistency. Batter should be very thick but not like a dough. If it appears too thick, mix in a tablespoon of water.

Add all the spices, curry leaves, and salt to the batter. Stir a couple of times then keep aside for 2 hours.

Place a heavy adai madaku pan (or a very large flat pan) over medium heat. Pour about an inch of ghee–oil mixture on the madaku.

When the oil is hot, pour a cup of the batter and spread it out to make an 8-inch round dosai. Pour 4 tablespoons of the ghee–oil mixture on top.

Fry till the base is golden. Flip over and fry the other side until golden as well.

Make the remaining dosai in the same way and serve hot.

# KEDGEREE

JANE CHURCHILL                                    TAMIL NADU

SERVES: 4–5                          PREPARATION TIME: 30 MINUTES

INGREDIENTS

| | |
|---|---|
| Poached flaked salmon (or smoked haddock) | 250 gms |
| Long grain rice | 500 gms, cooked |
| Hard boiled eggs | 4, peeled and cut into eighths |
| Double cream | 500 ml |
| Madras curry powder | a big pinch |
| Salt and pepper | to taste |
| Paprika | to serve |

METHOD

Lightly whisk the curry powder into the cream. Place over a high heat and bring the cream to the boil. Turn down the heat and let the cream simmer for a few minutes to on take the flavour from the curry powder.

Stir in the rice and reheat gently for a few more minutes until it starts to bubble a little at the edges. Gently fold in the salmon, reheat again for a few more minutes. Finally, add the boiled eggs, season to taste and serve sprinkled with a little paprika. This is great served with a very simple leaf salad.


# ADAI

ARUNA SAIRAM                              CHENNAI, TAMIL NADU

SERVES: 6                            PREPARATION TIME: 30 MINUTES
                                     (PLUS SOAKING TIME 3 HOURS)

INGREDIENTS

| | |
|---|---|
| Rice | 1 cup |
| Yellow split pigeon pea lentils | ¼ cup |

| | |
|---|---|
| Split black gram | ¼ cup |
| Yellow skinned gram | ¼ cup |
| Split Bengal gram | ¼ cup |
| Red chilli powder | 1 tsp |
| Coconut | ½, grated |
| Any greens e.g. spinach or moringa leaves | 2 cups, chopped |
| Green chillies | 2, chopped |
| Ginger | 1 tbsp, chopped |
| Curry leaves | 4–5, finely chopped |
| Coriander leaves | handful, chopped |
| Oil or ghee | as needed |
| Salt | to taste |

## METHOD

Soak the rice and all dals for 3 hours in water. Drain.

In a mixer, add salt, green chilli, ginger, red chilli powder, and the soaked rice and dals. Add enough water to grind to a thick coarse paste.

Next add the grated coconut and your choice of greens and give just two short spins to the mixer.

Add the chopped curry leaves and coriander and mix well. You will have a somewhat grainy paste that can be spread into a thick dosa.

Heat a flat pan and grease it generously with oil or ghee. Take a ladleful of batter and spread it on the tawa in a continuous circular motion. Drizzle oil on the edges and cook for couple of minutes until light golden. Now flip it over and cook for a few minutes on the other side too. Remove and store in a hot case.

Serve with avial or jaggery and butter.

# AKKARA ADISIL

SUDHA AND N. RAVI                                    CHENNAI, TAMIL NADU

SERVES: 8                                    PREPARATION TIME: 45 MINUTES

INGREDIENTS

| | |
|---|---|
| Milk | 4 cups |
| Yellow skinned gram | ⅓ cup |
| Rice | ½ cup, washed |
| Jaggery | 2½ cups, grated |
| Ghee | 4 tbsp |
| Cashew nuts | 4 tbsp |
| Almonds | 4 tbsp |
| Raisins | 2 tbsp |
| Cardamom | ½ tsp |
| Nutmeg | ½ tsp |
| Saffron strands | few |

METHOD

Take two cups of milk in a heavy bottomed vessel, bring to boil, stirring all the while, till the milk thickens. Remove from heat and set aside.

Soak almonds in boiling water for 15 minutes. Drain, peel, and cut into slivers.

Fry cashews in 1 tablespoon of ghee and set aside.

Boil the remaining two cups of milk with one cup water in a rice cooker. Add nutmeg, cardamom, washed rice, and dal to the boiling milk and cook well until both rice and dal are softened.

Dissolve jaggery in water and strain. Add to the cooked rice, mix and cook for a few more minutes. Keep stirring, adding 2 tablespoons of ghee.

Add slivered almonds, fried cashews, raisins, and the thickened milk to the cooked rice.

Finally, add saffron and the remaining ghee. Stir well and serve hot.

# BEETROOT PORIYAL

## (SAUTEED BEETROOT)

VISALAKSHI RAMASWAMY                    CHETTINAD, TAMIL NADU

SERVES: 4                              PREPARATION TIME: 25 MINUTES

INGREDIENTS

| | |
|---|---|
| Beetroot | ¾ kg |
| Groundnuts | 100 gms, roasted |
| Curry leaves | 2 handfuls, on the stalk |
| Dried red chillies | 2, torn into small pieces |
| Salt | to taste |
| Vegetable oil | 10 tbsp (for roasting and sautéing) |

METHOD

Peel and grate the beetroot. Squeeze the grated beetroot to remove excess moisture.

Heat oil in an iron wok.

Add the stalks of curry leaves and sauté for a few seconds until softened. Remove from oil and drain well. Strip the leaves from the stalk and keep aside.

Add the groundnuts to the wok and sauté till they turn golden brown. Remove from oil and keep aside.

In the same wok, add the red chillies and stir fry for a couple of minutes till the flavour seeps into the oil.

Add the grated beetroot and salt, stirring well.

Sauté until cooked but not mushy. Garnish with the fried curry leaves and groundnuts and serve hot.

# KOZHI UPPU KARI

## (SPICY DRY CHICKEN)

VISALAKSHI RAMASWAMY                    CHETTINAD, TAMIL NADU

SERVES: 4                              PREPARATION TIME: 45 MINUTES

INGREDIENTS

| | |
|---|---|
| Chicken | ½ kg, washed and cut into cubes |
| Cinnamon stick | ½ inch |
| Bay leaf | ½ |
| Aniseed | 1 tsp |
| Curry leaves | a few |
| Dried red chillies | 40, torn into small pieces |
| Onions | 30-35, small, peeled |
| Tomato | 1 medium size, finely chopped |
| Garlic | 10 cloves, peeled |
| Ginger | 1½ inch, finely chopped |
| Rock salt | to taste |
| Water | 2 cups |
| Vegetable oil | ¼ cup |

METHOD

Heat oil in a wok.

Add cinnamon stick, bay leaf, aniseed, and curry leaves; sauté for a few seconds on medium heat. When they start to splutter, add dried red chillies, each torn into two to three pieces. Fry until the flavour of the chillies seeps into oil.

Add onions, tomato, garlic and ginger and sauté till the onions are golden.

Add the chicken pieces and salt, and gently stir fry until the meat starts releasing liquid.

Add water and cook covered on low heat until chicken is cooked through, about 25 minutes. Adjust the amount of water added at this stage depending on the amount of stock released by the chicken.

Remove the lid and cook uncovered on high heat until all the liquid is absorbed.

Garnish with chopped coriander leaves.

**Note:** The Uppu Kari can also be made using mutton instead of chicken. In traditional Chettinad cuisine, mutton is the meat of choice for this recipe.

# ELANEER PAYASAM

## (TENDER COCONUT KHEER)

VISALAKSHI RAMASWAMY                         CHETTINAD, TAMIL NADU

SERVES: 8–10                    PREPARATION TIME: 40 MINUTES

INGREDIENTS

| | |
|---|---|
| Whole tender coconuts | 4 |
| Milk | 4½ cups |
| Condensed milk | ½ cup or to taste |
| Sugar | to taste |

METHOD

Boil the milk in a heavy bottomed vessel, stirring frequently, until it reduces by half. This should take about 15 minutes. Remove from heat.

Add the condensed milk and then the sugar. Let the milk cool.

In the meantime, break open the coconuts and extract the coconut water. Set aside after reserving half a cup.

Remove the flesh from the coconuts. Grind the pieces in a mixer grinder with upto a half cup of coconut water.

In a double boiler, heat the tender coconut mixture until warm. Add this tender coconut to the milk mixture and stir well to combine.

Adjust the consistency of the payasam with the reserved coconut water.

Serve chilled.

# KALONJI KE BAIGAN

SUNAINA MALHOTRA

ANDHRA PRADESH

SERVES: 6–8

PREPARATION TIME: 1 HOUR 10 MINUTES

INGREDIENTS

| | |
|---|---|
| Aubergines | 12 small |
| Tomatoes | 4 large |
| Red onions | 2 medium, finely chopped |
| Nigella seeds | 1 tsp |
| Garlic paste | 1 tsp |
| Turmeric | 2 tsp |
| Coriander seeds | 2 tsp, ground |
| Chilli powder | 1 tsp |
| Sambhar masala or curry powder | 1 tsp |
| Red Kashmiri powder | 1 tsp |
| Dry red chillies | 3–4, fried |
| Salt | to taste |
| Sugar | a pinch |

METHOD

Slice the aubergines lengthwise into halves, keeping them joined at the stem.

Combine the turmeric power, coriander powder, and chilli powder and place them between the sliced aubergines.

Heat the mustard oil in a medium size wok or frying pan and cook the aubergine until tender. Remove them from the wok.

Meanwhile boil the tomatoes and peel them. Purée them into a thick sauce.

Heat the mustard oil in the wok over medium heat. Add the nigella seeds and fry for a minute or until the seeds start to sputter. Add the chopped onions and garlic and cook until translucent. Add the tomato sauce curry powder, coriander powder, and red Kashmiri powder (which helps to enhance the red colour of the sauce). Season with salt and a pinch of sugar. Cook for about 6–7 minutes and add the aubergines, taking care to not break them in the sauce.

Garnish with dry fried red chillies.

*The India Cookbook*

# CHICKEN CHETTINAD PEPPER MASALA

MEENAKSHI MEYYAPPAN                                CHETTINAD, TAMIL NADU

SERVES: 4–6                                        PREPARATION TIME: 1 HOUR

INGREDIENTS

| | |
|---|---|
| Vegetable oil | ½ cup |
| Cinnamon | 1, 2-inch piece |
| Green cardamom pods | 2 |
| Onions | 1½ medium size, finely chopped (about 150 gms) |
| Fresh tomato purée | ½ cup, from about 2 medium tomatoes |
| Sea salt | 1 tsp, or to taste |
| Chicken | 600 grams (1 small or ½ medium chicken), cut into 8 pieces |

For the wet paste

| | |
|---|---|
| Fennel seeds | 1 tsp |
| Black peppercorns | 2 tsp |
| Cumin seeds | 1 tsp |
| Whole dried red chillies, mild, preferably goondumilagai | 4 |
| Coriander seeds | 1 tsp |
| Turmeric powder | ½ tsp |
| Garlic | 1 tsp, peeled and grated |
| Ginger | ½ tsp, peeled and grated |

METHOD

Place a heavy flat pan on low heat and dry roast the fennel seeds, peppercorns, cumin seeds, dried red chillies, and coriander seeds until fragrant and slightly darkened. Grind them using a mortar–pestle, adding a little water, or in a wet grinder/blender to make a paste. Add turmeric, garlic and ginger to the wet paste and mix well. Set aside.

Place a large wok over high heat and add oil. When hot but not smoking, add cinnamon, cardamom, and onion and stir. Reduce heat to medium and sauté for about 4 minutes or until onion is lightly coloured before adding the tomato purée. Sauté for an additional minute.

Add the wet masala paste to the wok, breaking it apart with a spoon, stirring well to incorporate. Continue to cook for 10–12 minutes, scraping the bottom of the wok, till the oil separates from the masala. The mixture should look well cooked and should have darkened.

Sprinkle the sea salt and stir. Then add the chicken, stirring to coat well with the mixture. Continue cooking for 1–2 minutes before adding 1½ cups of water. Scrape the bottom of the kadhai to deglaze and bring to a boil on high heat. Turn the heat down to low and cook for 15–20 minutes, covered; stir occasionally.

Uncover and reduce till the sauce thickens to coat the chicken.

Remove from heat. Serve immediately.

**Note:** For a healthier alternative, reduce the quantity of oil to ¼ cup to begin, and then add more oil if needed to prevent the masala from sticking and burning. For a quail Chettinad pepper masala, substitute an equal weight of quail (around six quails) for the chicken. Cut the quail into two pieces each, separating the breast from the legs and follow the recipe above. Also try this masala with potatoes or mushrooms for a vegetarian Chettinad pepper masala.

## CRAB MASALA

NALINI AND P. CHIDAMBARAM                    CHETTINAD, TAMIL NADU

SERVES: 4–6                              PREPARATION TIME: 40 MINUTES

INGREDIENTS

| | |
|---|---|
| Crab | 1 kg, washed and cleaned |
| Onion | 3 large, chopped |
| Tomato | 2 medium, roughly chopped |
| Refined oil | 5 tbsp |
| Green chillies | 2, finely chopped |
| Ginger garlic paste | 3 tbsp |
| Dessicated coconut | ½ cup |
| Turmeric powder | ¼ tsp |
| Curry leaves | 4–5 |
| Coriander powder | 2 tbsp |
| Red chilli powder | 1 tbsp |

| | |
|---|---|
| Ground pepper | 2 tbsp |
| Moringa leaves | 2 handfuls |
| Coriander leaves | a handful |
| Salt | to taste |

METHOD

Heat oil in a pan. Add the onions and sauté until browned.

Add ginger garlic paste, green chillies, and curry leaves. Cook for a couple of minutes while stirring.

Add the chopped tomato, coriander and chilli powders, coriander leaves, turmeric, and salt. Cook for 5 minutes or until the tomato has softened.

Add the desiccated coconut and mix well. Now add crab, pour enough water to cover and bring the gravy to a boil.

Add the moringa leaves and pepper and mix well. Cover and cook for 15 minutes on low heat. Serve hot.

# SAGO AND POTATO VADA

RAJSHREE PATHY                    COIMBATORE, TAMIL NADU

SERVES: 4                    PREPARATION TIME: 30 MINUTES

INGREDIENTS

| | |
|---|---|
| Sago | ¼ cup |
| Potatoes | 3 medium sized, boiled and peeled |
| Onion | 1 large |
| Green chillies | 2 |
| Coriander leaves | a handful |
| Bengal gram flour | 1 tbsp |
| Peanuts | ¼ cup, roasted |
| Turmeric powder | ¼ tsp |
| Cumin seeds | ¼ tsp |
| Oil | to deep fry |
| Salt | to taste |

METHOD

Soak sago in salted water for a minute. Drain and set aside.

Mash potatoes until tender. Add salt to taste.

Peel and grind peanuts to a coarse powder.

Finely chop coriander leaves, onions, and green chillies.

Mix all ingredients together in a bowl. Knead well then divide into small portions.

Oil your palm and flatten each portion into a disc. Make a hole in the centre of each vada.

Heat enough oil for deep frying. Fry the prepared vadas until golden brown and serve hot.


# KANDA PULSU

SHARAN SONU APPARAO                    ANDHRA PRADESH

SERVES: 4                    PREPARATION TIME: 30 MINUTES


INGREDIENTS

| | |
|---|---|
| Yam | 500 gms, diced into large pieces |
| Garlic pods | 4, finely chopped |
| Onions | 4, finely chopped |
| Tomatoes | 2, chopped and skinned |
| Dry red chilli | 1, quartered |
| Tamarind water | 1 cup (made from ½ cup of tamarind) |
| Fenugreek seeds | ½ tsp |
| Mustard seeds | ½ tsp |
| Coriander powder | 1 tsp |
| Cumin powder | ½ tsp |
| Turmeric powder | ¼ tsp |
| Red chilli powder | ½ tsp |
| Groundnut oil | 3-4 tbsp |
| Powdered jaggery | 2 tbsp |
| Curry leaves | a few |
| Coriander leaves | a small bunch |

## METHOD

Boil the yam with salt. It should be soft but not squishy. Set aside.

Heat a heavy bottomed cooking vessel. Heat the oil (do not let it smoke). Fry the boiled yam in this oil till the sides get coated but not crisp. Remove and set aside.

In the same oil, fry the fenugreek seeds, then add garlic. Brown the garlic and add mustard seeds. Once the mustard starts popping add the chopped onions and half the curry leaves. Let the onions brown— this will give colour to your pulusu. Once the onions brown, add the cumin and coriander powder and cook for couple of minutes.

Then add the turmeric powder and tomato. Add the red chilli powder. Cook until the tomatoes become soft. Now add the tamarind and start mixing. Add a cup of water or more to make a thick but liquid gravy. Allow this mixture to heat up and once it starts bubbling add the boiled fried yam. Add more water if it's too thick. Allow it to boil, about 10-15 minutes. Add the some of the curry leaves as it's cooking. Add salt to taste

Finally add the jaggery, do not cook for more than five minutes. Garnish with chopped coriander and curry leaves. Serve with rice and a dollop of ghee.


# KACHIYA MORU

## (COOKED BUTTERMILK)

ANNU PALAKUNNATHU MATTHEW                    KERALA

SERVES: 4                         PREPARATION TIME: 25 MINUTES

INGREDIENTS

|  |  |
|---|---|
| Yoghurt | 2 cups |
| Salt | to taste |

For ground masala

|  |  |
|---|---|
| Coconut | 2 tbsp, (optional) |
| Turmeric powder | ¾ tsp |
| Cumin seeds | ½ tsp |

| | |
|---:|:---|
| Onions | 3 small |
| Green chillies | 2 |
| Coconut oil | 2 tbsp |
| Fenugreek seeds | ½ tsp |
| Mustard seeds | ½ tsp |
| Garlic | 3, sliced |
| Ginger | 1 inch piece, sliced into long thin strips |
| Curry leaves | few leaves (1 stalk ) |
| Whole dried red chillies | 3 |
| Red chilli powder | ¼ tsp |

## METHOD

Prepare the ground masala by grinding all the listed ingredients. Whisk the yoghurt till smooth, add a cup of water and beat well. Mix in the masala and salt and keep aside.

Heat oil in a deep vessel. Add fenugreek and mustard seeds and red chillies. When they splutter, add onions, garlic, and ginger. Keep stirring till the onions turn golden brown. Add curry leaves and red chilli powder. Stir, then remove the vessel from heat and allow to cool for a few minutes.

Now pour the buttermilk mixture into the vessel. Stir with a wooden spatula or spoon. Put the vessel back on the heat and cook while stirring all the time. Do not let the buttermilk boil.

Keep lifting the wooden spatula or spoon to check if steam is emitting from it. When this happens remove from the flame. Continue to stir till the buttermilk cools down.

Transfer to a china or glass bowl to prevent curdling or splitting of the mixture before serving.

# MEEN VEVICHATHU

## (KERALA SYRIAN FISH CURRY)

ANNU PALAKUNNATHU MATTHEW                          KERALA

SERVES: 4–6                              PREPARATION TIME: 1 HOUR

### INGREDIENTS

| | |
|---|---|
| Fish (any fleshy fish) | 1 kg, cut into thick uniform pieces |
| Kerala kokum | 3 |

### For masala paste

| | |
|---|---|
| Turmeric powder | ¾ tsp |
| Kashmiri red chilli powder | 5 tbsp |
| Fenugreek seeds | ¾ tsp, roasted and powdered |
| Mustard powder | ¼ tsp |
| Salt | to taste |

### For seasoning

| | |
|---|---|
| Coconut oil | ¼ cup |
| Fenugreek seeds | ½ tsp |
| Mustard seeds | 1 tsp |
| Onions | 2 tbsp, sliced |
| Garlic | 1 tbsp, sliced |
| Ginger | 1 tbsp, sliced |
| Curry leaves | 3 stalks |

### METHOD

Soak kokum in ½ cup warm water. Make the masala paste with warm water and set aside.

Clean and wash the fish and keep in a vessel filled with clean water.

Heat the oil in a shallow vessel (preferably earthen) with a wide mouth. Add the fenugreek and mustard seeds and let them splutter.

Add curry leaves and the sliced onions, garlic, and ginger. When the onions become soft add the masala paste and cook until oil appears on the surface of the masala.

Now add enough hot water to get a runny gravy. Once it boils, drop the fish pieces gently around the vessel such that the gravy covers every piece of fish. Drop the soaked kokum into the gravy.

Do not stir the gravy once the fish is added. But you may lift the vessel and move it in circles to mix the gravy. Bring to a boil by covering the vessel with a lid.

Add salt and do the same circular motion to mix the gravy. Now lower the flame and cook till the fish is done and the gravy reduces.

When the oil surfaces and floats on the top the dish is ready to serve.

# PRAWN CURRY

SIMRAN AND NEERAJ KANWAR                                        KERALA

SERVES: 6–8                        PREPARATION TIME: 2 HOURS 30 MINUTES

INGREDIENTS

| | |
|---|---|
| Green cardamom pods | 8 |
| Cloves | 8 |
| Cinnamon | 2½ sticks |
| Fenugreek seeds | 2½ heaped tbsp |
| Fennel seeds | 3–4 tbsp |
| Coconut oil | 3–4 tbsp |
| Garlic | 3 heaped tbsp, grated |
| Ginger | 2½ heaped tbsp, grated |
| Onions | 4 medium |
| Tomatoes | 8 medium |
| Coconut cream or coconut milk | 600 ml |
| Curry leaves | around 40 |
| Coriander | the stalks of a bunch |
| Prawns | 1 kg, shelled (keep shells aside if possible) |
| Coriander powder, cumin, and paprika | 3 tbsp each |
| Turmeric powder | 2 tbsp |
| Hot chilli powder | 1 tbsp (optional) |
| Salt | to taste |
| Green chillies | 3 |
| Lemons | 2, juiced |

METHOD

Take a nice wide frying pan and on a medium flame throw in the whole spices i.e. cardamom, clove, cinnamon, fenugreek, and fennel. Dry roast until they begin to pop around the pan; be careful not to burn them. This should take about 5 minutes.

Add 2–3 tablespoons of coconut oil and throw in the garlic and ginger followed by the onions, curry leaves, and coriander stalks. Cook until you get some nice golden colour on the onions.

If you have the prawn shells, add them now. Add all the ground spices. Toss these around until the shells are a nice pinkish hue. This should all take about 20 minutes or so.

Add in all the coconut milk. Stir well and cover. Allow this to cook for about 30–40 minutes. Now take this all off the flame and sieve into another saucepan. Make sure you squeeze out all the juices. Pour a little hot water into the sieve and, wearing a pair of rubber gloves, squeeze out the juices three to four times in order to get all the flavour contained inside.

Now you have a nice curry in one saucepan. Put this back on a medium flame and allow to cook.

In a second saucepan add a tablespoon of coconut oil and throw in all the prawns. Keep turning over so they are all evenly coloured. The prawns should be cooked for about 10 minutes until they release water. Now strain all the water from the prawns into the main pot of curry and keep the prawns aside.

Chop up the tomatoes. Heat a non-stick frying pan and cook the tomatoes in it until they are properly reduced. Once done add this to the main saucepan of curry. Now you will need to allow the curry to bubble and cook on medium heat for about 40 minutes until the froth at the top disappears altogether.

Now sieve the whole thing again. Put the reduced gravy back on the stove, and throw in the cooked prawns. This should cook together for about 15–20 minutes. Mix in the lemon juice; the dish is now ready to serve.

Garnish with coriander, a slice of lime, and some green chillies. Serve hot with idlis if possible, else with rice.

# AMMA'S RED FISH CURRY

## (KOTTAYAM-STYLE)

DILIP CHERIAN

KERALA

SERVES: 4

PREPARATION TIME: 40 MINUTES
(PLUS 4 HOURS RESTING TIME)

INGREDIENTS

| | |
|---|---|
| Fish (surmai/yellow tuna/ayala) | ½ kg |
| Coconut oil | 4 tbsp, plus extra for garnishing |
| Mustard seeds | 1 tsp |
| Fenugreek seeds | ¼ tsp |
| Shallots/sambar onion | 20, peeled and sliced thinly |
| Garlic cloves | 5, finely chopped |
| Ginger | 2-cm piece chopped finely |
| Green chillies | 2, slit lengthwise |
| Curry leaves | a handful |
| Kashmiri red chilli powder | 4 tbsp (for colour) |
| Black pepper powder | 1 tsp |
| Turmeric powder | 1 tsp |
| Fenugreek seed powder | a big pinch |
| Salt | to taste |
| Malabar tamarind or tamarind pulp | 3 pieces or 2 tbsp |

METHOD

Heat the coconut oil in a wok, ideally an earthenware wok. Add mustard and fenugreek seeds and let them sizzle.

After they turn dark, add the shallots, garlic, ginger, curry leaves, and turmeric powder. Sauté for 3 minutes or so.

Lower the flame and add in the Kashmiri chilli powder and pepper powder. Sauté on low heat for about 5–6 minutes until the spices get toasted and their colour darkens to a fiery red.

Add the tamarind pulp and 2 cups water. Add the salt and bring to a full boil.

Add the fish and mix well until the pieces are fully immersed in the gravy. You may temper some extra curry leaves in coconut oil and add here if you like.

Cook this partially covered on a medium-high flame. It will take 8–10 minutes for the fish to get cooked.

Add a big pinch of fenugreek seed powder and pepper powder, as per your taste. Garnish generously with more curry leaves. Finally, drizzle in a tablespoon of coconut oil on top while the fish is still hot (this is vital).

Now take off the heat and cover. Let it sit for 4 hours for the flavours to fully emerge and seep through. The dish will taste wonderful only if it sits for a while. Serve with brown rice.

# ROASTED COCONUT CURRY

PADMA MUKUNDAN AND
SHAILJA AND SUMANT JAYAKRISHNAN                          KERALA

SERVES: 4–6                         PREPARATION TIME: 40 MINUTES

INGREDIENTS

| | |
|---|---|
| Cooking oil | 1 tsp |
| Grated coconut | 1 cup |
| Cumin seeds | 1 tsp |
| Whole peppercorns | ½ tsp |
| Coriander powder | 4 tsp |
| Red chilli powder | 1 tsp |
| Oil | 2 tbsp |
| Cardamom pod | 1 |
| Cloves | 2–3 |
| Onions | 1–2, sliced |
| Tomatoes | 1–2, chopped |
| Potatoes | 4–5, peeled and cut into cubes |
| Curry leaves | 1 bunch |

METHOD

In a heavy bottomed wok, heat a teaspoon of oil. Add the grated coconut and roast over medium heat until the coconut turns deep brown. Lower the heat and add cumin seeds, peppercorns, chilli powder, and coriander powder. Stir together until the smell of raw masala disappears. Cool and grind to a smooth paste.

Heat 2 tablespoons of oil in another pan. Add cardamom pods and cloves. Add onions and fry till golden brown. Add tomatoes and fry till they are softened. Add potatoes and the masala paste and stir all together. Add water to form a gravy. Add salt to taste and curry leaves. Cook till potatoes turn soft. Remove from heat and serve with rice or appams.

**Note:** A variety of vegetables may be added to the potatoes. Mutton may be used instead of vegetables to make a delicious mutton curry.

# MANGO PULISSERY

## (RIPE MANGO CURRY)

PADMA MUKUNDAN AND
SHAILJA AND SUMANT JAYAKRISHNAN                          KERALA

SERVES: 4                                    PREPARATION TIME: 30 MINUTES

INGREDIENTS

| | |
|---|---|
| Ripe mangoes of any variety | 5–6 small, cut into large slices with the skin |
| Turmeric powder | ½ tsp |
| Red chilli powder | 1 tsp |
| Salt | to taste |
| Grated coconut | 1 cup |
| Green chillies | 2–3 |
| Cumin seeds | 1 tsp |
| Yoghurt | ½ cup, beaten smooth |
| Oil | 1 tbsp |
| Fenugreek seeds | ½ tsp |
| Mustard seeds | ½ tsp |
| Curry leaves | a sprig |

METHOD

Place the mangoes in a pot with the turmeric powder, red chilli powder, and salt and cook over a medium flame. Be careful not to overcook them.

Grind the grated coconut with green chillies and cumin seeds. Mix this into the cooked mango with a little water, and boil for a minute. Reduce flame to simmer.

Mix the beaten yoghurt into the mangoes, stirring all the time without bringing to the boiling point. Remove from fire.

Heat the oil in a separate pan. Splutter the fenugreek seeds, mustard seeds, and curry leaves in this. Temper the mangoes with this and serve.

# IDLIS

SHASHI THAROOR                                              KERALA

SERVES: 4–6                              PREPARATION TIME: 20 MINUTES
                                  (PLUS SOAKING AND FERMENTATION TIME)

INGREDIENTS

| | |
|---|---|
| Rice | 1 cup |
| Husked black gram | ½ cup |
| Salt | 1 tsp, or to taste |
| Oil | to grease idli moulds |
| Sour yoghurt | 1 tablespoon (optional) |
| Carom seeds or cumin seeds or fenugreek seeds | 1 tsp (optional) |

METHOD

Soak the rice and black gram in water overnight. You may scale up this recipe by increasing quantities of both in a 2:1 ratio.

Grind the soaked rice and gram together to medium coarseness; add water if needed to make a thick but pourable batter. Mix in salt and leave the batter outside to ferment until the batter rises and becomes slightly sour (24 hours in summer, 36 hours in winter). The time can be shortened somewhat by adding some slightly sour dahi to the batter instead. Some cooks add carom and/or cumin seeds to the batter; my mother puts fenugreek seeds in sometimes.

Once the batter is ready, generously grease the moulds of an idli maker and spoon the batter into the moulds.

Take a deep pot or a large pressure cooker and add about 2 cups of water. Heat the pot until the water begins to boil slightly. Place the idli maker into the pot gently and cover. Steam the idlis for about 12 minutes. The idlis are ready when a wooden toothpick or skewer inserted into the centres comes out clean.

**Note:** The perfect idli is soft, fluffy, slightly sour, melts in your mouth. Flavour comes from the accompaniments—coconut chutney; 'gunpowder' with melted ghee; and my own favourite, a paste called ulli samandhi made of grinding small onions or shallots with red chillies and salt and just a dash of tamarind, and roasting the results.

# TARA'S BISCUIT ROTI

NIRUPAMA MENON RAO                                         KARNATAKA

SERVES: 4–6                               PREPARATION TIME: 45 MINUTES

INGREDIENTS

| | |
|---|---|
| Gram flour | 1 cup |
| Lemons | 2, juiced |
| Coriander leaves | a bunch |
| Green chillies | to taste |
| Grated coconut | ½ cup |
| Asafoetida | a pinch, dissolved in water |
| Whole wheat flour | 1 cup |
| All-purpose flour | ½ cup |
| Vegetable oil | for frying |

METHOD

Coarsely grind the coriander leaves, asafoetida water, coconut, and green chillies together. Add salt to taste. Add the gram flour and lemon juice. Make into walnut-sized balls and set aside.

Mix the two flours together with a little oil, salt, and water. Knead well, for about 7–10 minutes.

Shape the dough into balls, slightly larger than the walnut-sized ones you've made already. You should have equal numbers of these balls and the gram flour balls.

Roll out the flour balls into puris. Place the gram flour balls in the centre and fold the outer layer, pinching to close. Roll these filled balls out into discs.

Heat enough oil for deep frying and fry the discs until they are golden brown. Serve hot.


# PONGAL

LATHA REDDY                           BANGALORE, KARNATAKA

SERVES: 4                          PREPARATION TIME: 30 MINUTES

INGREDIENTS

| | |
|---|---|
| Rice | 2 cups |
| Split yellow lentils | 2 cups |
| Turmeric powder | 2 tsp |
| Curry leaves | 4 sprigs |
| Cumin seeds | 2 tbsp |
| Vegetable oil | 4 tbsp |
| Ghee | 2 tbsp |
| Whole peppercorns | 2 tbsp |
| Fresh ginger | 2 tbsp, finely grated |
| Asafoetida | a pinch |
| Cashew nuts | 12, broken into halves |
| Salt | to taste |

METHOD

Crush the peppercorns gently to get roughly cracked pepper after keeping aside 1 teaspoon of whole peppercorns.

Wash rice and yellow lentils well and add turmeric, 1 tablespoon oil, salt to taste, and 4 cups water.

Cook briefly in a pressure cooker or for a longer time in a large dish on the stovetop until the rice and lentil mixture is mushy and well cooked.

Heat the remaining oil and ghee. Add the cumin seeds, curry leaves, and grated ginger. When the cumin seeds and curry leaves crackle, add the asafoetida, cashew nuts, cracked and whole pepper, and switch off heat. The cashew nuts should be light brown.

Add the tempered cumin seeds and spice mixture to the cooked rice and lentils.

Serve with a dollop of ghee and chutney of your choice.

# SPINACH THOREN

SHOBITA PUNJA                                                          KERALA

SERVES: 4                                        PREPARATION TIME: 30 MINUTES

INGREDIENTS
For the masala

|  |  |
|---|---|
| Green chillies | ½ tsp, chopped |
| Cumin seeds | a pinch |
| Garlic | 2 cloves |
| Onion | 1 small |
| Dry chilli seeds | ¼ tsp |
| Grated coconut | ½ cup, plus extra for garnishing |
| Spinach | 3 cups, finely chopped |
| Salt | to taste |

For the seasoning

|  |  |
|---|---|
| Oil | ½ tbsp |
| Mustard seeds | ¼ tsp |
| Raw rice | ¼ tsp |
| Whole dried red chillies | 1, broken into 2–3 pieces |
| Curry leaves | 3–4 |
| Onions | 1 tsp, thinly sliced |

METHOD
Grind all the ingredients for the masala. Mix the ground masala with the coconut.

Lightly cook the chopped spinach with a pinch of salt and a little water. Make sure the spinach is not overcooked.

Make a well in the centre of the spinach in the pan and put the ground masala into it. Cover the pan. When the ground masala is cooked through (about 5 minutes), stir the mixture and remove from heat when all the water has been absorbed.

Prepare the seasoning by heating the cooking oil and frying all the listed ingredients in it. Pour over the cooked spinach and stir.

Garnish with a little fresh grated coconut over the dish to bring out the contrast of the greens and white. Serve hot or cold.

# KODAVA PANDI CURRY

KAVERI PONAPPA                                          COORG, KARNATAKA

SERVES: 4–6                                    PREPARATION TIME: 1 HOUR
                                        (PLUS OVERNIGHT MARINATION TIME)

INGREDIENTS

| | |
|---|---|
| Pork | 1 kg (200 gms combined fat and bones, some meat on the bone), cut into cubes |
| Turmeric powder | 2 tsp |
| Red chilli powder | to taste |
| Whole black peppercorns | 1 tbsp, heaped or to taste |
| Cumin seeds | 2 tbsp |
| Mustard seeds | 1½ tbsp |
| Coriander powder | 2 tbsp |
| Fenugreek seeds | ½ tsp |
| Ginger | 4-inch piece |
| Garlic | 8–10 cloves |
| Oil | 2 tbsp |
| Onions | 2–3 large, chopped fine |
| Salt | to taste |
| Green chillies or fresh bird's eye chillies | 3–4, slit lengthwise |
| Kachampuli (tart, dark Kodava vinegar) | 1–1½ tbsp (Substitutes are thick tamarind paste/malt vinegar or extract |

| | from soaked, dried kokum. You will not get the dark rich colour and distinctive flavour of kachampuli and thick gravy, though). |
|---|---|
| Lime | 1, sliced |

METHOD

Wash and drain the pork, pat dry. Mix in the turmeric powder and red chilli powder and marinate overnight in the fridge. Bring the pork to room temperature before cooking.

Dry roast each of the spices separately on a hot griddle. Begin with the black peppercorns, followed by coriander seeds. Mustard seeds should begin to crackle; cumin seeds and fenugreek should turn dark brown and begin to release their aromas. Fenugreek seeds tend to burn very quickly, so turn off the heat and roast gently. Allow spices to cool completely. Grind each separately to a fine powder and bottle. Roasting and grinding the spices a day or two ahead will make this step easier. The powdered spices are best made in small batches and stored in an airtight container for short periods.

Grind the ginger and garlic to a coarse paste. Heat the oil in a pressure cooker and fry the chopped onions until lightly browned. Add the garlic ginger paste, and fry for a few minutes.

Add the pork, and fry until the meat changes colour. Sprinkle over all the dry roasted spices. Stir thoroughly and fry for a few minutes. Add salt to taste.

Add about 2 cups of hot water or according to the gravy required. You should have a thick gravy. Pressure cook for 20 minutes over medium-low heat. Remove from the heat after 20 minutes, allow the pressure to release on its own before opening the pressure cooker.

Add about 1½ tablespoons of kachampuli, stir well and simmer gently for about 10 minutes. Taste for seasoning and finally add a few fresh green chillies, slit lengthwise. Serve with additional squeezes of lime, according to taste. Eat with kadambuttus (steamed rice balls). Pandi curry tastes better if allowed to rest for a day or two.

# SAVJI KEEMA CURRY

NAYANA DHONGADI                                    HUBBALLI, KARNATAKA
COURTESY SAGARI AND AJAY HANDA

SERVES: 4                              PREPARATION TIME: 1 HOUR

INGREDIENTS

| | |
|---|---|
| Coconut paste | ½ cup |
| Whole wheat flour | 2 tsp |

For the meatballs

| | |
|---|---|
| Minced meat | 500 gms |
| Salt | 1 tsp |
| Turmeric powder | ½ tsp |
| Red chilli powder (mirgut) | 1 tsp |
| Coriander powder (haavez) | 1 tsp, roasted |
| Grated dry coconut | 2 tbsp |
| Whole wheat flour | 1 tsp |
| Coriander leaves | 4 tsp, chopped |
| Ginger garlic paste | 2 tsp |
| Coriander leaves paste | 2 tsp |
| Oil | 2 tbsp |

For the curry

| | |
|---|---|
| Tomatoes | 2, finely chopped |
| Ginger garlic paste | 2 tbsp |
| Salt | 1 tsp, or to taste |
| Turmeric powder | ½ tsp |
| Coriander powder | 2 tbsp, roasted |
| Garam masala | 1½ tbsp |
| Oil | 1 cup |
| Red chilli powder | 8 tbsp |

METHOD

To prepare the meatballs, add all the listed ingredients in a bowl and mix well. Let the meat rest for about 20 minutes.

Blend together the prepared mix in a food processor/mixer to a soft doughy consistency. Roll them into small balls using lightly oiled hands. Set aside.

Heat oil in a wok. Mix all the ingredients listed under 'for the curry' with a little water (enough to make a thick paste) and fry it in the oil.

Add ½ cup water to the wok. Add the prepared meatballs and cook for 10 minutes on a low flame.

Meanwhile, in a separate pan mix ½ cup of water with the coconut paste and cook on low for 10 minutes. This coconut mix can also be prepared earlier.

Mix 2 tablespoons of this coconut mixture with 2 teaspoons of whole wheat flour and ½ cup water. Add this to the curry and cook for 5 minutes. The dish is now ready to serve.


# PODI KURA MAAMSAM
## (CRISPY SHREDDED LAMB)

VIDYA GAJAPATHY RAJU                          VIZAG, ANDHRA PRADESH

SERVES: 4                                     PREPARATION TIME: 1 HOUR

INGREDIENTS

| | |
|---|---|
| Mutton | ½ kg, boneless |
| Ginger garlic paste | 1 tbsp |
| Turmeric powder | ¼ tsp |
| Coriander powder | 2 tbsp |
| Red chilli powder | 1–1½ tsp |
| Salt | to taste |
| Coarse Bengal gram powder | 5 tbsp, roasted |
| Poppy seeds | 1 tbsp |
| Oil | ¾ tbsp |
| Cinnamon | 1 small piece |
| Cloves | 4 |

METHOD

Put the mutton with the turmeric, salt, coriander, and ginger garlic paste in a pressure cooker with a little water. Place on medium heat and cook for three whistles.

Remove the lid and cook till all the water evaporates. Shred the mutton using a fork.

In a pan, heat the oil and add the cinnamon and cloves. Then add the shredded mutton and fry till it changes colour to a light brown. Add the chilli powder and keep frying for some more time.

Keep adding small amounts of the coarsely powdered gram. The mutton should start to get dry and crispy. At this stage add the poppy seeds.

Keep frying in the pan till the mutton turns a dark brown colour. Serve hot with chapattis or rice.

# PICKLED AVAKKAI BIRYANI

PREETHA REDDY                                          ANDHRA PRADESH

SERVES: 6                                    PREPARATION TIME: 2 HOURS
                                        (PLUS EXTRA TIME TO MAKE PICKLE)

INGREDIENTS

| | |
|---|---|
| Basmati rice | 1 kg |
| Onion | ½ kg, sliced |
| Tomato | ¼ kg, chopped |
| Yoghurt | 200 gms |
| Red chilli powder | 50 gms |
| Garam masala powder | 1 tbsp |
| Avakkai (Andhra mango pickle) | 600 gms |
| Soya chunks | 100 gms, soaked |
| Mint leaves | 1 cup, chopped |
| Mint leaves for layering | ½ cup |
| Coriander leaves | 1 cup, chopped |
| Fresh ghee | 200 gms |
| Ginger and garlic paste | 1 tbsp |
| Salt | to taste |

METHOD

Wash the basmati rice 2–3 times using only cold water. Then transfer the washed rice into a large vessel, pour water into it until the rice is fully covered and set it aside to soak for at least 25 minutes.

Meanwhile, blanch the soya nuggets in salted water for 5 minutes and then, grind them to a coarse paste using a blender (to resemble minced meat).

Heat the ghee (reserving a tablespoon) in a heavy bottomed pan; add sliced onions and sauté until golden brown. Set aside half the quantity for layering the biryani.

Add the ginger and garlic paste, red chilli powder, and garam masala powder, and sauté until the raw flavour goes away.

Add chopped mint and coriander leaves, then the chopped tomato, coarsely blended soya nuggets, and cook for 3–4 minutes. Add the yoghurt, salt to taste and simmer for 3–4 minutes.

Strain the soaked rice. Separately, heat water in a vessel to cook the rice. Add salt to the water and gently add in the rice. Cook until the rice is parboiled.

Preheat oven at a temperature of 176°C. Once the rice is cooked, it is time to start layering to prepare the biryani. In a heavy bottomed pot, arrange a thin layer of the gravy, then layer with a third of the biryani rice, add a third of the avakkai pickle, and top it with a third of the biryani masala. Keep adding 4–5 mint leaves between each layer.

Repeat as above twice and finally add in a large tablespoon of ghee along with the fried onions and fresh mint leaves. Cover with a lid and to make the vessel completely airtight, seal the edges with chapatti or bread dough, or aluminium foil. This will preserve the aroma of the biryani.

Now place the biryani pot in the preheated oven for 10–12 minutes. Once done, remove from the oven and serve hot along with some raita.

**Note:** Pickles have considerable salt, so keep in mind while adding salt to the biryani.

If you want to make your own pickle, follow the steps below.

For the avakkai

| | |
|---|---|
| Whole raw mangoes (known as avakkai mangoes) | 2 kg |
| Red chilli powder | 750 gms |
| Fenugreek seeds | 100 gms |
| Turmeric powder | 3 tbsp |
| Asafoetida powder | 3 tbsp |
| Sesame oil | 1 kg |
| Garlic cloves | 200 gms, peeled and crushed |
| Garlic cloves | 100 gms whole peeled |
| Cumin powder | 2 tbsp |
| Salt | to taste |

METHOD

Wash the mangoes thoroughly and then soak them in a large bowl for an hour to remove any mud that might be deposited on them.

After an hour, wash them again under running water and then pat them dry individually with a clean cloth to ensure that they are completely moisture free.

Cut the mangoes in half with the seed and kernel intact. Remove the kernel using a spoon and wipe it dry.

Powder the fenugreek seeds and set aside.

In a thick bottomed pan, heat the sesame oil, add in the powdered fenugreek seeds, then the cumin powder, crushed garlic and finally the turmeric and chilli powders and immediately remove from heat.

Add the cut avakkai mangoes, peeled whole garlic, asafoetida, and salt to taste.

Transfer them into a dry ceramic container and store them in cool dry place. Allow 3–4 days for maceration before using the avakkai.

# BILGRAMI STEW

NAJMA CURRIMJEE                                         HYDERABAD

SERVES: 6                              PREPARATION TIME: 45–50 MINUTES

INGREDIENTS

| | |
|---|---|
| Vegetable oil | ½ cup |
| Ghee | ½ cup |
| Chicken (use either a whole chicken cut up, or specific cuts as desired) | 700 gms |
| New yellow potatoes | 5–6, peeled and halved if needed |
| Cauliflower | large, ½ |
| Green peas | 1 cup |
| Eggs (hardboiled) | 4 |
| Onions | 2 medium, finely chopped |
| Ginger garlic paste | 2 tbsp |
| Black pepper | 1 tsp, finely ground |
| Black pepper | 1 tsp, coarsely ground |
| Coriander leaves | ½ cup, chopped |
| Green chillies | 2–3, to taste |
| Salt | to taste |

METHOD

Cut the cauliflower into medium size florets.

Heat the ghee on medium–high heat in a large saucepan or deep frying pan. Fry the cauliflower in the ghee till golden brown but not soft. Remove and set aside. Fry the potatoes in the ghee till golden brown but not soft; remove and set aside. Carefully fry the hard-boiled eggs in the ghee till golden brown. Remove from the ghee and set aside.

Top up the ghee with a little oil and heat. Fry the chicken pieces, adding a little salt, until golden but not cooked through. Remove from oil and set aside.

Add any remaining oil to the pan and heat. Add the onions to the hot oil and cook till transparent and light golden. Do not let them brown.

Add the ginger garlic paste and cook till fragrant. Lower the heat.

Add the black pepper, salt, green chillies, and chopped coriander and fry gently till the masala is lightly fragrant.

Add the chicken back in and add 1½ cups of water. Cook the chicken till it is tender.

Add the potatoes and cauliflower and cook for a few minutes till they are cooked through.

Add the eggs and the peas, and simmer for a few minutes till everything is warmed through. Stir occasionally but be gentle so that the meat and vegetable pieces stay whole and do not disintegrate.

Remove from heat. Garnish with finely chopped fresh coriander leaves and serve immediately with hot basmati rice or warm crusty bakery bread.

# BIBI MARIAM KI ROTI

NAJMA CURRIMJEE                                           HYDERABAD

SERVES: 6                              PREPARATION TIME: 45–50 MINUTES

INGREDIENTS
For lamb boti

| | |
|---|---|
| Vegetable oil | ½ cup |
| Lamb | 500 gms, boneless, cut into 1-inch pieces |
| Onion | 1 medium-sized |
| Cinnamon | 1 stick |
| Bay leaf | 1 |
| Ginger garlic paste | 1 tbsp |
| Salt | 1 tsp, or to taste |
| Red chilli powder | 1 tsp |
| Turmeric powder | 1 tsp |
| Coriander leaves | ½ cup, chopped |
| Green chillies | 2–3, to taste |

For the roghni roti

| | |
|---|---|
| Whole wheat flour | 1 cup |

| | |
|---|---|
| Ghee | ¼ cup |
| Salt | a pinch |
| Water or warm milk | 2 tbsp |

For the yoghurt chutney

| | |
|---|---|
| Full-fat yoghurt | 1 cup, whipped into smooth, thick consistency |
| Fresh coriander leaves | ½ cup, finely chopped |
| Green chillies | 1–2, finely chopped |
| Cucumber | ¼ cup, diced |
| Mint leaves | 2–3 sprigs, finely chopped |
| Salt | to taste |

METHOD

First, make the lamb botis:

Finely chop the onions.

Heat the oil in a heavy frying pan. Add the onions, bay leaf, and cinnamon to the oil and fry until the onions are pale golden.

Cut the lamb into small cubes and pat dry. Add the meat to the fried onions and fry for about 5 minutes.

Add the ginger garlic paste and fry for a few more minutes. Add red chilli powder, turmeric, and salt to taste. Fry until the mixture is fragrant, then add the green chillies.

Continue frying on medium heat until the meat is well browned and quite dry, then stir in the chopped coriander. Remove from heat.

Check the seasoning and adjust as needed. Allow to rest while you make the roti and yoghurt chutney.

For the yoghurt chutney, stir together all the listed ingredients for the chutney, adding salt and green chilli to taste. Keep cool. This can also be made in advance. To make the roti, begin by stirring together the flour and salt. Add the ghee and mix to a consistency of soft moist breadcrumbs. Add the water or milk and knead into a stiff dough.

Portion the dough into small balls as for chapattis. Roll out, without dusting with any additional flour, into rounds less than ¼ inch (5 mm) thick and approximately 4½ inches (10–11cm) wide.

If the edges of the roti are rough, use a biscuit cutter or knife to smoothen. Prick with a fork and set aside. Keep rolled rotis covered with a damp cloth till all are rolled before cooking.

Heat an iron pan and add a drizzle of ghee. Place a roti in the centre of the hot tawa and press down to cook evenly.

It should not rise or puff up, so keep rotating and pressing down to cook quickly. Turn over and add a drizzle of ghee at the edges if needed, till the roti is golden and cooked. Cook the rest of the rotis similarly.

Before assembling the dish, briefly reheat the lamb if needed. Top a generous spoonful of lamb on each hot roti, then pour the yoghurt mixture over the top.

Garnish with additional fresh coriander as desired and enjoy.

# LAMB PASINDAS

SELMA BILGRAMI AND NAJMA CURRIMJEE                HYDERABAD

SERVES: 4                      PREPARATION TIME: 1 HOUR 15 MINUTES
                               (PLUS 2 HOURS MARINATION TIME)

INGREDIENTS

| | |
|---|---|
| Lamb pasindas (meat cubes flattened by a heavy butcher's knife or meat mallet) | 500 gms |
| Vegetable oil | ¾ cup |
| Onions | 1 large or 2 medium |
| Yoghurt | 1 cup |
| Ginger garlic paste | 1 tbsp |
| Salt | 1 tsp, or to taste |
| Red chilli powder | 1 tsp |
| Turmeric powder | 1 tsp |
| Almonds | 5–6, ground |
| Peanuts | 2 tbsp |
| Poppy seeds | 1 tsp |
| Fresh coriander leaves | 50 gms |
| Fresh mint | 25 gms |
| Green chillies | 2 |
| Lemon | 1 |

| Garam masala | ½ tsp |
|---|---|
| Dry coconut | 1 tsp |

## METHOD

Heat the oil in a pan. Finely slice and fry the onions in the vegetable oil till they are evenly crisp and golden brown. While the onions are frying, add ginger garlic paste to the flat pieces of meat, squeeze a lemon over the meat, combine well, and keep aside.

Once the onions are ready, drain them and set aside. Keep the oil aside.

Lightly toast the poppy seeds, almonds, and peanuts, and grind to a fine powder. Grind the fresh coriander, mint, and green chillies separately. Beat the yoghurt to a smooth consistency. Add salt, chilli powder, turmeric, and ground greens to the yoghurt.

Crush the fried onions and add to the yoghurt mixture, combining well.

Add the yoghurt mixture to the lamb, fold in thoroughly until it is well coated. Marinate for 2 hours.

Take a shallow, wide, heavy bottomed pan and pour in the oil (in which the onions were fried). Place the meat and yoghurt mixture in the oil.

Cook on high heat for ten minutes or until the juices are hot and bubbling.

Cover tightly and reduce the heat to medium or low. When it smells fragrant, check that the meat is tender and the water has reduced. With a flat spoon turn the pieces of meat over to evenly brown all the meat and masala.

Transfer the cooked pasindas to a shallow heatproof serving dish. Place under a hot grill to further brown the meat on top if you so desire.

To give the dish a smoky flavour, take half an onion skin or a round cup of foil, pour a teaspoon of ghee in it and place in the centre of the dish, on top of the meat. Light a piece of charcoal and place in the ghee. Immediately cover the dish so that the fragrant smoke is absorbed into the meat. Remove the cover and the foil cup or onion skin after a few minutes.

Garnish with finely sliced onion rings, lemon wedges, and mint. Pasindas are best served with naan or rice.

# TOMATO CHUTNEY

SELMA BILGRAMI AND NAJMA CURRIMJEE                    HYDERABAD

SERVES: 4–6                    PREPARATION TIME: 30–40 MINUTES

INGREDIENTS

| | |
|---|---|
| Tomatoes (ripe) | 500 gms |
| Garlic paste | 1 tsp |
| Salt | 1 tsp, or to taste |
| Red chilli powder | 1 tsp |
| Turmeric powder | 1 tsp |
| Cumin seeds | 1 tsp, freshly toasted and ground |
| Coriander seeds | 1 tsp, freshly toasted and ground |
| Curry leaves | 2–3 stalks |
| Coriander leaves | 50 gms, chopped |
| Green chillies | 2–3 |

For tempering

| | |
|---|---|
| Vegetable oil | 100 ml |
| Cumin seeds | ½ tsp |
| Fenugreek seeds | ¼ tsp |
| Whole dried red chillies | 3–4 |
| Whole garlic cloves | 3–4, peeled |

METHOD

Wash and chop the ripe tomatoes into small pieces. Place in a medium saucepan and add garlic paste, salt, red chilli powder, turmeric, ground cumin, and ground coriander. Stir well and start cooking on a medium heat.

Wash and roughly chop coriander leaves; wash the curry leaves. Add both to tomato mixture and continue cooking uncovered.

When the tomatoes are soft and the water has almost dried, remove from heat.

In a separate frying pan, prepare the temper by heating the oil to a high heat. When the oil is hot, add ingredients in this order: garlic, cumin, dry red chillies, and lastly fenugreek seeds. Fry until the fenugreek is dark brown but not burnt.

Pour over the cooked tomatoes. Transfer into a dish and garnish with a fresh green chilli and a few curry leaves.

# HIRVAY MASALEY CHA KOMBDI PULAO

NITA KHANNA                                                    HYDERABAD

SERVES: 6                                   PREPARATION TIME: 1 HOUR
                                (PLUS 30 MINUTES MARINATION TIME)

INGREDIENTS
For the chicken layer

| | | |
|---|---|---|
| Chicken | 1 kg, bone in, skinned, and cut into 12 pieces | |
| Thick yoghurt | 2 cups | |
| Ginger garlic paste | 2 tbsp | |
| Fresh coriander leaves | ½ cup | |
| Fresh mint | ½ cup | |
| Green chillies | 4, finely chopped | |
| Onions | 6, sliced and deep fried till golden brown, plus extra for garnish | |
| Salt | to taste | |
| Nutmeg powder | ½ tsp | |
| Shredded khoya | 2–3 tbsp | |
| Spanish saffron | 6 strands | |
| Ghee | ½ cup, melted | |

For the spice paste (dry roast and grind to a powder)

| | |
|---|---|
| Green cardamom pods | 5, seeds only |
| Cloves | 5 |
| Cinnamon sticks | 2, about 1 inch each |
| Black peppercorns | 1 tsp |
| Coriander seeds | 1 tsp |

For the rice

| | | |
|---|---|---|
| Basmati rice | 1 kg | |
| Black cumin seeds | 1½ tsp | |
| Cinnamon sticks | 3, 1 inch each | |
| Cloves | 8 | |
| Bay leaves | 2 | |
| Salt | to taste | |
| Ghee | ½ cup, melted | |

METHOD

Very coarsely grind the coriander and mint leaves and green chillies together with the fried onions. Whisk the yoghurt in a bowl with the nutmeg and salt and stir in the coriander–mint–chilli–onion mixture. Add the chicken to this mixture and then add in the melted ghee. Mix gently and let the chicken marinate in this for 30 minutes.

In a large vessel, heat about 2 litres of water with salt, the black cumin seeds, cinnamon, cloves, and bay leaves. When the water comes to a boil, add the rice and cook it till half done. (The grain should have plenty of bite in it.) Drain thoroughly and immediately and spread the rice out in a large tray to prevent further cooking.

Grease a deep and heavy bottomed vessel with a little ghee and spread the rice as the bottom layer. If using an oven for cooking then use an oven proof deep dish like French enamelled iron ware. Spread the marinated chicken on top of the layer of rice. Lightly sprinkle the khoya and saffron over the chicken. Pour the remaining ½ cup melted ghee over the chicken. Cover with a tight lid and make a dough seal to prevent the steam from escaping.

Place the vessel on a large griddle or iron pan and cook on a medium low flame for 45 minutes and then on low flame for 15 minutes. Alternatively, preheat the oven to 180°C. Place the ovenproof dish inside and cook for an hour. Turn off the oven and let sit for 15 minutes.

To serve, open the dish and ladle the pulao from the bottom onto a large rice plate or silver tray and garnish with some fried onions. Serve piping hot with a cucumber and onion raita.

# HYDERABADI BIRYANI

SHABANA AZMI                                          HYDERABAD

SERVES: 8–10                    PREPARATION TIME: 1 HOUR 15 MINUTES
                                (PLUS 1 HOUR MARINATION TIME)

INGREDIENTS

| | |
|---|---|
| Mutton (gol boti or raan) | 1 kg |
| Basmati rice | 1 kg, washed and soaked |
| Ghee | ¼ kg |
| Onions | 5–6, thinly sliced |
| Lemons | 2, juiced |
| Saffron | 2 pinches, soaked in some water |
| Cold milk | 3 tbsp |

For marination

| | |
|---|---|
| Yoghurt | ½ kg |
| Ginger garlic paste | 1½ tbsp |
| Mint leaves | a bunch |
| Coriander leaves | a bunch |
| Green chillies | 4–6, finely chopped |
| Red chilli powder | ½ tsp |
| Black cumin seeds | ¼ tsp, slightly crushed |
| Green cardamom pods | 14, ground after removing shells |
| Green cardamom pods | 4 |
| Cinnamon | 4 small sticks |
| Whole peppercorns | 20–25 |
| Cloves | 5–6 |
| Garam masala | ½ tsp |
| Salt | to taste |

METHOD

Marinate the mutton for at least 1 hour in the ingredients listed.

Heat the ghee in a large wok. Fry the sliced onions until they are browned. Drain and set aside.

In the same ghee (you may take some out if you choose), fry the marinated meat.

Add three-fourths of the fried onion and 1½ teaspoon of salt and fry on high heat, stirring continuously so the meat doesn't stick.

When the meat has mostly cooked through and the onions appear dry, remove from heat.

Take a deep pan. Add enough water to fill up half of the vessel and add a pinch of salt and the garam masala. Bring to a boil.

Once the water starts boiling, add the rice and stir intermittently.

Wait till the rice is about fully cooked, then drain and layer half of it in a large and deep pan. On top of this layer all the cooked meat. If you removed any ghee while frying the meat, add it here. Also add the reserved fried onions and finally layer the remaining rice on top.

Sprinkle the saffron—water mixture and lemon juice on top, and then add the cold milk.

Now tightly cover the dish and weigh the lid down with a pestle. Put on high heat for a minute, then reduce heat.

Carefully place an iron griddle or tawa under the dish and leave to cook for 10 minutes. Take off the heat, but let the dish remain on the griddle until it is time to serve.

# HALEEM

DOREEN AND PETER HASSAN · HYDERABAD

SERVES: 10 · PREPARATION TIME: 2 HOURS
(PLUS SOAKING TIME OVERNIGHT)

## INGREDIENTS

| | |
|---|---|
| Boneless meat | 2 kg |
| Wheat | 1 kg |
| Sour yoghurt | ½ kg |
| Ghee | 200 gms |
| Water | 4 cups |
| Oil | ¼ cup |
| Onions | 6 large, sliced |
| Cashew nuts | 4 tbsp |
| Ginger garlic paste | 4 tsp |
| Red chilli powder | 2 tsp |

| | | |
|---|---|---|
| Turmeric powder | 1 tsp | |
| Garam masala powder | 1 tsp | |
| Salt | to taste | |

For spice mix (lightly roasted and ground together)

| | | |
|---|---|---|
| Cardamom pods | 8 | |
| Poppy seeds | 2 tbsp | |
| Chironji | 2 tbsp | |
| Black cumin seeds | 1 tbsp | |
| Coriander powder | ½ tbsp | |

For garnish

| | | |
|---|---|---|
| Fried onions | as needed | |
| Lemon | 1, juiced | |

METHOD

Fill a large pan to the brim with water and soak the wheat in it overnight. The next morning, de-husk the wheat and pressure cook it until soft. Let it cool and then grind to as fine a consistency as possible. Ideally, it should resemble a thick porridge.

Heat oil and fry the onions until golden brown. Then, add ginger garlic paste and chilli and turmeric powders. Fry until aromatic. Now, add the meat and fry until the water dries up. Then, add the spice mix that you made and allow the mixture to brown.

Add the yoghurt and as much water as required for the gravy. I usually use 5 cups of water. When the meat is cooked, add the garam masala and simmer for a few minutes. Remove the pieces of meat and grind to a fine paste.

Heat 200 grams of ghee in another pan. Add the black cumin seeds and cardamom. Lastly, add the ground meat and gravy and mix well. Leave to simmer for 15 minutes. Garnish the haleem with fried onions and lemon juice. Serve with accompaniments of your choice. Suggested accompaniments: whites of spring onions, mint leaves, radishes sliced into strips, fried onions, halved lemons.

**Note:** Make sure you eat this dish as soon as it is made; you cannot store it even in the fridge for more than a day because the wheat will begin fermenting.

# KHATTA MEETHA AAM CHUTNEY

DOREEN AND PETER HASSAN                                    HYDERABAD

SERVES: 25–28                              PREPARATION TIME: 25 MINUTES

INGREDIENTS

| | | |
|---|---|---|
| Semi-ripe mangoes | 1 kg | |
| Jaggery | 100 gms | |
| Tamarind juice | 2 tbsp | |
| Oil | 1 tbsp | |
| Chilli powder | 2 tsp | |
| Salt | to taste | |

METHOD

Peel the mangoes and cube them.

Heat oil in a pan and add the mangoes and chilli powder. Let the mixture cook for 5 minutes before adding in jaggery, tamarind juice, and salt. Mix well to combine all the flavours and let the chutney come to a boil. Lower the flame and let it cook for 5 minutes. Take the pan off the flame and let the chutney cool before you serve it.

# VATHA KULAMBU

POONAM MUTTREJA AND DR SHIV KUMAR                          TAMIL NADU

SERVES: 6                                  PREPARATION TIME: 45 MINS

INGREDIENTS

| | |
|---|---|
| Garlic | 50 gms |
| Onion | 400 gms |
| Tamarind | 50 gms, soaked in water |
| Jaggery | 25 gms |
| Whole red chillies | 2 |
| Red chilli powder | ½ tsp |
| Curry leaves | 8 |
| small onion | 400 gms |

|       |           |
|-------|-----------|
| Oil   | 25 gms    |
| Atta  | 2 tsp     |
| Salt  | to taste  |

## METHOD

Heat oil in a pan and add garlic. Lightly brown. Add the onions and sauté for two minutes. Add the whole red chillies, red chilli powder and curry leaves for two minutes. Then add the tamarind water, salt, and jaggery. Then add atta to thicken the gravy. It's ready serve.

# JUMMAN KA KORMA

SYEDA BILGRAMI AND ASKARI IMAM                    HYDERABAD

SERVES: 6–8                          PREPARATION TIME: 2 HOURS

## INGREDIENTS

| | |
|---|---|
| Mutton | 1 kg |
| Yoghurt | 250 gms |
| Onions | 250 gms, sliced |
| Ghee or oil | 250 gms |
| Coriander seeds | 4 tsp, roasted and ground to paste |
| Coriander leaves | a bunch, chopped |
| Cardamom pods | 2 |
| Cloves | 4 |
| Black cumin | a pinch, ground into fine powder |
| Ginger paste | 2 tsp, heaped |
| Garlic paste | 2 tsp, heaped |
| Red chilli powder | 1 tsp or to taste |
| Salt | to taste |

## METHOD

Wash the mutton well and place in a bowl. Add half of the ginger and garlic pastes, chopped coriander leaves, and a little salt, cover and set aside.

Heat the ghee in a pan. Fry the onions until brown; remove and strain. Spread the fried onions out on a plate and then grind to a fine consistency.

In the remaining ghee, fry the remaining ginger and garlic pastes and red chilli powder until fragrant. Sprinkle a little water and then add the meat. Mix well and cook on low heat.

Cook until the water dries up.

Add yoghurt and coriander paste. Mix well and cover and cook on medium heat till the moisture of the yoghurt is reduced entirely.

Lower the heat, and then add the ground fried onion. Sprinkle in some water and then fry until everything is nicely browned but not burnt.

Once the ghee begins coming up on the sides, test the meat for doneness and add enough water to allow the meat to tenderize without making it too watery.

When the meat is cooked, lower the heat. Add the cardamom pods, cloves, and black cumin powder; mix and serve hot.

**Note:** Chicken korma can be made in the same way. Add 3–4 teaspoons of roasted and ground cashew nuts or almonds to the korma.

## KACHCHEY GOSHT KI BIRYANI

FALAKNUMA PALACE-EZRA JAH                                    HYDERABAD

SERVES: 8–10                          PREPARATION TIME: 1 HOUR 15 MINUTES
                                      (PLUS 18 HOURS MARINATION TIME)

INGREDIENTS

| | |
|---|---|
| Lamb boti | 500 gms |
| Lamb curry cut (with bone) | 500 gms |
| Red chilli powder | 30 gms |
| Green cardamom powder | 2 gms |
| Raw papaya paste | 200 gms skin and seeds removed |
| Salt | 10 gms |
| Ginger garlic paste | 100 gms |
| Mint leaves | 50 gms, chopped |
| Coriander leaves | 100 gms, chopped |

| | |
|---|---|
| Fresh garam masala [homemade] | 10 gms |
| Green chillies | 20 gms, slit lengthwise |
| Green cardamom | 5 gms |
| Cloves | 5 gms |
| Cinnamon stick | 2 gms |
| Desi ghee | 200 gms |
| Rose water | 20 ml |
| Fried onion | 300 gms |
| Yoghurt | 500 gms |
| Saffron | 2 gms |
| Salt | 20 gms, or to taste |
| Rice | 1 kg |
| Oil | 20 ml |

METHOD

Marinate lamb with ginger garlic paste, raw papaya, salt, and Kashmiri red chilli powder for 18–20 hours.

Mix garam masala, chopped mint, chopped coriander, slit green chillies, fried onion, and yoghurt in a copper vessel.

In a large and deep vessel, heat enough water to cook 1 kilogram of rice. When it comes to a boil add the whole spices, salt, and the oil. Drain and set aside.

Now begin layering the biryani in a large dish. Place the marinated lamb first, then spoon all the rice over it. Top with saffron, rose water, and ghee. Cover tightly.

Put the dish on a hot plate or iron pan placed on a low flame and cook for 1 hour. Let it rest covered for 30 minutes before serving.

# East

~

# DRY CABBAGE CURRY WITH SHRIMP

REBA AND HIMACHAL SOM

KOLKATA, WEST BENGAL

SERVES: 4–6

PREPARATION TIME: 1 HOUR

INGREDIENTS

| | |
|---|---|
| Cabbage | 500 gms, chopped fine |
| Potatoes | 2, cut into small cubes |
| Shelled shrimp | 150 gms |
| Oil | 2 tbsp |
| Coriander powder | 1 tbsp |
| Cumin powder | 1 tbsp |
| Turmeric powder | 1 tsp |
| Chilli powder | ½ tsp |
| Ginger paste | 1 tsp |
| Cow's milk ghee | 1 tbsp |
| Bay leaves | 2 |
| Cumin seeds | ¼ tsp |
| Water | ½ cup |
| Green chillies | 1 or 2, slit lengthwise (optional) |
| Salt and sugar | to taste |

METHOD

Fry the cubed potatoes in hot oil until lightly browned and keep aside. Lightly sauté the shrimps in the same oil and keep aside. To the same pan, add cabbage, sprinkle with salt, and simmer covered for 5 minutes. Mix together all the masala powders with a little water to form a paste. Remove the cover and add the masala paste and stir fry. Add ginger paste. Add ½ cup water, stir in the potatoes and shrimps. Adjust salt and add sugar to taste.

Simmer over low heat until potatoes are cooked and there is practically no gravy in the pan. Add green chillies (optional). In a separate frying pan, heat ghee, add bay leaves and cumin seeds. Pour over the cabbage curry and remove from the stove.

# CHITOL MACHER MUITHA

## (FISH DUMPLINGS IN GRAVY)

MADHU AND HARSHVARDHAN NEOTIA                    KOLKATA, BENGAL

SERVES: 4–6                              PREPARATION TIME: 45 MINUTES

INGREDIENTS

| | |
|---|---|
| Chitol (knifefish) or singhara | 250 grams, boneless |
| Green cardamoms | 4 |
| Cloves | 4 |
| Cinnamon sticks | 2, medium size |
| Grated garlic | 1 tbsp |
| Grated ginger | 1 tbsp |
| Ginger-garlic paste | 1 tbsp |
| Green chillies | 2 |
| Mustard oil | 1 tbsp |
| Onions | 50 gms |
| Cumin powder | 1 tsp |
| Refined oil | 2 tbsp |
| Potatoes | 3, medium sized, mashed |
| Red chilli powder | a pinch |
| Turmeric powder | 1 tsp |
| Tomato purée | 1 to 2 tbsp |
| Cashew nut paste | 3 tbsp |
| Ghee | 1 tbsp |
| Sugar | 1 tsp |
| Salt | to taste |
| Water | 2 cups |

METHOD

To prepare the dumplings, take the boneless fish and add to it mashed potatoes, grated ginger, garlic, onion, and green chillies. Make small dumplings, then steam and fry them.

For the gravy, heat the refined oil, add onion paste followed by ginger–garlic paste, tomato purée, cashew nut paste, and water. Add cumin powder, chilli powder, turmeric powder, sugar, and salt to taste.

Once the gravy is ready, finish with green cardamoms, cloves and cinnamon sticks.

Slip the dumplings into the gravy and drizzle with ghee before serving.

# CHINGRI MALAIKARI

SAGARIKA GHOSE                                                    WEST BENGAL

SERVES: 4–6                                          PREPARATION TIME: 45 MINUTES

INGREDIENTS

| | |
|---|---|
| Golda prawns* | 1 kg (ten pieces) whole, with heads cleaned and intact |
| Coconut | ½, grated and ground to a paste |
| Coconut milk | 200 gms dry coconut mixed with 2 cups of water |
| Onions | 3, ground to a paste |
| Ginger | 30 gms, ground to a paste |
| Cloves | 6 |
| Green cardamom | 6 |
| Cinnamon | 2 small pieces |
| Cumin powder | 2 tsp |
| Coriander powder | 2 tsp |
| Turmeric powder | 2 tsp |
| Kashmiri red chilli powder | 2 tsp |
| Mustard oil | 2 tbsp |
| Pure ghee | 3 tbsp |

METHOD

Coat the pieces of prawn with a bit of salt and turmeric powder. Fry until the shells turn red and keep aside.

Heat mustard oil in a kadhai (Indian wok), add the whole garam masalas. When the masalas start to sputter add the onion paste and fry until golden brown. Add the ginger paste and fry. Mix together the

*Giant freshwater prawns

masala powders with water to form a paste Add the masala paste and fry until the water evaporates. At this stage, add the ghee and coconut paste and fry. Next add the coconut milk and simmer. Add the fried prawns, reduce heat, cover and simmer. Serve hot.

# DAL PITHA

## (STEAMED RICE DUMPLINGS FILLED WITH BENGAL GRAM FLOUR STUFFING)

SHOVONA NARAYAN AND HERBERT
TRAXL COURTESY SANGEETA SATYAMURTY                          BIHAR

SERVES: 4–6                     PREPARATION TIME: 45 MINUTES (PLUS 4 HOURS FOR
                                                            SOAKING)

INGREDIENTS:
For the rice dough

| | | |
|---|---|---|
| Rice flour | 2 cups |
| Oil | 1 tsp |
| Salt | a pinch |

For the chana dal stuffing

| | |
|---|---|
| Chana Dal | 1 cup |
| Green or red Chillies | 4 or 5, chopped |
| Garlic | cloves 10 |
| Turmeric powder | ½ tsp |
| Cumin seeds | ½ tsp |
| Oil | 1 tsp |
| Salt | to taste |
| Coriander leaves | a bunch, finely chopped, for garnishing |
| Black mustard and whole red chilli | for seasoning |
| Oil | 1 tsp, for greasing |

METHOD
To make the rice dough for the pitha: Knead the rice flour with hot water to make a dough. Keep the rice dough covered with a damp cloth to keep it moist.

To make the chana dal filling: Soak the chana dal in water for 4 hours. Grind the soaked chana dal with little water into a coarse paste. Mix into it the crushed chillies, crushed garlic, and turmeric powder. Add salt to taste. Add chopped cilantro leaves. The stuffing is now ready.

To make the pithas: Grease a steam vessel with oil. Make small lemon sized balls from the rice dough and roll the balls into thin round shapes with the help of a rolling pin, of 3–4 inches in diameter. Fill these rice dough discs with the dal stuffing/ filling and close the edges. Traditionally, the dumplings are shaped like gujiyas. Fill all the pithas with the dal filling.

Place the pithas in the greased vessel and steam them for about 10 minutes. For the seasoning, in a pan, heat a teaspoon of oil over low flame, add whole black mustard seeds and whole red chillies. Turn them lightly till they turn golden brown.

Before serving, pour the seasoning over the pithas. If desired, additional garnishing of chopped green chillies and coriander leaves can also be used. The pithas can be served either as a whole dumpling or cut into half.

Serve with green coriander chutney or tangy tomato chutney.

# CARROT SOUFFLÉ

SUNITA KUMAR AND PREAH NARANG          KOLKATA, WEST BENGAL

SERVES: 4                                    PREPARATION TIME: 1 HOUR 30 MINUTES

INGREDIENTS

| | |
|---|---|
| Carrots | 500 gms |
| Eggs | 2, separated |
| Milk | ½ cup |
| Flour | 1 tbsp |
| Onion | 1 |
| Cream | 2 tbsp |
| Butter | 1 tbsp |
| Mustard paste | ½ tsp |
| Tomato sauce | 1 tsp |

|              |            |
|--------------|------------|
| Black pepper | ¼–½ tsp    |
| Lemon juice  | ¼ tsp      |
| Nutmeg       | a pinch    |

## METHOD

Boil and blend the carrots, set aside. Beat the egg whites, set aside. Brown the onion in a little butter. Then add the flour and cook it. Now add the milk, mustard, black pepper, lemon juice, and nutmeg and cook to make a white sauce. Add a little tomato sauce, cream, blended carrots with the two egg yolks and cook for a while. Cool a little and add the beaten egg whites.

Warm the dish for 10 minutes before pouring the mixture to bake in a preheated oven at 175°C.

# CHEESE SOUFFLÉ

SUNITA KUMAR AND PREAH NARANG          KOLKATA, WEST BENGAL

SERVES: 4                              PREPARATION TIME: 1 HOUR 30 MINUTES

## INGREDIENTS

|                      |                 |
|----------------------|-----------------|
| Cheddar cheese       | 50 gms, grated  |
| Eggs                 | 4, separated    |
| Milk                 | 1 cup           |
| Flour                | 1 tbsp          |
| Butter               | 25 gms          |
| Mustard powder       | ½ tsp           |
| Black pepper powder  | ½ tsp           |
| Salt                 | to taste        |

## METHOD

Melt butter in a pan. Add flour and stir on low flame till the smell of raw flour is gone. Add milk, black pepper, mustard powder, and salt to taste. Add grated cheese and egg yolks. Keep mixing on low flame. Cool a little, then add the beaten egg white.

Butter the baking dish, then pour mix into it. Bake at 150°C for 15 minutes.

Serve hot.

# AWADHI CALCUTTA BIRYANI WITH POTATOES

SHAHENSHAH MIRZA

KOLKATA, WEST BENGAL

SERVES: 4–6

PREPARATION TIME: 2 HOURS

INGREDIENTS

| | |
|---|---|
| Mutton | 500 gms |
| Basmati rice | 500 gms |
| Potatoes | 5–6 (large) |
| Ginger garlic paste | 4 tsp |
| Coriander powder | 1 tsp |
| Onions | 2 medium size, finely sliced |
| Onion | 1 medium size, made into a paste |
| Cloves | 5 |
| Cardamom pods | 5 |
| Cinnamon | 2 pieces |
| Bay leaves | 2 |
| Nutmeg paste | ½ tsp |
| Mace | 1 small blade |
| Curd | 100 gms |
| Saffron | a few strands |
| Milk | ½ cup |
| Rose water | 4 tbsp |
| Orange food colour | a little |
| Ghee | 150 gms |
| Salt | To taste |

METHOD

Fry the onions in ghee and keep aside. Peel the potatoes, cut into halves. Prick them with a fork. Fry the potatoes till half done. Heat ghee and add three cloves, three cardamom pods, a cinnamon, and a bay leaf. Add the meat pieces, then ginger-garlic paste, onion paste, coriander powder, nutmeg paste, mace, curd and fry well. Now add the previously fried onions and cook the meat till tender.

Wash and soak the rice for 30 minutes to an hour. Heat the ghee and add two cloves, two cardamom pods, a cinnamon, and a bay leaf. Fry for a few minutes and add the soaked and drained rice. Add boiled water and cook the rice till half done. Now spread a layer of rice in a heavy bottomed pan, then place a layer of mutton and potatoes and top it with rice. Sprinkle saffron mixed with rose water, milk, and orange food colour.

Place the pan on a low flame for 30 minutes and seal the lid tight with kneaded dough so that the steam does not escape. Serve hot, preferably with raita.

# DAAB BHAPA SONDESH
## (STEAMED TENDER COCONUT SONDESH)

SUNDEEP BHUTORIA                    KOLKATA, WEST BENGAL

SERVES: 6                          PREPARATION TIME: 1 HOUR

INGREDIENTS

| | |
|---|---|
| Chhaana or cottage cheese | 700 gms |
| Tender coconut malai | 300 gms |
| Rabri | 300 gms |
| Plain curd | 25 gms, lightly beaten |
| Powdered sugar | 30 gms |

METHOD

Crumble the cottage cheese using your fingertips into a large cooking vessel. Add the rabri to the vessel as well as the tender coconut malai, powdered sugar, and beaten curd. Mix all the ingredients together until they form a homogenous paste. Pour the mixture into a dish and steam for about 45 minutes. Pour out into individual bowls and serve with crushed nuts of your choice.

# MISHTI DOI

SUNDEEP BHUTORIA                                    KOLKATA, WEST BENGAL

SERVES: 6                        PREPARATION TIME: 1 HOUR (PLUS 12 HOURS TO SET)

INGREDIENTS

| | |
|---|---|
| Full cream milk | 1 litre |
| Granulated white sugar | 150 gms |
| Thick sour yoghurt | 240 gms |

For the caramel

| | |
|---|---|
| Water | 50 ml |
| Granulated white sugar | 100 gms |

METHOD

In a saucepan, add the sugar and milk. Bring to a quick boil over high heat. Then reduce the heat to medium and keep stirring until the mixture has reduced to half (about 40 minutes). Remove from the heat and set aside.

In another saucepan make the caramel. Add sugar into a pan on low heat. Keep stirring with a fork until the sugar melts, turns sticky and rich brown in colour. Ensure that the caramel doesn't burn. Remove from the heat and carefully add water. The caramel will become hard. Place the saucepan over a low flame and keep stirring quickly until all the caramel that has become stuck to the bottom of the pan dissolves (1 or 2 minutes). Pour this caramel into the reduced milk mixture. Mix well and keep aside.

Whisk the yoghurt until smooth. Once the milk mixture has cooled to lukewarm, add the yoghurt in. Mix with a hand whisk. Pour the yoghurt mixture into an earthen pot, close with a lid and keep overnight in a warm place and leave undisturbed for 10 to 12 hours. Once the mishti doi sets, place in the refrigerator for a couple of hours and serve cold or at room temperature.

# SANTULA

RAGHUNATH MAHAPATRA

ODISHA

SERVES: 4

PREPARATION TIME: 1 HOUR 20 MINUTES

## INGREDIENTS

| | |
|---|---|
| Potatoes | 250 gms, diced |
| Raw papaya | 100 gms, chopped |
| Aubergines | 3, halved |
| Turmeric powder | 1 tbsp |
| Coriander powder | ½ tbsp |
| Ginger | small piece |
| Refined oil | 2 tbsp |
| Onion | 1, sliced |
| Garlic | 2 cloves |
| Mustard seeds | ½ tbsp |
| Milk | 1 cup |
| Asafoetida | ½ tsp |
| Green chillies | 2 whole, slit and deseeded |
| Coriander leaves | small bunch |
| Sea salt | to taste |

## METHOD

Place the diced potatoes, raw papaya, and aubergines in a pressure cooker with 2 tablespoons of water. Add turmeric powder, cumin powder, salt, and ginger.

In a pan, sauté the sliced onions with mustard. Add chopped ginger, garlic, turmeric powder, coriander powder, asafoetida, salt, and water. Transfer the potatoes, raw papaya, and aubergine to the pan. Pour the milk over it. Add some coriander leaves and the green chillies.

Simmer for 5 to 7 minutes. Serve hot.

# MUTTON KATHI ROLL

ANITA BEHL                                           KOLKATA, WEST BENGAL

SERVES: 4                          PREPARATION TIME: 1 HOUR 20 MINUTES

INGREDIENTS

For the mutton filling

| | |
|---|---|
| Mutton | 400 gms, boneless, cut into small pieces |
| Yoghurt | 100 gms |
| Ginger paste | 50 gms |
| Garlic paste | 50 gms |
| Salt | 1 tsp |
| Kashmiri red chilli powder | ½ tsp |
| Coriander powder | ½ tsp |
| Turmeric | ½ tsp |
| Refined vegetable oil | 2 tbsp |
| Dried fenugreek leaves | ½ tsp |
| Garam masala | ½ tsp, freshly ground |
| Onion | 1, large, diced finely |

For the kathi roll dough

| | |
|---|---|
| Wheat flour | 1 cup |
| All-purpose flour | 2 cups |
| Eggs | 3 medium, each whisked separately |
| Salt | a pinch |
| Carom seeds | a pinch |
| Oil | 1 tsp |

For the garnish

| | |
|---|---|
| Onion | 1 large, sliced |
| Coriander leaves | small bunch |
| Green chilli | 1, chopped |
| Chaat masala | to taste |
| Lemon | ½ |
| Oil | 1 tsp |

METHOD

Mix all the ingredients except the mutton into the yoghurt. Then add the mutton and mix thoroughly. Keep aside for 30 minutes.

Stir fry the diced onion in a kadhai using vegetable oil. Add the marinated mutton mixture to the onion and cook for 5 to 7 minutes. In a pressure cooker, heat 3 tablespoons of oil. Cook the onions and mutton in the pressure cooker with one cup of water until the mutton is soft. Remove the cooked mutton mixture and keep aside.

For kathi roll: use both wheat flour and all-purpose flour to make a soft dough. Roll out 4 parathas and fry them on a tawa with oil. Add the whisked egg to one side of the paratha and cook till the required consistency is reached.

Assemble the roll by adding the prepared mutton on the roti. Add the onion garnish, squeeze some lemon juice, sprinkle chaat masala, and roll up the paratha to make the kathi roll.

# PRAWN CURRY

CRISTINA AND PREM PATNAIK                                                      ODISHA

SERVES: 4                                       PREPARATION TIME: 45 MINUTES

INGREDIENTS

| | |
|---|---|
| Prawns | 16, medium |
| Garlic | 1 large |
| Curry leaves | 10–12 |
| Tomato | 1 large, julienned |
| Small mustard seeds | 2 tsp |
| Cumin seeds | 1 tsp |
| Salt | to taste |
| Red chilli + Turmeric powder | 1 tbsp (for colour) |
| Mustard oil | 4 tbsp |
| Potato | 1 large, diced (optional) |
| Green chillies | 2 |
| Lemon | ½ |

METHOD

Grind the garlic and mustard seeds with 1 tablespoon water. Once paste is ready, add 2 tablespoons water to the paste. Heat mustard oil till it smokes, add curry leaves, and cumin. Then add salt, turmeric + chilli powder. After 1 minute add tomatoes and green chillies. Cook for about 3 minutes, then add prawns and the juice of ½ lemon. Cook for a few more minutes and add about 25 millilitres of water. Add the diced potatoes if you are using them. Taste the gravy—if it is too bitter add ¾ tablespoon of tamarind juice. Cook until the prawns and potatoes are cooked through. Serve hot.

# GARLIC-HERB CARROT SLIVERS

NALINI SINGH                                                                BIHAR

SERVES: 6                                    PREPARATION TIME: 25 MINUTES

INGREDIENTS

| | |
|---|---|
| Red carrots | 500–600 gms, washed and peeled |
| Garlic | 10 cloves |
| Olive oil or refined cooking oil | 2 tbsp |
| Dried rosemary and oregano | ¼ tsp (optional) |
| Salt and chunky-crushed pepper | to taste |

METHOD

Simmer the carrots in boiling water for 5 minutes. Drain and spread the boiled carrots on a flat steel surface to semi-dry. While the carrots are drying, peel the garlic and dice finely. Rub 1 tablespoon oil on a clean baking tray and spread the diced garlic and dried herbs (reserve 2 teaspoons). Sprinkle a pinch of salt and pepper on it. Slice each boiled carrot into four long pieces and place on the garlic bed in the baking tray. Sprinkle 1 teaspoon of the diced garlic and herbs on the long carrot slivers. Drizzle a little oil on the dressed carrots.

Bake on medium–high heat for 7–10 minutes. Turn the carrot slivers over, sprinkle the remaining garlic and herbs and some more oil and bake for 5 more minutes.

Serve hot or cold on a platter as a delicious and nutritious side dish.

# NIMONA

RENUKA AND PAVAN VARMA

SERVES: 4                                    PREPARATION TIME: 1 HOUR

INGREDIENTS

| | | |
|---|---|---|
| Fresh peas* | 500 gms, shelled |
| Onions | 4, medium size |
| Garlic | 8–10 cloves |
| Ginger | 2 inch |
| Mustard oil | 4 tbsp |
| Urad dal badi | 2 |
| Cloves | 8 |
| Whole black peppercorns | 8–10 |
| Black cardamom | 2 |
| Bay leaves | 2–4 |
| Cumin seeds | 2 tsp |
| Potato | 2, cubed |
| Salt | to taste |
| Red chilli powder | to taste |

For tempering

| | | |
|---|---|---|
| Desi ghee | 4 tbsp |
| Onion | 2, finely chopped |
| Cloves | 8 |

METHOD

Grind the peas coarsely on a grinding stone or in a food processor (do not make it into a smooth paste) and set aside. Make a smooth paste with the onions, garlic, and ginger in a food processor.

Heat 4 tablespoons of mustard oil in a pressure cooker. Add the badi and fry till golden. Set aside. Now add all the whole spices to the hot oil and wait till the cumin seeds have sputtered. Add the onion-ginger-garlic paste and fry till golden brown. Add the ground peas and fry for another 5 minutes.

Now smash the badi and add to the peas along with the cubed

---

*Use the hard peas available at the end of pea season.

*The India Cookbook*

potatoes. Then add salt and red chilli powder to taste and enough water to make the peas into a dal consistency. Close the lid and pressure cook for one whistle on high and the second whistle on a low flame. Once the pressure releases naturally open the cooker.

In a tempering pan, add 4 tablespoons ghee. When hot add the cloves and fry till the colour changes, then remove the cloves and crush into a paste. Now into the same ghee add a finely chopped onion and fry till golden. Return the fried clove paste to the ghee and onion tempering and pour over the nimona. Serve hot with rice and extra ghee on the side.

## JIMMIKAND (ELEPHANT FOOT YAM) BHARTA OR CHOKHA

RENUKA AND PAVAN VARMA                                             BIHAR

SERVES: 4–6                                        PREPARATION TIME: 40 MINUTES

INGREDIENTS

| | |
|---|---|
| Elephant foot yam (jimmikand) | 1 kg |
| Garlic | 10 cloves |
| Raw mustard oil | 3 tbsp |
| Green chillies | 3, finely chopped |
| Coriander leaves | 2 tbsp, finely chopped |
| Lemon | 1, juiced |
| Salt | to taste |

METHOD

Wash and steam the yam well and mash it. Add 5 cloves of garlic chopped fine and 5 cloves of crushed garlic. Now add all the remaining ingredients and mix well. If the consistency is too thick then add 2–3 tablespoons of boiled water. Adjust salt, lemon juice. and raw mustard oil according to personal taste.

Tip: Keep refrigerated in the summer and at room temperature in the winter.

**Note:** Replace jimmikand with potatoes and adjust quantities to make this into aloo chokha or replace with flame roasted and peeled tomatoes to make tamatar chokha or flame roasted and peeled aubergine for baingan chokha.

# KHAR FISH CURRY

NILA MEHTA                                                    ASSAM

SERVES: 8                                    PREPARATION TIME: 1 HOUR

INGREDIENTS

| | |
|---|---|
| Rohu | ½ kg, cut for curry |
| Rohu head | 1, about 1–1½ kg, cleaned and cut into pieces |
| Raw papaya | 1, cut into 1-inch cubes |
| Red pumpkin | ½ kg, cut into 1-inch cubes |
| Sweet potatoes | 2, cut into 1-inch cubes |
| Ash gourd | ½ kg, cut into 1-inch cubes |
| Potatoes | 2, cut into 1-inch cubes |
| Fresh coriander | 2 tsp |
| Green chillies | 2 |
| Ginger, sliced | ½-inch piece |
| Turmeric powder | ½ tsp |
| Mustard oil | for frying |
| Salt | to taste |
| Khar or cooking soda | 2 tbsp or 1 tsp |

METHOD

Marinate the fish and the fish head by rubbing turmeric powder and salt into the pieces. In a large wok or frying pan heat some mustard oil until it smokes. Fry the fish, a few pieces at a time, and set aside. In the same oil (add a little more if needed) add the ginger, green chillies, and turmeric powder. Do not let them brown.

Then add all the vegetables and stir well. Stir the vegetables and make sure they don't burn.

Now add the khar or cooking soda. Then for about 5 minutes, reduce the flame to low, cover the wok and let it cook into own juices. After about 30 minutes, the vegetables will become soft.

When the water from the vegetables have almost evaporated, add about a cup of hot water.

Bring the flame up high. When it starts simmering, add the fish, fish head, and coriander and let it boil through. Add salt if necessary, then cook 10 more minutes.

Serve with hot steamed Joha rice.

**Note:** Khar (alkaline soda) is a traditional Assamese ingredient. It is a concentrate that is made by passing water through the ashes of burnt dry plantain peels. The preferred variety of plantain, bhimkol (*Musa balbisiana*), has large seeds and is believed to have the highest nutritional value of all the local banana varieties. It has a thick skin. This concentrate is alkaline in nature and is believed to aid digestion and cleanse the stomach. Dishes made using khar are the first item consumed in a multi-course Assamese meal. Khar is cooked with an assortment of leaves, vegetables and even split black gram (maatimah). The prepared dish is also called khar, after its star ingredient. Being alkaline, it does not combine well with acidic foods; the Assamese do not mix khar with sour food.

Cooking soda may be used as a substitute for khar, but no self-respecting Assamese would use it! As with all soda, it is important to use only small quantities, to avoid an unpleasant aftertaste—this is not an issue when using authentic khar.

# BASTANGA GAHORI MANGSHO
## (BAMBOO SHOOT PORK)

ORENO LOTHA                                          NAGALAND

SERVES: 4                         PREPARATION TIME: 1 HOUR 10 MINUTES

INGREDIENTS

| | |
|---|---|
| Pork loin with skin | 600 gms |
| Dry red chillies | 4 to 5 |
| Shredded bamboo shoots | a handful (dry or wet) |
| Mongmong Tu/schezwan | a handful pepper leaves |
| Mustard leaves | a handful |
| Hot water | 1½ cups |
| Ginger paste | 2 tsp |
| Garlic paste | 2 tsp |
| Salt | to taste |

## METHOD

In a tiny bowl take some hot boiling water. Break the dry red chillies in it. (Discard the seeds for less heat.) Cover and soak for about 10 minutes. Drain the water and pound or grind the chillies in a blender into a fine paste.

Heat up a deep pan and cook the pork till it releases its own oil. Add the chilli paste, salt, and enough hot water to cover the pork. Bring it to a boil and cook till the pork is half-cooked. Now add the shredded bamboo shoots and continue to cook till the pork is completely cooked. Add the leafy vegetables.

Once the water starts to evaporate, add the ginger and garlic paste and cook for 10 minutes till the raw smell is gone. Stir till the oil separates from the meat. Serve with rice, dal, and a spicy chutney.


# NGANAM
## (STEAMED FISH)

BOBBY URIPOK                                              MANIPUR

SERVES: 4                          PREPARATION TIME: 1 HOUR 10 MINUTES


### INGREDIENTS

| | |
|---|---|
| Small fish (mukkak nga or nga sang) | 500 gms* |
| Turmeric leaves | 8 to 10 |
| Banana leaves | 4 |
| Maroi napakpi (chives)/ maroi-nakuppi (garlic chives)/ spring onions | a small bunch, chopped |
| Green chillies | 7 to 8, halved |
| Turmeric powder | 2 tsp |
| Mustard oil | 1 tsp (optional) |
| Salt | to taste |

---

*If not available, substitute with fresh mackerel, tuna, hilsa, or pomfret. If using big fish, either cut into pieces or cook whole.

METHOD

Wash the fish gently and thoroughly and drain the excess water. On a plate place a layer of turmeric leaves and then the banana leaves.

Boil some water in a rice cooker with the steamer on top. Mix the fish gently with the other ingredients—cut chillies, chives or onions, turmeric powder and salt. Add a teaspoon of mustard oil so that the fish do not stick to each other. Spread the mixture on the leaves, wrap gently and put on a steel or aluminium quarter plate. Place the plate with the wrapped fish on the steamer and close the lid, steam for about 15 minutes.

Remove the wrapped fish from the steamer and place it on a frying pan on the gas stove. Place a heavy utensil on top of it, then heat it on low flame for about 15 minutes on each side, turning it carefully. This is to remove excess water from the leaves. Now open the wrapped fish. The nganam is ready to serve.

# ROASTED FISH SALAD

CHANDA CHOUDHURY                                        TRIPURA

SERVES: 4                          PREPARATION TIME: 30 MINUTES

INGREDIENTS

| | |
|---|---|
| River fish | 4, medium-sized |
| Green chillies | 6–8 |
| Ginger | 1 inch, chopped |
| Onion | 1, chopped |
| Lemon | ½ |
| Local green herbs | a small handful |
| Black pepper powder | a pinch |
| Salt | to taste |

METHOD

Clean the fish well, rub salt on them and roast for at least 5 minutes in an oven (or better still, over firewood.) Once the fish is properly cooked, debone and set aside.

Roast the green chillies, then grind to a paste. Add the ginger, onions, and fresh green herbs of your choice. Season with salt, pepper, chilli paste, and lemon juice before serving.

## DOH NEI IONG
### (PORK BELLY WITH BLACK SESAME PASTE)

CHEF HAMMAR                                    MEGHALAYA

SERVES: 4                        PREPARATION TIME: 1 HOUR 10 MINUTES

INGREDIENTS

| | | |
|---|---|---|
| Pork belly | ½ kg, cut into 1 or ½ inch pieces |
| Red onions | 4, medium sized, grated |
| Ginger paste | 1 tsp |
| Garlic paste | 2 tbsp |
| Turmeric powder | 2 tsp |
| Roasted black sesame paste | 2 tbsp |
| Mustard oil | 2½ tbsp |
| Salt | 1 to 2 tsp or to taste |

METHOD

Roast the sesame seeds in a pan. When they start to smoke, remove them and grind well using a traditional stone grinder (or food processor). Add a few drops of water if needed. The paste should be thick. Set aside.

In a medium-sized wok (preferably non-stick) heat the mustard oil. When it starts to smoke lower the heat. Add the grated onions and stir gently till they brown (use a flat wooden ladle if possible). After a couple of minutes, add garlic paste and turmeric powder. Continue stirring.

Add the pork belly and increase heat. Stir to mix thoroughly. The meat should cook in its own fat too (this greatly enhances the flavour). Add a teaspoon of salt and sprinkle in a little water if needed.

Mix in the ginger paste and cook for a few minutes. Now add the black sesame paste and spread it evenly over the meat. Be careful that it doesn't burn. Add 2½ cups of warm water (you can add this in increments). Bring the pot to a boil, stir well, and then simmer covered for 40 minutes or till meat is tender

Check regularly to ensure that the gravy doesn't dry out. Add more water if needed and adjust salt. The final texture should be thick, not soupy and the colour, a rich dark green.

# RAWTUAI LEH BEHLAWI NHAH BAI
## (BAMBOO SHOOT AND LONG BEAN LEAF STEW)

HAMMARSING KHARHMAR SAWYAN                    MIZORAM

SERVES: 4                    PREPARATION TIME: 1 HOUR 10 MINUTES

INGREDIENTS

| | |
|---|---|
| Young bamboo shoot (rawtuai) | 500 gms, peeled and chopped into rings |
| Long bean leaf (behlawi nhah) | 10 medium sized leaves, sliced in half |
| Sawtooth coriander (Burma dhaniya) | 5 leaves, diced |
| Green chilli | 5, slightly bruised or broken in half |
| Fermented pork fat (saoum) | 2 tsp |
| Baking soda | 1 tsp |
| Water | 500 ml |
| Salt | 1 tsp |

METHOD

Boil the bamboo shoots till they are soft (around 40 to 60 minutes depending on the hardness of the young shoots). Drain water and set aside.

In a medium-sized sauce pan bring 500 millilitres of water to a boil. Add chillies and soon after add the bamboo shoots with a pinch of salt. Stir well. (Use a large soup ladle if possible. Lift the contents, drop them back down and stir constantly.)

After a few minutes add baking soda. Adjust heat if needed (soda may cause the mixture to foam to the top of the pot).

Add the fermented pork fat and let it dissolve fully into the broth. Throw in the long bean leaves. Cook until they soften and turn darker green (around 2–3 minutes).

Right before serving add the coriander.

This dish must be eaten immediately. The colours will be vibrant, the aroma of the herbs fresh and the flavours strong! It's always eaten with rice.


# STEAMED RICE CAKE

SINAWATI AND SUWANA MUNGYAK          ARUNACHAL PRADESH

SERVES: 4–6                          PREPARATION TIME: 1 HOUR

INGREDIENTS

| | | |
|---|---|---|
| Rice powder | 500 gms |
| Jaggery | 200 gms |
| Sesame seed | 2 tbsp, roasted |
| Dry coconut | 2 tsp, chopped |
| Raisins | 1 tsp (optional) |
| Cashews | 1 tsp (optional) |
| Kopaat | 20 leaves |
| Water | 1 cup |
| Salt | a pinch |

METHOD

In a bowl mix together the rice powder, salt, jaggery, sesame seeds, and dry fruits. Add water and knead to a soft dough. Take clean leaves and tear into triangular shape. Make cones of the leaves place a spoonful of dough into it and fold it. Flatten it by pressing softly so it spreads all over the leaf. Steam for 30–35 minutes or till it is cooked.

**Note:** A momo utensil can be used for steaming though we use our traditional steamer.

# PAACHAW
## (FRESH FISH WITH DRIED BAMBOO SHOOT)

SINAWATI AND SUWANA MUNGYAK                    ARUNACHAL PRADESH

SERVES: 4                              PREPARATION TIME: 30 MINUTES

INGREDIENTS

|  |  |
|---|---|
| Fresh water fish | 500 gms |
| Dried fermented bamboo shoot | 2 tbsp |
| Garlic | 6 cloves |
| Green chilli | 3 |
| Pichimkhim (white basil) | a bunch |
| Pofoihom | 7–8 leaves |
| Makat | 7–8 leaves |
| Water | 1 cup |
| Salt | to taste |

METHOD

Clean the fresh water fish and cut into pieces. In a mortar and pestle or a food processor, grind the garlic, green chillies, and herbs together.

In a pan, place the pieces of fish, dried bamboo shoot, the pounded herbs, salt, and water. Mix well and cook on medium heat. Serve with steamed rice.

# TIBETAN THUKPA SOUP

WANGCHUK DENSAPA                                      SIKKIM

SERVES: 4                              PREPARATION TIME: 40 MINS

INGREDIENTS

|  |  |
|---|---|
| Chinese egg noodles (thin) | 300 gms |
| Onion | 1, medium, sliced |
| Mushrooms | 100 gms, sliced |
| Carrot | 1, finely sliced |
| Cabbage | ½ cup, chopped |

| | |
|---|---|
| Red bell pepper | 1, finely sliced |
| Ginger | 1 tsp, minced |
| Green chillies | 2, slit, deseeded and sliced |
| Garlic cloves | 3 |
| Cumin powder | 1 tsp |
| Turmeric powder | ½ tsp |
| Coriander seeds | 2 tsp |
| Soy sauce | 2 tbsp |
| Rice wine vinegar, or plain vinegar | 1 tsp |
| Vegetable stock | 1 litre |
| Vegetable oil | 3 tbsp |
| Onion | 1, finely chopped, for garnishing |
| Spicy chilli sauce | to taste, optional |
| Salt | to taste |

METHOD

Cook noodles in boiling water until al dente. Strain and set aside.

In a large pot, over medium heat, add oil. Saute garlic, ginger and green chilli for 1 or 2 minutes until brown. Add onions, mushrooms, bell pepper, carrots, cabbage and stir for 3 to 5 minutes until vegetables are tender.

Add cumin, turmeric, salt, coriander seeds, soy sauce and vinegar. Mix well.

Add vegetable stock and let it simmer on low heat for 5 minutes.

Serve the thukpa soup by placing 2 tablespoons of noodles in each soup bowl. Then ladle soup broth into the bowl and garnish with finely chopped onion and spicy chilli sauce to taste.

# West

~

# VANGI BATH
(BRINJAL RICE)

GITA ABHYANKAR                                    MAHARASHTRA

SERVES: 8                              PREPARATION TIME: 30 MINUTES

INGREDIENTS

| | |
|---|---|
| Rice | 1½ cups |
| Brinjal | 500 gms, small, cut lengthwise |
| Red chillies | 6 |
| Bengal gram | 3 tbsp |
| Coriander seeds | 2 tsp |
| Clove | 3 |
| Cinnamon | 1-inch |
| Dry coconut powder | 3 tbsp |
| Oil | ¼ cup |
| Onion | 1, roughly chopped |
| Mustard seeds | 1 tsp |
| Curry leaves | 8 to 10 |
| Turmeric powder | ½ tsp |
| Salt | to taste |
| Cashews | 2 tsp |
| Peanuts | 2 tsp |

METHOD

Cook the rice and keep aside.

Add the chillies, Bengal gram, coriander seeds, cloves, cinnamon, dry coconut powder with 1 teaspoon oil in a processor and make into a powder.

Heat oil in frying pan, add curry leaves, mustard seeds, onion, and turmeric. Add the aubergine and salt, and cook till tender.

Add this to rice along with the prepared powder and mix well. Garnish with roasted cashews and peanuts.

# KOLHAPURI SUKKA MUTTON

NITA KHANNA                                      KOLHAPUR, MAHARASHTRA

SERVES: 6                                      PREPARATION TIME: 1 HOUR

INGREDIENTS

| | |
|---|---|
| Mutton | 1 kg goat meat on the bone, cut into 1½-inch pieces |
| Ginger garlic paste | 2 tbsp |
| Turmeric powder | 1 tbsp |
| Red chilli powder | 1 tbsp |
| Cooking oil | 4 tbsp |
| Fresh coriander leaves | a small bunch |
| Salt | to taste |

For the spice paste

| | |
|---|---|
| Oil | 1 tbsp |
| Coriander seeds | 1 ½ tsp |
| Cinnamon | 3–4 sticks, about 1-inch each |
| Black cardamom | 5 |
| Cloves | 8 |
| Peppercorns | 8 |
| Dried coconut | 1½ tbsp, grated and roasted |
| Poppy seeds | 1½ tbsp, roasted |
| Onions | 6, sliced, deep fried and drained off on paper towels (birista) |

METHOD

First prepare the spice paste: heat the oil in a flat pan over medium low heat. Sauté the coriander seeds, cinnamon, cardamom pods, and cloves till fragrant. Take care not to burn them. Dry grind the sautéed spices to a fine powder. Roast and dry grind the poppy seeds finely and mix with the spice powder. Grind the fried onions and coconut. Mix together the dry spice powder and the poppy seed powder with some water to form a well-integrated paste. Combine the spice paste, ginger garlic paste, turmeric powder, chilli powder, and salt well. Marinate the mutton in this mixture for about 30 to 45 minutes.

Heat the oil in a pan and add the marinated mutton to it. Lightly sauté the meat for 3 to 5 minutes on a medium-low flame till the oil coats the meat thoroughly but the meat does not start browning. Add 2 cups of water, cover tightly and cook on a low flame, stirring from time to time to ensure the meat does not stick to the bottom of the pan, and until the meat is tender, the water has dried up from the gravy, the oil has separated, and a glisten of oil coats the meat (about 1–1½ hours). Garnish with chopped coriander leaves and serve with hot bajra (millet) chapattis and the onion birista on the side.

## MASALE BHAAT

SHOBHAA DE                                    MAHARASHTRA

SERVES: 4–6                          PREPARATION TIME: 1 HOUR

INGREDIENTS

|  |  |
|---|---|
| Rice | 1 cup |
| Onion | 1 medium, diced |
| Brinjal | ½ cup, small, sweetish, cut into quarters |
| Tendli | ½ cup sliced |
| Cumin seeds | ½ tsp |
| Hing | a pinch |
| Turmeric powder | ½ tsp |
| Green chillies | 1 tsp, finely chopped |
| Ginger | ½ tsp, grated |
| Coconut | freshly grated |
| Ghee | 1 tsp |
| Fresh coriander | a small bunch |
| Cashews | 8–10, roasted |

For the dry masala mix

|  |  |
|---|---|
| Cumin seeds | ½ tsp |
| Coriander seeds | ½ tsp |
| Black peppercorns | 5–6 |
| Cloves | 3 |

METHOD

Soak the rice for about 30 minutes, then drain the water and set aside.

Dry roast the spices for the mix. Set aside.

Heat ghee in a heavy-bottomed pan, add cumin seeds, turmeric, hing, green chillies, and ginger. Once they sputter, add the onions and brown them. Then add the tendli and aubergine and cook so that they are crisp and firm. Then add the soaked and drained rice, add water and cook over a medium flame. Cover the pan, place a weight on the cover and cook until the rice is done. Uncover the pan, separate the rice and add the masala mix. Top with coconut and garnish with fresh coriander and cashews.

# DAHI GUJIYA CHAAT WITH SPINACH AND DATE CHUTNEYS

SAMEER SETH AND FLOYD CARDOZ                BOMBAY, MAHARASHTRA

SERVES: 6–8                                PREPARATION TIME: 2 HOURS

(PLUS OVERNIGHT SOAKING)

INGREDIENTS

For the urad dal gujiya

| | | |
|---|---|---|
| Black gram (urad dal) | 250 gms | |
| Salt | ½ tsp | |
| Chironji seeds | 1 tbsp | |
| Cashew nuts | 2 tbsp, roughly chopped | |
| Golden raisins | 2 tbsp, roughly chopped | |
| Hing | 1 tsp | |
| Black salt | 1 tbsp | |
| Vegetable oil | for frying | |

For the seasoned curd

| | |
|---|---|
| Yoghurt | 500 gms |
| Salt | to taste |
| Castor sugar | 1 tbsp |

For the spinach chutney

| | |
|---|---|
| Onion | ½ cup |
| Cumin powder | ½ teaspoon, toasted |
| Green chillies | 1–2 pieces |

| | |
|---:|:---|
| Spinach | 2 cups |
| Coriander leaves | 1 cup |
| Dried mango powder | 1 tsp |
| Ginger | 1 tbsp |
| Vegetable oil | 2 tbsp |
| Lime juice | to taste |
| Salt | to taste |
| Crushed ice | 2–3 pieces |

For the date and tamarind chutney

| | |
|---:|:---|
| Dates | 200 gms, deseeded |
| Tamarind paste | 375 gms |
| Jaggery | 350 gms |
| Water | 500 ml |
| Dry ginger | 2 tbsp |
| Fennel seeds | 1 cup |
| Star anise | 3 tbsp |
| Coriander seeds | 1¼ cups |
| Cumin seeds | 5 tbsp |
| Dried Kashmiri chilli | 2 |
| Black peppercorns | 3 tbsp |
| Black cardamom | 5 |
| Green cardamom | 5 |
| Cloves | 5 |
| Cinnamon | 4-inch stick |
| Bay leaves | 3 |
| Salt | 2 tbsp |

To garnish

| | |
|---:|:---|
| Toasted cumin seed powder | ½ tsp |
| Toasted red chilli powder | ½ tsp |
| Jeeravan powder | ½ tsp |
| Pomegranate seeds | ½ tsp |
| Nylon sev | ½ tsp |
| Coriander microgreens | a small bunch |

METHOD

Wash the urad dal and soak it for 4–5 hours or overnight. Drain the excess water. Add to food processor with salt and make a thick paste without adding any water. Take the dal paste into a bowl and knead.

The mixture to make gujiya is ready.

In a small bowl, mix the cashews, raisins, and chironji seeds together. In a large mixing bowl, whisk together the water with the hing and black salt.

Heat the vegetable oil in a large pot. Spread out a plastic sheet on the rolling board and wet it with water. Take a lime-sized portion of the mixture and roll into a ball. Now press this ball with wet fingers making a flat disc of 2 inches. Put ½ teaspoon of the nut mixture over the rolled out gujiya and fold it from one side in a half-moon shape.

Gently transfer this gujiya into the hot oil for frying. Fry till golden brown on both sides and cooked through. Shake off excess oil and transfer the fried gujiya into the bowl of warm water. Repeat the process with more batter and filling to make all the gujiyas.

Allow the fried gujiyas to sit in the water for 20 to 25 minutes so that they soften. Keep refrigerated.

For the curd, whisk all the ingredients together and keep refrigerated.

To make the spinach chutney, blend all the listed ingredients together in a blender. Cool down using ice so it doesn't discolour. Keep refrigerated.

To make the date purée, put the deseeded dates in a pot with 200 millilitres water and bring to a boil. Reduce to a simmer and cook for 8–10 minutes till the dates are fully soft. Purée the mixture in a blender.

To make the tamarind chutney, place the jaggery in a pot, add 500 millilitres of water and bring slowly up to a boil. Cover until the jaggery melts.

Heat a heavy-bottomed skillet over medium heat and toast each spice (except dried ginger) separately until fragrant. Cool down all the spices and grind finely in a spice grinder.

Combine the date purée, tamarind, jaggery, dried ginger, and spice powder, cook on low heat for 20 minutes. Taste should be equal amounts of sweet and sour. Add more salt if needed.

Take out the soaked gujiyas from the bowl of water and press with hands to strain water from it. Repeat the step with all the gujiya and put them on a plate.

Dip each gujiya into the seasoned curd and place on the serving bowl. Garnish with toasted cumin powder, toasted red chilli powder, jeeravan powder, sev, pomegranate seeds, and coriander microgreens.

# BHUTTA CURRY

RINKE SARAN

MUMBAI, MAHARASHTRA

SERVES: 4

PREPARATION TIME: 30 MINUTES

INGREDIENTS

| | | |
|---|---|---|
| Corn | 2, cleaned and cut into roundels |
| Coriander powder | 1 tsp |
| Green chillies | 2 |
| Garlic cloves | 4–5 |
| Coconut | 1, grated |
| Coconut milk | from the flesh of 2 coconuts |
| Curd | ½ kg |
| Oil | 2 tsp |
| Mustard seeds | ½ tsp |
| Asafeotida | a punch |
| Curry leaves | 8–10 |
| Salt | to taste |

METHOD

Boil the corn with a bit of salt. Set aside.

Grind the coriander power, green chillies, garlic, grated coconut, and 3 or 4 pieces of boiled bhutta to a fine paste.

Grind together the coconut milk and curd.

In a vessel, add a little oil. Once hot, cook the spice paste and the coconut and curd mixture. Once cooked add the bhutta, salt to taste, and cook till the gravy thickens.

In a small pan add oil. Once hot add the mustard seeds, curry leaves, and hing and pour onto the curry.

# IRAQI DATE AND WALNUT CAKE WITH CARAMELIZED WALNUT TOPPING

RAMOLA BACHCHAN

MUMBAI, MAHARASHTRA

SERVES: 6–8

PREPARATION TIME: 1 HOUR 30 MINUTES

INGREDIENTS

To prepare the dates

| | |
|---|---|
| Iraqi dates | 8–10 |
| Baking soda | 1 tsp |
| Boiling water | 2 cups |

For the cake

| | |
|---|---|
| All-purpose flour | 2 cups |
| Baking powder | 1½ tsp |
| Baking soda | ½ tsp |
| Salt | ½ tsp |
| Eggs | 4, separated |
| Brown sugar | 1 cup |
| Vegetable oil | ¾ cup |
| Coffee powder | 1 tbsp |
| Cinnamon | 1 tsp |
| Vanilla extract | 1 tsp |
| Crushed walnuts | 1 cup |

For the topping

| | |
|---|---|
| Toasted walnuts | ½ cup |
| Granulated sugar | ¾ cup |
| Kosher salt | ½ tsp |

METHOD

Preheat the oven to 180°C. Grease a 9-inch springform cake pan.

Place the dates in a small saucepan with the baking soda and boiling water and leave to soak for 30 minutes to an hour. Drain and mash.

In a large bowl sift the flour, baking powder, baking soda, and salt together.

In another bowl, whisk together the yolks, sugar, and oil together.

Add a tablespoon of hot water to the coffee and add into the mixture along with the cinnamon powder and vanilla extract. Fold in the flour, a third at a time, till you have a smooth batter.

Whisk the egg whites till they form soft peaks and fold into the batter until absorbed. Bake for 45–50 minutes or until a toothpick comes out clean.

For the topping, toast the walnuts and keep aside.

Add sugar and 2–3 tablespoons of water in a small pan and caramelize over medium heat for five minutes or so, then add in the butter and salt and stir to prevent from burning. When it thickens, take the pan off the heat and add the toasted walnuts. Pour over the top of the cooled cake.

# BAKED EGGS

PHEROZA AND JAMSHED GODREJ                MUMBAI, MAHARASHTRA

SERVES: 12                                PREPARATION TIME: 30 MINUTES

INGREDIENTS

| | |
|---|---|
| Egg whites | 10 |
| Eggs yolks | 3 |
| Flour | ½ tbsp |
| Ghee | 1 tbsp |
| Green chillies | 6 |
| Coriander leaves | 1 big bunch |
| Garlic | 5 cloves, ground to a fine paste |
| Ginger | 1-inch piece |
| Cumin seeds | 1 tsp |
| Turmeric powder | ½ tsp |
| Salt | ½ tsp or to taste |

METHOD

Beat the egg whites till stiff. Add the egg yolks and beat again. Fold in the flour and the rest of the ingredients except ghee gradually. In a deep frying pan, heat the ghee. Pour in the mixture and when slightly set, put the pan into a hot oven (preheated at 180°C) till it has risen and is set.

## CHEESE AKURI

PHEROZA AND JAMSHED GODREJ      MUMBAI, MAHARASHTRA

SERVES: 8      PREPARATION TIME: 30 MINUTES

INGREDIENTS

| | |
|---|---|
| Eggs | 8 |
| Ghee | 2 tbsp |
| Salt | 1 tsp |
| Fresh coriander | small bunch |
| Onion | 1 small, chopped |
| Bacon | 3 strips, chopped fine |
| Green chillies | 6, chopped |
| Grated cheese | 1 tbsp |

METHOD

Beat the eggs, add onion, coriander, chillies, and bacon. Heat the ghee, pour in the egg mixture and stir on a low heat till the eggs are set. Add the grated cheese, stir, and remove from the fire. Serve on toast or with buttered toast.

## EGGS AKURI

PHEROZA AND JAMSHED GODREJ      MUMBAI, MAHARASHTRA

SERVES: 6      PREPARATION TIME: 30 MINUTES

INGREDIENTS

| | |
|---|---|
| Eggs | 6 |
| Onions | 6, medium sized, sliced |
| Green chillies | 5, finely chopped |
| Coriander leaves | 1 small bunch |

| | |
|---|---|
| Milk | ¼ cup |
| Ghee | 2 tbsp |
| Salt | to taste |
| Green chilli | 1, chopped and fried |
| Cumin seeds | ¼ tsp, for garnishing, fried |

METHOD

Break the eggs in a pan. Add salt and milk and mix lightly.

In a pan fry the onions until they turn a light golden colour. Add the chillies and coriander and fry for a few more minutes. Pour in the egg mixture and stir constantly till cooked like scrambled eggs.

Pour into a hot dish, garnish with the fried cumin seeds and chillies and serve immediately.

## RAVA KHEER

PHEROZA AND JAMSHED GODREJ            MUMBAI, MAHARASHTRA

SERVES: 8                              PREPARATION TIME: 30 MINUTES

INGREDIENTS

| | |
|---|---|
| Rava | 2 tbsp |
| Water or rose water | 2 cups |
| Milk | 1 cup |
| Sugar | to taste |
| Ghee | 2 tsp |
| Powdered cardamom and nutmeg | to taste |
| Silvered almonds | to decorate |

METHOD

Add rose water or water to rava, blending well. Cook on on medium flame, stirring constantly till thick. Add sugar and milk gradually, stirring all the time and cook till the mixture is thick. Add ghee and mix well, remove from fire, add powdered cardamom pods and nutmeg and pour into a bowl. Sprinkle with almonds. If water has been used, then add rose water for flavour or a few drops of rose essence.

# SEV

PHEROZA AND JAMSHED GODREJ       MUMBAI, MAHARASHTRA

SERVES: 8       PREPARATION TIME: 30 MINUTES

INGREDIENTS

| | |
|---|---|
| Sev | 400 gms (very fine vermicelli) |
| Ghee | 2–3 tbsp |
| Sugar | 6 tbsp |
| Water | 1½ cups |
| Rose water | 1 tbsp |
| Almonds | 8, blanched, sliced, and fried |
| Raisins | 1 tbsp, fried |

METHOD

Deep fry the sev in hot ghee till brown. Drain all the ghee. Dissolve sugar in water and boil to a thin syrup. Mix the sev in the syrup and cook covered over a low flame till the sev is soft and the water is absorbed. Add a little water if necessary. Stir occasionally so that the sev does not get lumpy. Mix in the rose water and remove from the fire. Serve hot or cold, sprinkled with the almonds and raisins.

It can also be cooked without frying by boiling with a little milk added to the syrup.

# COPRA PAK

PHEROZA AND JAMSHED GODREJ       MUMBAI, MAHARASHTRA

SERVES: 6–8       PREPARATION TIME: 25 MINUTES

INGREDIENTS

| | |
|---|---|
| Coconut | ½, grated (only the white part) |
| Rose water | 3 tbsp |
| Milk | ½ cup |
| Sugar | 225 gms |
| Ghee | 1 tsp |
| Almonds | 25 gms, blanched and slivered |

## METHOD

Mix the coconut, sugar, rose water, ghee, and milk into a pan and cook on a low fire, stirring constantly till it forms into a soft ball and no longer sticks to the pan.

Grease a marble surface, spread the mixture on it and roll it out to ¼-inch thickness. Sprinkle with sliced almonds and cut into cubes whilst hot.

Once cooled, store in a jar.


# PARSI STYLE MUTTON CURRY

ZARINE AND SANJAY KHAN                    MUMBAI-PARSI, MAHARASHTRA

SERVES: 8                                      PREPARATION TIME: 1 HOUR

## INGREDIENTS

| | |
|---|---|
| Mutton | 1 kg, cut into pieces |
| Potatoes | 4, cut into quarters |
| Ginger paste | 1 tsp |
| Garlic paste | 1½ tsp |
| Red Kashmiri chillies | 10, whole |
| Cumin seeds | 2 tsp |
| Sesame seeds | 2 tsp |
| Poppy seeds | 2 tsp |
| Coriander seeds | 2 tsp |
| Garlic cloves | 10 |
| Turmeric powder | 1 tsp |
| Red chilli powder | 1 tsp |
| Coconut | ½, grated |
| Coconut milk | 1 cup |
| Onions | 3, sliced |
| Curry leaves | 10 |
| Bay leaves | 2 |
| Lemon | 1, juiced |
| Oil | 4 tbsp |
| Salt | to taste |

## METHOD

Heat oil in a pan. Fry the mutton with ginger and garlic paste and salt until the mutton pieces turn brown. Place the mutton in a cooker with a little water and cook till tender.

Grind together the Kashmiri chillies, cumin, sesame, poppy, coriander, garlic, turmeric, red chilli powder, and grated coconut. Keep aside.

Fry the onion till light brown. Then add the ground masala and fry together with salt, curry leaves, and bay leaves. After the masala is well fried, add the mutton along with its stock. Do not add any water. Instead, add the coconut milk and simmer.

Boil the potatoes and add to the curry as it simmers (if more gravy is required, add some more coconut milk).

Finally, stir in the lemon juice and serve.


# YAKHNI

LAILA KHAN FURNITUREWALLA                    MUMBAI, MAHARASHTRA

SERVES: 4–6                         PREPARATION TIME: 2 HOURS 30 MINUTES

INGREDIENTS

| | | |
|---|---|---|
| Mutton | 1 kg, from the shoulder |
| Fennel seeds | 125 gms |
| Green cardamom | 25 gms, whole |
| Black cardamom | 25 gms, whole |
| Cinnamon stick | ½ |
| Cloves | 8 |
| Black pepper | 25 gms |
| Bay leaves | 2 |
| Star anise | 3 |
| Garlic and ginger | 125 gms, whole |
| Caraway seeds | 100 gms |
| Mint leaves | small bunch |
| Yoghurt | 1½ kg |
| Salt | to taste |

## METHOD

Wash and cut the mutton into pieces and place in a vessel.

Tie together all the spices in a muslin cloth and place with the mutton. Add salt and 3 cups of water. Cover and cook on high flame. When water has reduced to about 1 cup, then the mutton is cooked. Switch off the gas, remove the spices.

In another pan, cook the yoghurt for 2 hours on a slow fire, stirring continuously. Once it thickens and becomes difficult to stir, add the meat and water.

Place the mint leaves on a hot pan until they dry. Powder and then spread on top of the meat. The yakhni is ready.

Serve with an aromatic pulao loaded with dry fruits and nuts.


# MACHCHI NO SAAS
(FISH SAUCE)

BAPSI NARIMAN                                MUMBAI, MAHARASHTRA

SERVES: 6                                    PREPARATION TIME: 1 HOUR

## INGREDIENTS

| | |
|---|---|
| Pomfret | ½ kg, or any other firm fish cut into 8 pieces |
| Salt | 1½ tbsp |
| Vinegar | 4½ tbsp |
| Oil | 4 tbsp |
| Cumin seeds | ½ tsp |
| Green chillies | 2, finely chopped |
| Garlic | 8 cloves, finely chopped |
| Ginger | ½-inch piece, finely chopped |
| Onion | 1, sliced |
| Turmeric powder | ¼ tsp |
| Gram flour/plain flour | 2 tbsp |
| Sugar | 4 tsp |
| Eggs | 2 |
| Coriander leaves | 1 tbsp, freshly chopped |

## METHOD

Wash the fish and apply 1 tablespoon salt and ½ tablespoon vinegar. Keep aside for 30 minutes. Mix the eggs, sugar, and gram flour in the rest of the vinegar.

Heat oil, add cumin seeds, green chillies, garlic, ginger, and onion and fry until onion turns golden. Mix in turmeric and the remaining salt. Cook for a minute or two. Add 4 cups of water. Let it come to the boil and simmer for about 5 minutes. Keep aside. The rest of the cooking should be done when ready to serve. (Do not heat again or the mixture may curdle.)

Wash the fish again and mix in the pieces. Cook for 5 to 10 minutes, covered, turning over the pieces once.

Once the fish is cooked, remove and set aside.

Carefully add the egg mixture to the sauce. Slowly bring to a boil, shaking the pan from side to side so that no lumps are formed and it doesn't curdle. Place the fish back in the pan, making sure not to break the pieces. Garnish with fresh coriander and serve hot with khichri.

**Note:** You can use prawns instead of fish. In which case, shell and devein the prawns.

# SITAPHAL ICE CREAM

DEVIEKA AND SURESH BHOJWANI                              MUMBAI

SERVES: 6–8                              PREPARATION TIME: 30 MINUTES

## INGREDIENTS

| | | |
|---|---|---|
| Sitaphal | 1 kg | |
| Whole milk | 1 litre | |
| Condensed milk | ½ tin | |
| Ice and salt for freezing | as required | |

## METHOD

Deseed the sitaphal. Set aside. Boil the milk to reduce the quantity to little over half a litre. Let it cool. Mix together the milk, sitaphal flakes (reserve a few) and condensed milk in a blender. Pour the mixture into an Indian style ice cream maker that has been frozen with ice and salt. Add the reserved sitaphal flakes to the liquidized mixture before starting the ice cream maker. The ice cream should be ready to serve in 20-30 minutes, depending on the type of ice cream maker used.

## BIKANERI PARATHA

YAMINI AND ASHOK JAIPURIA                              RAJASTHAN

SERVES: 8–10                    PREPARATION TIME: 45 MINUTES (PLUS 3 HOURS FOR
                                                                SOAKING)

INGREDIENTS

| | |
|---|---|
| Moong dal | 200 gms |
| Deghi mirch | 10 gms |
| Moti Kuti mirch | 10 gms |
| Salt | 20 gms |
| Asafoetida | 10 gms |
| Refined oil | 100 gms |
| Ginger | 30 gms |
| Whole wheat flour | 400 gms |
| Maida | 200 gms |
| Milk | ½ litre |

METHOD

Soak moong dal for at least 3 hours prior to the cooking. Then grind it with ginger. Heat refined oil in a kadhai. Add salt, asafoetida, and red chilli powder to prepare a paste of the dal filling and roast it properly. Then leave it to cool.

In a big plate take maida and atta and mix with milk to make a dough. Roll out the parathas, stuff the dal paste in each, and close. Cook it on a tawa with oil.

# ARMENIAN SAMOSA

MALLIKA SARABHAI                                    AHMEDABAD, GUJARAT

SERVES: 5                                           PREPARATION TIME: 1 HOUR

INGREDIENTS

For the paste

| | | |
|---|---|---|
| Feta or paneer | 250 gms, grated |
| Cheese | 100 gms, grated |
| Fresh mint leaves | 50 gms, finely chopped |
| Coriander | 50 gms, finely chopped |
| Onions | 50 gms, finely chopped |
| Capsicum | ½, finely diced |
| Salt | to taste |
| Dried oregano | 1 tbsp |
| Lemon | 1, juiced |

For the dough

| | |
|---|---|
| Cornflour | 250 gms |
| Oil | as needed |

METHOD

Mix all the listed ingredients under 'for the paste' with your hands. Do
not use a grinder.

Make the dough with some oil, to a hard consistency. Roll it out
and cut into triangles. Stuff these with the paste and bake at medium
heat. Serve hot.


# PAKKI KERI NO AMBAKALIO
(RIPE MANGO RELISH)

BAPSI NARIMAN                                       MUMBAI, MAHARASHTRA

SERVES: 8                                           PREPARATION TIME: 30 MINUTES

INGREDIENTS

| | |
|---|---|
| Mangoes | 3 large, ripe |

| | |
|---|---|
| Desi ghee | 2 tbsp |
| Onions | 2 large, sliced |
| Cloves | 4 |
| Cinnamon | ½-inch piece |
| Cardamom pods | 6 |
| Dry red chill | 1, broken into 3 pieces, seeds removed |
| Jaggery | 250 gms |
| Salt | ½ tsp |

METHOD

Peel the mangoes, cut into large pieces, discarding the seed. Heat the ghee and fry the onions, cloves, cinnamon, cardamom, and chilli until onions are soft. Add jaggery, water, and salt and bring to a boil. Boil until the jaggery melts. Add the pieces of mango and cook further for 5 more minutes. Turn over the mango pieces once. Be careful when not to break the mango pieces. Serve hot or at room temperature as desired.

# GOAN FISH CURRY

ZARINE KHAN                                                                 GOA

SERVES: 4–6                                          PREPARATION TIME: 30 MINUTES

INGREDIENTS

| | |
|---|---|
| Pomfret | 2 large |
| Turmeric | 1 tsp |
| Onions | 2, finely chopped |
| Tomato | 1 large, finely chopped |
| Tamarind water | 1 tbsp |
| Green chillies | 5 to 6, half-slit |
| Coconut milk | 200 ml |
| Salt | to taste |
| Oil | 4 tbsp |

For the ground masala

| | |
|---|---|
| Cumin seeds | 1 tsp |
| Fenugreek seeds | ½ tsp |

| | |
|---|---|
| Red chilli powder | 2 tsp |
| Coriander powder | 1 tsp |
| Turmeric | ½ tsp |
| Coconut | 1 |
| Fresh coriander | ¼ bunch |
| Salt | to taste |

METHOD

Wash the fish thoroughly. Add turmeric and salt to the fish. Shallow-fry and keep aside.

Fry the finely chopped onions in another pan till light brown. Add the ground masala to the onions and cook till mixed well. Add the tomato and keep frying till it has cooked through. Add the tamarind water and then add 200 millilitres of coconut milk. (You could use water, but coconut milk is preferred.)

Bring to a boil. Add the fish and simmer for 10 to 15 minutes till the fish is cooked. Lastly, sprinkle some fresh coriander and slit green chillies and leave on a low flame till you see a thin layer of oil on the top of the gravy.

Serve with rice.

# BAKED CRABS

ANU AND IQBAL MALHOTRA                                                     GOA

SERVES: 6                                          PREPARATION TIME: 1 HOUR

INGREDIENTS

| | |
|---|---|
| Crabs | 3 kg, preferably live (at least 6 crabs) |
| Mayonnaise | 2 tbsp |
| Cheddar cheese | 150 gms, grated |
| Chilli sauce | 1 tbsp |
| Palm/date jaggery | 1 tbsp |
| Bread crumbs | 50 gms |
| Salt | to taste |

Boil the crabs for 30 minutes in a large pot of water. Once the shells turn red, remove the crabs. Clean out the shells; keep six aside. Collect the crab meat in a bowl. Crack the claws and add the crab meat in the same bowl.

Once all the crab meat has been collected, mix in the mayo, chilli sauce, cheese, and jaggery. Add salt to taste.

Pack the mixture into the shells with a spatula/spoon. Sprinkle bread crumbs over the packed shells. Place under a grill until brown.

Place on a serving platter and with freshly fried potato wafer chips.

# PRAWN CAKE

MARIA COUTO                                                              GOA

SERVES: 8–10                                          PREPARATION TIME: 1 HOUR

INGREDIENTS

| | |
|---|---|
| Semolina (rava) | ½ cup |
| Sugar | 1 cup |
| Butter | ¾ cup |
| Eggs | 3 large |
| Salt | 1 tsp |
| All-purpose flour | 2 cups and more for dusting |
| Baking powder | 2 tsp |
| Coconut | ½, grated fine (reserve water from coconut) |
| Milk | ½ cup |
| Vanilla or almond essence | 1 tsp (halve quantity if using extract) |
| Oil | for greasing |

For the filling

| | |
|---|---|
| Oil | 2 tbsp |
| Onions | 2 medium, finely sliced |
| Prawns | 4 cups, shelled, cleaned, and deveined |
| Salt | 1 tsp |
| Coconut milk | thick, from half a coconut |
| Sugar | 3–4 tbsp |

| | |
|---|---|
| Vinegar | to taste |
| Dried Kashmiri red chillies | 10–12, finely ground with 1 tbsp vinegar |

For the garnish

| | |
|---|---|
| Tomato wedges | as needed |
| Coriander leaves | a handful |

METHOD

Soak the semolina in the reserved coconut water and set aside.

In the meantime, beat sugar and butter together until light and fluffy. Beat in the eggs one at a time. Stir in salt.

Sift the flour with baking powder and add this to the above mixture alternating with coconut, soaked semolina, and milk. If needed, add a little coconut water or regular water to obtain a batter that is thick but pourable. Stir in the essence of your choice.

For the filling, heat oil in a pan and fry onions till browned. Add the ground chillies, stir, and add prawns and salt. Add coconut milk, sugar, and vinegar to taste. Set aside. Preheat oven at 190°C.

Prepare a deep 9-inch baking tin by greasing with oil or butter and dusting with flour. Pour in half the prepared batter, then layer the prawns on top. Spread the remaining batter on top evenly, then bake this in the oven for 30 minutes or until the top is browned. Insert a wooden skewer into the middle to check for doneness; it should come out clean.

Let cool slightly, then turn the prawn cake out on a serving dish. Garnish with tomato wedges and coriander and serve.

# KORI KACHPU
## (CHICKEN CURRY)

MONIKA AND CHARLES CORREA                                        GOA

SERVES: 4–6                                       PREPARATION TIME: 45 MINUTES

INGREDIENTS

| | |
|---|---|
| Chicken | 1 kg, cut into bite-sized pieces |
| Coconut | 1, shredded |

| | | |
|---|---|---|
| Oil | 1 tbsp | |

For the masala

| | | |
|---|---|---|
| Red chillies | 10 (to make 2 heaped tbsp powder) |
| Cumin powder | 2 tsp |
| Garlic | 6 cloves |
| Mustard powder | ½ tsp |
| Turmeric powder | ¾ tsp |
| Black peppercorns | 10 |
| Cinnamon | 1 inch |
| Cloves | 3 |
| Tamarind | a lemon-sized ball |

METHOD

Grind together all the masalas into a paste.

In a kadhai, add cooking oil. Sauté the onion till soft, the add the masala paste.

Fry the masala for about 20 minutes. Add the chicken pieces, add salt to taste, mixing the masala over the chicken until the chicken is cooked (add some water if needed) and the masala has dried, leaving a little gravy for the coconut to absorb.

Now, add the shredded coconut. Mix well with the curried chicken.

The kori kachpu can be served with panpole or neer dosas.

# PANPOLE/NEER DOSA

MONIKA AND CHARLES CORREA                                          GOA

SERVES: 10–12                              PREPARATION TIME: 45 MINUTES

INGREDIENTS

| | | |
|---|---|---|
| Rice | ¾ kg |
| Coconut | 2 tbsp, shredded |

METHOD

Soak rice for 30 minutes. Drain the rice, keeping the water aside.

Grind in a food processor along with the coconut and a little of the water that was kept aside. Add salt to taste. Add only as much water only as necessary to make pancakes of a fine consistency.

Grease a cast-iron dosa pan. Add a spoonful of the batter on the pan. Cover the pan. Cook for 2 minutes. Take off the pan. Serve hot.

# BIKANER MOHAN MASS
## (WHITE MEAT)

PRINCESS RAJYASHREE · BIKANER, RAJASTHAN

SERVES: 4–6 · PREPARATION TIME: 1 HOUR

INGREDIENTS

| | |
|---|---|
| Chicken | 1 kg |
| Dried coconut powder | 100 gms |
| Poppy seeds | 50 gms |
| Ginger | 100 gms |
| Garlic | 100 gms |
| Onion | 200 gms, sliced |
| Salt | 2 tsp |
| Black pepper powder | 1 tsp |
| Cloves | 10 gms |
| Green cardamom pods | 10 gms |
| Green chillies | 50 gms |
| Yoghurt | 250 gms |
| Milk | 250 gms |
| Desi ghee | 250 gms |
| Khoya | 100 gms |
| Lemons | 2 |

METHOD

Cut meat into 1 inch cubes, wash and pat dry.

Make a fine paste of coconut powder, poppy seeds, ginger, garlic, black pepper powder, cloves, cardamom pods, and green chilli.

Heat ghee in a deep vessel. Sauté onions in ghee till transparent. Add meat and salt, simmer on very low flame. When water dries, add spice paste and sauté further. Add khoya and milk. Strain yoghurt through muslin cloth into this and sauté.

If meat is not cooked by now, add hot water, cover and cook until meat is done.

Gravy should be thick. If not cover vessel and cook on high flame till gravy thickens.

Add lemon juice after taking the vessel off the fire.

The dish is ready to be served.

# SABUDANA KHICHARI

NAYANA GARODIA                                          AHMEDABAD, GUJARAT

SERVES: 4                    PREPARATION TIME: 10 MINUTES (PLUS 6 HOURS FOR
                                                                   SOAKING)

INGREDIENTS

| | |
|---|---|
| Sago | 1 cup |
| Boiled potato | ½ cup |
| Roasted peanut | ¾ cup |
| Curry leaves | a few |
| Cumin seeds | a pinch |
| Asafoetida | a pinch |
| Oil or ghee | 1 tbsp |
| Ginger paste | 1 tsp |
| Green chillies | 1 to 2, chopped |
| Lime juice, sugar and salt | to taste |

METHOD

Thoroughly wash the sago and soak in a large bowl for 6 hours. Drain the water thoroughly and spread the sago evenly on a clean dish cloth to dry. Now chop the potato into small juliennes and gently crush the roasted peanuts, making sure they do not turn into powder.

Once the sago is dry, add the potato pieces and the crushed peanuts and gently mix on the dish cloth using a fork. This is to prevent the sago from sticking.

Put the pan on a low fire, add oil or ghee. When it warms add the cumin seeds and asafoetida. When they splutter, add curry leaves, ginger paste, and green chillies. Lightly sauté the mixture for a minute, take it off the fire and add the sago mix. Gently stir in the salt and sugar. After 2 to 3 minutes take it off the fire and add the lime juice.

Garnish with finely chopped coriander leaves and freshly grated coconut and serve warm.

## BICHHUBOOTI SOUP

AMAN NATH                    NEEMRANA, TEJARA, RAJASTHAN

SERVES: 8                    PREPARATION TIME: 30 MINUTES

INGREDIENTS

|  |  |
|---:|:---|
| Nettle leaves | ½ kg |
| Garlic | 1 large pod or 50 gms |
| Butter | 50 gms |
| Chicken stock | 1 litre |
| Salt and pepper | to taste |
| Cream | as needed |

METHOD

Wash the nettle leaves carefully and pressure-cook with salt for 10 minutes.

Wash the cooked leaves in a sieve under cool running water.

Purée the leaves with the garlic.

In a large pot, add 2 litres of water, chicken stock, butter, and salt. Add the nettle and garlic purée and boil for 10 minutes.

Season with pepper and a swirl of cream.

# INSTANT RAVA DHOKLA

MALLIKA AND CHIRAYU AMIN                    GUJARAT

SERVES: 4–6                    PREPARATION TIME: 1 HOUR

INGREDIENTS

| | |
|---|---|
| Rava | 1 cup |
| Yoghurt | 1 cup, thick, slightly sour |
| Sugar | ½ tsp |
| Ginger | 1 tsp, grated |
| Chilli paste | 1 tsp |
| Oil | 2 tsp |
| Salt | to taste |
| Eno fruit salt | 1 tsp |
| Baking soda | ¾ tsp |

For tempering

| | |
|---|---|
| Oil | 2 tsp |
| Mustard seeds | 1 tsp |
| Cumin seeds | ½ tsp |
| Sesame seeds | ½ tsp |
| Asafoetida | a pinch |
| Curry leaves | 7–8 |
| Green chilli | 2, slit |
| Coriander leaves | 2 tbsp, finely chopped |

METHOD

In a large mixing bowl take the rava and curd. Add sugar, ginger, chilli paste, and salt. Mix well to form a thick batter. Rest the batter for 30 minutes or till rava absorbs all the moisture. Then add water to get an idli batter consistency.

Add Eno fruit salt, mix in gently. Immediately pour the batter into a 7-inch greased thali and spread batter evenly. You can add black crushed pepper or red chilli powder on the batter and steam for about 10–12 minutes.

Heat the oil. Add the mustard seeds, cumin seeds, sesame seeds, and asafoetida. Once the mustard seeds splutter add curry leaves and green chilli. Pour over the dhokla. Sprinkle coriander leaves and cut the dhokla into desired shapes.

Serve soft and spongy rava dhokla with green chutney.

# Central

~

# MUTTON KEBABS

SHARMILA TAGORE

BHOPAL, MADHYA PRADESH

SERVES: 6–8

PREPARATION TIME: 1 HOUR 15 MINUTES

## INGREDIENTS

| | |
|---|---|
| Mutton (parche) | 1 kg |
| Papaya | 2 tbsp, ground |
| Yoghurt | 250 gms |
| Onion | 500 gms, sliced |
| Garlic cloves | 2–3 |
| Ginger | 4 inch piece or 25 gms |
| Chickpeas | 200 gms, roasted |
| Poppy seeds | 15 gms |
| Red chilli powder | to taste |
| Salt | to taste |
| Oil | 250 ml |
| Coconut | 2–3 inches |
| Cinnamon sticks | 2–3 |
| Black cardamom pods | 4 |
| Whole black peppercorn | 8–10 |
| Black cumin | 1 tsp |
| Cloves | 3 |
| Green cardamom | 4 |

## METHOD

Crush mutton pieces with a mallet or something similar. Add ground papaya, mix, and cover. Set aside.

Heat oil in a wok and fry the sliced onion. Take out half the fried onion and grind with the chickpeas, coconut, and poppy seeds to a fine consistency.

To the onions in the wok add the above mixture, whole spices, and the marinated mutton. Stir and cook for 15 minutes. Continue cooking till the dish releases aroma.

Add the yoghurt and cook for 10 minutes. Cover and simmer on low heat for 15 minutes.

Serve hot with finely sliced raw onions, fresh mint leaves, lemon wedges, and green chillies.

# CHICKEN KORMA

SUBHALAKSHMI AND AMJAD ALI KHAN

GWALIOR,
MADHYA PRADESH

SERVES: 4                    PREPARATION TIME: 1 HOUR 10 MINUTES

INGREDIENTS

| | |
|---|---|
| Oil | 1 cup |
| Ghee | 2–3 tsp |
| Onions | 2, sliced |
| Yoghurt | 1 cup |
| Green cardamom pods | 8–10 |
| Chicken | ½ kg |
| Cloves | 6–7 |
| Garlic | 2 tbsp |
| Coriander powder | 1 tbsp |
| Chilli powder | 1 tbsp |
| Ginger paste | 1 tsp |
| Garam masala | 1 tsp |
| Saffron | few strands mixed in 3 tsp water |
| Coriander leaves for garnishing | chopped |
| Salt | to taste |

METHOD

Heat 6 tablespoons of oil in a pan and fry the sliced onions in it. Purée the fried onions with the yoghurt and set aside.

Heat the remaining oil in a pan on medium flame. To this, add the ghee. Once sufficiently hot, add cardamom, cloves, and garlic, and fry until golden.

Add the chicken and let it cook for about 2–3 minutes, stirring continuously. Once the chicken has browned, add the coriander and chilli powders. Add salt to taste and mix.

Add ginger paste and the onion–and–yoghurt mixture, stir and cook for a minute.

Add the garam masala and the saffron.

If the gravy is too thick at this stage, add some water to thin it out.

Cover and simmer on a low flame for about 10–15 minutes. Stir occasionally.

Garnish with coriander leaves and serve hot.


# POHA

VISHAKHA KAWETKAR                                                    BHOPAL

SERVES: 4                                    PREPARATION TIME: 20 MINUTES

### INGREDIENTS

| | |
|---|---|
| Poha | 200 gms 1½ cup |
| Peanuts | ½ cup |
| Red onion | 1 small, finely diced |
| Curry leaves | 20 |
| Green chillies | 2, finely chopped |
| Jaggery | 4 tsp, finely powdered |
| Fennel seeds | ½ tsp |
| Cumin seeds | ½ tsp |
| Mustard seeds | ½ tsp |
| Turmeric powder | ½ tsp |
| Coriander powder | ¼ tsp |
| Groundnut oil | 2 tbsp |
| Lime or lemon | 1, juiced |
| Salt | to taste |

### METHOD

Put the poha into a sieve, run water through it. Gently move the poha around with your hands, ensuring that it all gets wet. Once the water comes out clean, let the excess water drip. Place the poha aside and let it drain fully.

Heat the oil in a pan on medium to low heat and once hot, add the peanuts. Stir and fry for about 3 minutes, or until the peanuts are golden in colour. Then add the curry leaves, green chilli, mustard seeds, fennel seeds, cumin seeds, chopped onions, other spices and salt. Stir and sauté for about 2 minutes.

Now add the drained poha and the powdered jaggery. Mix well. Switch off the heat. Then add lemon juice. Serve hot.

## CHIRONJI KI BARFI

NITA KHANNA                                   SAGAR, MADHYA PRADESH

SERVES: 6–8                                   PREPARATION TIME: 2 HOURS

INGREDIENTS

| | | |
|---|---|---|
| Chironji or charoli | 500 gms |
| Sugar | 350 gms |
| Full fat cow milk | 3 litres |
| Desi ghee | 100 gms |

METHOD

Boil the full fat milk and allow it to cool down to a lukewarm temperature. Dry roast the chironji very lightly and rub between the palms of your hands to remove some of the outer husk from the seed nut.

Dry grind the chironji to a medium density powder in a grinder. Traditionally, a mortar pestle was used to pound it to a powder form, ensuring a richer and nuttier flavor in the final product.

In a large iron wok, on low heat, add the chironji powder and warm it very lightly while stirring.

To the chironji powder, add the warm milk gradually, stirring continuously to avoid any lumps till the milk and powder form a smooth consistency. On medium heat, stir the mixture continuously until it comes to a full boil. Continue stirring the mixture and reduce it down to a solid khoya-like consistency, until both, the chironji and the full fat milk, start to release their fats and fill the kitchen with the distinct, nutty aroma of khoya and chironji. Add the sugar gradually, stirring continuously to incorporate it without burning.

When the sugar has integrated completely into the reduction, turning it into a rich glossy brown, gradually add the desi ghee. Continue to stir the reduction vigorously until the combined fats are released and the reduction starts leaving the sides of the wok.

Take the reduction off from the heat and ladle it, while still hot, into an 8 x 8 or 9 x 5 inch shallow-sided, baking tin, smoothening it to a flat and even surface. Raise the tin from both sides, and gently tap its bottom against the counter to release any air bubbles. Let cool completely.

Score square pieces to your desired size upon cooling. Lift gently and place each barfi in small, individual paper containers available for sweets, or in mini muffin cups. Place in a silver dish and serve. The barfis will keep for upto a week in the refrigerator.

# CHUHARA

## (DRIED DATES) KHEER

NITA KHANNA                                SAGAR, MADHYA PRADESH

SERVES: 4                                  PREPARATION TIME: 30 MINUTES

INGREDIENTS

| | |
|---|---|
| Dried dates | 24, pitted and chopped finely |
| Milk | 8 cups |
| Sugar | 1 cup, or to taste |
| Green cardamom pods | 4, ground to powder |

METHOD

Heat the milk in a pot.

Warm a cup of water slightly and soak the dates in it.

When the milk comes to a boil add the soaked dates. Reduce the heat and let the milk and dates cook until your desired level of softness is achieved.

Add sugar and cook until all the sugar melts. Cool and serve.


# MURGI SURVEDAR

RICHARD HOLKAR

MAHESHWAR/INDORE,
MADHYA PRADESH

SERVES: 4–6

PREPARATION TIME: 1 HOUR 30 MINUTES

INGREDIENTS

| | | |
|---|---|---|
| Ghee | 6 tbsp |
| Onion | 1/3 cup, chopped |
| Yoghurt | 1/4 cup |
| Thick coconut cream | 1 cup |
| Poppy seed | 1 tbsp |

For the chicken

| | |
|---|---|
| Minced garlic | 2 tsp |
| Minced ginger | 1 tbsp |
| Vegetable oil or ghee | 1 tbsp |
| Chicken pieces | 700 gms |
| Salt | 2 tsp |
| Turmeric | ½ tsp |
| Cashews | 30, unsalted |

For the masala

| | |
|---|---|
| Clove powder | ½ tsp |
| Cinnamon powder | ½ tsp |
| Cardamom powder | ½ tsp |
| Black pepper powder | ½ tsp |
| Minced ginger | 2 tsp |
| Garlic cloves | 8 |
| Onion | 2½ tbsp, minced |

METHOD

Begin by preparing the chicken (see ingredients listed under 'for the chicken'). Drop garlic, ginger, and oil into a blender and purée. Pour this purée into a heavy, medium sized pot and sauté over medium heat for 5 minutes. Ensure that the masala does not stick; add a little water as needed. Add all remaining ingredients in this section. Stir to mix well. Increase heat and continue frying, adding a little water from time to time, until the chicken is golden and all liquid has evaporated. Add 3 cups of boiling water. Cover and simmer until just tender. Remove chicken and nuts, drain, and reserve. Strain broth, reduce to 1 cup, and reserve.

One by one drop all the ingredients listed for the masala into a blender; pulverize each before adding the next. Add ¼ cup water and blend to a smooth, thick paste. Set masala aside next to stove.

In a heavy, medium sized saucepan, heat the clarified butter and fry onions until they just turn colour. Take off the heat, stir in the masala mixture, yoghurt, coconut cream, and poppy seeds. Return to heat and continue frying, scraping the bottom of the pan and stirring with a spatula. Add 1 tablespoon of boiling water whenever necessary to prevent sticking.

Continue thus until butter bubbles up to the top of the paste and the masala moves as a single mass when stirred. Add the reserved broth, cooked chicken, and nuts, mix and heat until warmed through. Do not allow to boil.

Sprinkle 2 tablespoons of fresh chopped coriander on top to serve.

# Subcontinental India

~

# CHICKEN KARAHI

RAZI AND SAIRA AHMED                                    LAHORE

SERVES: 4–6                               PREPARATION TIME: 1 HOUR

INGREDIENTS

| | |
|---|---|
| Chicken | 1 kg, curry cut |
| Ghee | ½ cup |
| Garlic | 2 tbsp, crushed |
| Red chilli powder | ½ tbsp |
| Black pepper | ½ tbsp |
| Rock salt | 1 tbsp |
| Turmeric powder | 1 tsp |
| Hung curd | 1 cup |
| Tomatoes | 4 medium, quartered |
| Ginger | ½ tsp, julienned |
| Coriander leaves | a bunch, chopped |
| Green chilli | 1, chopped |
| Garam masala | ½ tsp |

METHOD

Heat ghee in a wok. Add the crushed garlic; sauté till golden brown.

Add the chicken pieces and toss with a ladle. Add the red chilli powder, black pepper, rock salt, turmeric, and hung curd, and stir. Cook for 5 minutes or until the chicken has absorbed the yoghurt.

Add the tomatoes. Cover and cook on a low simmer for at least 30 minutes. Keep checking to see if the chicken is done and the gravy is a consistency you prefer. Add water if needed. Remove from heat once the chicken is done.

Add the julienned ginger, fresh coriander leaves, green chilli, and garam masala. Stir and serve hot.

# BIHARI ALOO

RAZI AND SAIRA AHMED                                    LAHORE

SERVES: 4–6                              PREPARATION TIME: 1 HOUR

INGREDIENTS

| | |
|---|---|
| Potatoes | 1 kg, peeled and cubed |
| Salt | to taste |
| Ghee | 6 tbsp |
| Onions | 4 medium, chopped |
| Whole dried red chillies | 12 |
| Mustard oil | 2 tbsp |

METHOD

In a pot, place the cubed potatoes. Add a tablespoon of salt and enough water to cover, place on the heat, and bring to a boil. Once the potatoes are cooked, remove them and drain.

Heat a frying pan; add ghee. As soon as the ghee starts sizzling, throw in the potatoes. Cook until golden brown.

In a separate pan, fry the onion until golden. Then add the red chillies and fry until they are toasted. Remove from heat, strain the onions and chillies, and leave to cool for 5 minutes.

In a mortar and pestle, lightly crush the onion and chilli mix, then add to the already hot potatoes.

Before serving, drizzle mustard oil on top of the dish to enhance the flavour.

# LAMB BIHARI KEBABS

RAZI AND SAIRA AHMED                                    LAHORE

SERVES: 6–8                  PREPARATION TIME: 3 HOURS (PLUS 24 HOURS
                                               MARINATION TIME)

INGREDIENTS

| | |
|---|---|
| Lamb pasandas | 1 kg |

| | |
|---|---|
| Papaya juice or powder | 2 tbsp |
| Mace | ½ tbsp |
| Hung curd | 1½ cups |
| Mustard oil | ½ cup |
| Himalayan pink salt | 1½ tbsp |
| Poppy seeds | 4 tbsp |
| Mustard oil | 1 tbsp |
| Coal | 2 kg |

METHOD

With a cleaver, flatten the pasandas and score them along their lengths. Place them in a bowl and add the papaya juice/powder, mace, and hung curd. Massage and mix well for 5 minutes. Add the mustard oil and mix.

On a skillet, toast whole red chillies till they darken. Crush the chillies with the poppy seeds in a mortar and pestle. Add to the pasandas with pink salt. Keep massaging and mixing for 5 minutes.

Cover with foil and after 2 hours lightly mix again. Let the meat marinate for 24 hours in the fridge.

Skewer the meat and grill over burning charcoal until cooked.

Brush your serving dish with mustard oil before placing the kebabs on top.

**Note:** Lamb can be easily substituted with mutton or chicken.


# AUBERGINE BORANI RAITA

MOMINA AIJAZUDDIN                                          LAHORE

SERVES: 4–6                              PREPARATION TIME: 45 MINUTES

INGREDIENTS

| | |
|---|---|
| Round aubergines | 4 medium sized |
| Yoghurt | ½ kg |
| Salt | 1 tsp |
| Cumin seeds | 1 tsp, roasted |
| Onions | 2 medium, chopped |

| | |
|---|---|
| Onion | 1, whole |
| Ginger garlic paste | 2 tsp |
| Garlic paste | 1 tsp |
| Tomatoes | 3–4 medium size |
| Turmeric powder | ½ tsp |
| Cumin powder | ½ tsp |
| Red chillies | ½ tsp, ground |
| Vegetable oil | ⅓ tbsp |
| Mint leaves | to garnish |

METHOD

Cut aubergines into 2-cm round slices and retain stalks. Prick slices lightly with a fork, salt them, and place them in a colander for drainage, preferably in the sun, for at least one hour. Fry them in hot oil until golden brown or for the diet conscious you can chargrill them for about 15 minutes on each side. Drain on paper.

Brown the chopped onions in oil. Add garlic ginger paste, turmeric, ground red chilli, cumin powder, and chopped tomatoes. Add one cup of water and one whole peeled onion. Cook over medium heat until the tomato curry thickens and the whole onion is tender.

In a separate bowl, mix the garlic paste, roasted cumin seeds, and salt to taste with the yoghurt.

To assemble, use a beautiful plate or platter, spread a layer of yoghurt mixture as the base. Arrange fried aubergine slices in a circle at the edges of the platter and some inside. Place the whole cooked onion in the middle. Spread some yoghurt on the slices. Spoon the tomato curry over the aubergine slices. Spoon remaining yoghurt and garnish with fresh mint leaves. This can be served at room temperature.

# GICHAY

## (TARO LEAF) CUTLETS

RASHID RANA                                                                      LAHORE

SERVES: 4                                             PREPARATION TIME: 45 MINUTES

## INGREDIENTS

| | |
|---|---|
| Taro leaves | 8, chopped |
| Gram flour | 250 gms |
| Salt | 1 tbsp |
| Red chilli powder | 1 tbsp |
| Turmeric powder | 1 tsp |
| Coriander powder | 1 tbsp |
| All spice powder | 1 tbsp |
| Onion | ½ cup, chopped |

## METHOD

In a bowl, mix all the spices, gram flour, chopped onion, and chopped taro leaves. Now gradually add water and make a paste. Make the mixture very thick, almost dough-like, so you can make rolls out of it.

After making the rolls, take a steamer and place all rolls in it. Steam the rolls for 30 minutes on a medium flame. Check for doneness and cook for longer if needed.

After steaming the rolls, slice them in the shape of cutlets and shallow fry in a pan from both sides until golden.

Taro leaf cutlets are ready to be served with any sauce you desire.

# SPICY CORN

SYED YAWAR ALI                                           LAHORE

SERVES: 4                              PREPARATION TIME: 25 MINUTES

## INGREDIENTS

| | |
|---|---|
| Sweet corn | 1 large tin |
| Mustard seeds | ½ tsp |
| Curry leaves | 8 |
| Fenugreek seeds | ½ tsp |
| Cumin seeds | ½ tsp |
| Tomatoes | 5, sliced |
| Garlic | 1 tbsp, crushed |
| Red chilli powder | to taste |
| Salt | to taste |

|  | Oil | 2 tbsp |
|---|---|---|

To garnish

|  |  |  |
|---|---|---|
| Lemon | 1, juiced |
| Green chillies | 4, chopped |
| Coriander leaves | a bunch |

## METHOD

Heat oil in a pan. Add the mustard, fenugreek and cumin seeds, garlic, and curry leaves, and brown lightly.

Add the tomatoes and the corn with its water. Add salt and red chilli powder to taste. Cook till tender.

Add the lemon juice and garnish with green chillies and coriander leaves before serving.

# SHAKARKANDI KA HALWA

MINNAL AND SHAHRYAR KHAN                               LAHORE

SERVES: 4–5                                    PREPARATION TIME: 30 MINUTES

## INGREDIENTS

|  |  |
|---|---|
| Sweet potatoes | 3 cups, boiled and mashed |
| Full fat milk | 6 cups |
| Ghee | 2 cups |
| Green cardamom pods | 2–3, crushed |
| Sugar | 1 cup |

## METHOD

Pour the full cream milk into a heavy bottomed pan. Drop in the sweet potato and place on a low flame. Keep stirring from time to time. When the mixture has thickened, add the ghee and throw in a few green cardamom pods. Keep stirring and cooking until the ghee starts leaving the mixture. Add a cup of sugar. Stir and cook until the sugar dissolves and serve.

# LAHORE RIVER FISH, RAHU (WHOLE)

SABENE, SEHYR, AND NASEEM SAIGOL                                    LAHORE

SERVES: 8–10                    PREPARATION TIME: 2 HOURS 30 MINUTES (PLUS 1 HOUR
                                                              MARINATION TIME)

INGREDIENTS

| | |
|---|---|
| Rahu, or any mid-size river fish | 6–7 kg |
| Ginger juice | ¼ cup |
| Tamarind pulp | ½ cup |

For the sauce

| | |
|---|---|
| Tamarind pulp | 1 cup |
| Ginger juice | ¼ cup |
| Soy sauce | 2 tbsp |
| Sweet soy sauce | 2 tbsp |
| Red chilli paste | to taste |
| Palm sugar | 2 tbsp |

To garnish (as needed)

| | |
|---|---|
| Ginger | julienned |
| Green chillies | finely chopped |
| Spring onions | chopped |
| Coriander | a bunch |

METHOD

Marinate the fish whole in ¼ cup ginger juice and ½ cup tamarind pulp for at least an hour.

Steam to cook for approximately 2 hours.

To make the sauce, heat all the ingredients in a saucepan and cook on medium heat until you get a thick sauce.

Pour this sauce over the prepared fish. Garnish with ginger, chillies, spring onions, and coriander and serve.

# GAJAR KI BHUJIA/CHUQANDAR KI BHUJIA

NAAZISH ATA-ULLAH                                      LAHORE

SERVES: 4                                 PREPARATION TIME: 30 MINUTES

INGREDIENTS

| | |
|---|---|
| Carrot/beetroot | ½ kg, grated |
| Onions | ½ kg, thinly sliced |
| Oil | 4 tbsp |
| Turmeric powder | ½ tsp |
| Red chilli powder | 1 tsp, or to taste |
| Cumin seeds | 1 tsp |
| Salt | to taste |
| Green chillies | 2, stems removed |
| Curry leaves | 2 sprigs |
| Coriander leaves | to garnish |

METHOD

In a heavy-bottomed wok or pan heat the oil. Add the carrots/beetroot and onions together and mix. Add the turmeric and red chilli powders, cumin seeds, and salt. Mix and let this cook until the vegetables release some water.

Add whole green chillies and curry leaves. Cover and cook on low heat for 20 minutes. Serve with a garnish of fresh coriander leaves.

# DOLI ROTI

NILOFER AFRIDI                                  QUETTA, BALOCHISTAN

SERVES: 15                    PREPARATION TIME: 5 HOURS (PLUS OVERNIGHT)

INGREDIENTS

| | |
|---|---|
| Black cardamom pods | 2 |
| Cinnamon | 1 inch piece |
| Nutmeg | 1–2 |
| Cloves | 5–10 |

| | |
|---|---|
| Fennel seeds | 1 tbsp |
| Split Bengal gram | 1 tbsp |
| Poppy seeds | 1 + 2 tbsp |
| All-purpose flour | 1 + 4 cups |
| Sugar | 1 cup |
| Shredded coconut | ½ cup |
| Ghee/clarified butter | 2 tbsp |
| Cooking oil | 2–3 cups |

## METHOD

In a saucepan, boil one glass of water with the fennel seeds, Bengal gram, and a tablespoon of poppy seeds for 2–3 minutes. Cool and store this liquid in an airtight container. Cover it with a napkin and leave it for at least 12 hours or preferably overnight in a warm area.

To make the khameer, take the above prepared liquid in a bowl. Add a cup of the flour and a cup of lukewarm water to make a liquid paste. You may need a little less than a cup of water, so add the water in little by little. Mix all ingredients well and keep it in a warm place for about 30 minutes.

To make the sugar syrup: in a bowl add the sugar and half cup of lukewarm water and mix well until the sugar dissolves.

In a wide shallow bowl add 4 four cups of flour and add the khameer mixture. Mix together. Then pour in the sugar syrup and continue kneading to make a dough.

Add the shredded coconut and knead well.

Spread the dough evenly in a dish and on top of the dough dab a layer of desi ghee.

Add a layer of poppy seeds on top of the ghee. Cover and leave it in a warm place for 3 hours.

After 3 hours, use the dough to make rounds 4–5 inches in diameter. In a wok, heat enough oil for deep frying. Individually fry the rounds in the oil until each puffs up from the middle. Serve hot. Traditionally, this is eaten as breakfast with chana bhajji/chutney.

# KHADDA KEBAB

NILOFER AFRIDI                                    QUETTA, BALOCHISTAN

SERVES: 10–12                                     PREPARATION TIME: 4 HOURS

INGREDIENTS

| | |
|---|---|
| Young lamb | 11–12 kg |
| Salt | to taste |
| Lamb fat from the liver area and the cavity | ½ kg |
| Garlic paste | 2 tbsp |
| Ginger paste | 2 tbsp |
| Red chilli powder | 2 tbsp |
| Coriander powder | 2 tbsp |
| Cumin powder | 1 tbsp |
| Garam masala powder | 1 tbsp |

For the pulao

| | |
|---|---|
| Sela rice | 1 kg, soaked in water for an hour |
| Onion | 1 medium |
| Cinnamon | 3–4 sticks |
| Cardamom | ½ tsp |
| Nutmeg | 2 |
| Salt | 1 tbsp |

For the garnish

| | |
|---|---|
| Carrots | 2, julienned |
| Golden raisins | 1 cup |
| Almonds | ½ cup, sliced |
| Walnuts | ½ cup, chopped |
| Sugar | 2 tsp |
| Saffron or food colouring | 2 strands or 1 tsp |

METHOD

To make Khadda Kebab the lamb meat has to be young. In Pashto, the term they use is bara, which means a young lamb, which hasn't teethed yet. It is also important that the lamb has sufficient fat. The preferred lamb comes from Khyber Pakhtun Khwa and Baluchistan provinces where the varieties and breeds of lamb are appropriate. Once the lamb is slaughtered, it is cleaned and skinned. The cavity is emptied and cleansed, keeping aside the fat around the liver and the layers from within. This is the only source of cooking fat for the lamb. Once the lamb is cleaned, slits and cuts are made along the bone regions. Also 6-inch slits are made across the breast and leg meat areas.

Slather and rub salt over the lamb inside and outside and leave to dry and soak for an hour or two. In the mean time in the 3½ feet by 2½ feet hole (khadda) that has been dug out to cook the lamb, put about 50 kilograms of wood and light a fire. The idea is to create embers and make an oven like environment; this should take about 1½ to 2 hours.

If you wish to make the Khadda Kebab spicy then after an hour after adding the remainder of the condiments as a rub on the lamb meat one at a time all over and inside.

Once the wood has all burned down into red-hot embers, remove half of them with a shovel and keep aside.

Take 3–4 inch thick long skewer, longer than the length of the lamb, and insert it right through the lamb so you are able to hang the lamb horizontally.

First place a layer of the fat from the liver, which is like a series of thin lines attached to each another on the shoulder of the lamb. Completely cover the shoulder area with the fat. On top of this thin fat, add larger sliced chunks of fat on the shoulder blade right across the length of the lamb.

Use a thick cotton string to keep the fat in place. Wind the cotton thread in a circular manner from the stomach to the shoulder keeping the fat in place. Tie the two front legs together with the strings tightly and also tie the hind legs together.

Take the silver foil and cover the two leg areas widely along the length of the legs so you can pick the lamb up easily. This will also help to remove it from the khadda later.

Place the prepared lamb down in the khadda with the rod suspending the meat half way down in the middle. Close the lid of the khadda. Seal the lid with wet mud on all sides of the lid ensuring it is airtight inside. With your hands smooth the mud over with wet hands to ensure there are no cracks. Place the remaining embers set aside on top of the khadda lid. Place weights to keep the lid down.

For the pulao, sauté the onion in oil until slightly caramel in colour. Add cinnamon, red chilli cardamom, nutmeg, and salt and fry until the oil separates. Take the soaked rice and boil it until it is cooked through about 70 per cent and set aside. Add the cooked rice to the masala and continue cooking it with a couple of glasses of water. Let it cook until the water is absorbed and the rice is cooked perfectly. Keep it covered and warm.

Make a syrup with the sugar and ⅓ cup water. Mix the nuts together and pour the sugar syrup on top with a little of the saffron.

After 3 hours start removing the embers from the khadda lid, then the weights. Take the lamb out of the khadda and remove by sliding it out of the pipe using the foil legs for safety.

Place the cooked lamb on a large flat serving dish. Place the prepared warm rice all around it. Add the garnish on top of the lamb. Finally sprinkle the julienned fresh carrots on top.

# FISH CAUIFLOWER RICE

RAANA SHAIKH                                                          KARACHI

SERVES: 6                    PREPARATION TIME: 1 HOUR 15 MINUTES (PLUS 1 HOUR
                                                          MARINATION TIME)

INGREDIENTS
For rice

| | |
|---|---|
| Cauliflower florets | ¼ cup |
| Peas | ¼ kg, shelled |
| Paneer | 100 gms, cubed |
| Almonds | 2 tbsp |
| Raisins | 1 tbsp |
| Rice | 1 kg, parboiled and strained |
| Amchur powder | a pinch |
| White cumin seeds | a pinch |
| Olive oil | as needed |

| | |
|---|---|
| Food colouring | as needed |
| (green, orange, red) | |

For fish

| | |
|---|---|
| Any white river fish | 1 kg, whole |
| Whole coriander seeds | 1 tbsp, crushed |
| Dried pomegranate seeds | 1 tbsp, crushed |
| Dried red chillies | 1 tbsp, crushed |
| Tamarind pulp | as per taste |
| Garlic cloves | 6 |
| Green chillies | 2 |
| Coriander leaves | a bunch (and more to garnish) |
| Salt | to taste |

METHOD

Prepare the masala for the fish by blending together all ingredients (except the fish) listed under 'for fish'. Take the cleaned fish and generously rub salt on both sides. Then pat the ground masala into each side of the fish. Tightly cover and refrigerate for an hour.

Boil cauliflower florets and peas in salted water with the white cumin seeds, amchur, and a tablespoon of oil. Once the cauliflower is partially cooked, remove both vegetables and strain.

In a pan, heat enough oil and shallow fry the almonds, raisins, and paneer separately.

Divide the cooked vegetables into three parts and dip into the three food colourings separately.

In a deep pan, heat a few tablespoons of olive oil. Add a layer of rice, then place half the vegetables on top. Add another a layer of rice and top with the remaining veggies.

Scatter paneer over the veggies. Cover and steam cook for 15 minutes.

Take the cooked pulao and scatter fried almonds and raisins on top. Set aside.

Take a large pan and heat 2 tablespoons of olive oil in it. Place the marinated fish in the pan; cover and cook for 3–4 minutes. Uncover and flip the fish and let it cook on the other side, covered, for another 3–4 minutes.

Place fish in a large platter and garnish with fried tomato and onion rings. Sprinkle green coriander leaves. Serve with the pulao.

**Note:** If you want, you can add some soaked saffron to the pulao after it's cooked.

## TIL ANDE KA ACHAAR

CHITRANGADA RAJE SINGH                    GWALIOR, KASHMIR

SERVES: 8                                          TIME: 20 MINUTES

### INGREDIENTS

| | |
|---|---|
| Hard-boiled eggs | 5, halved lengthwise |
| Timur peppercorn and jambu (Nepali spices) | 6 pieces |
| Cumin seeds | ½ tsp |
| Whole dried red chillies | 4 |
| Sesame seeds | ¼ cup |
| Garlic cloves | 4 |
| Ginger | ½-inch |
| Salt | to taste |
| Yoghurt | ½ cup |
| Lemons | 2, juiced |
| Mustard oil | 1 tbsp |
| Fenugreek seeds | ½ tsp |
| Green chillies | 4 |
| Turmeric powder | ½ tsp |
| Red chilli powder | ⅓ tsp |
| Coriander leaves | Few sprigs |

### METHOD

Place the halved hard-boiled eggs on a serving dish.

Dry roast the timur, jambu, and cumin seeds until fragrant in an iron pan. Transfer to a separate bowl. In the pan roast the whole red chillies, sesame seeds, garlic, and ginger until toasted and fragrant. Take off the heat and remove the skin of the garlic pods. Put all the roasted ingredients with some salt into a food processor and blend them until they reach a fine consistency.

Combine the yoghurt and lemon juice in a separate bowl. Add the blended mixture to this and stir until well combined.

In the pan, heat mustard oil for tempering the spices. To this, add fenugreek seeds, green chillies, turmeric, red chilli powder, and coriander leaves. Once the fenugreek seeds change colour, take the pan off the heat and pour its contents over the yoghurt mixture.

Pour the above mixture over the eggs in the serving dish. Refrigerate, and serve cold.

## BANGLADESHI MOOLI CURRY WITH SHRIMP

NASRIN AND FAROOQ SOBHAN

DHAKA/MURSHIDABAD,
BANGLADESH

SERVES: 4

PREPARATION TIME: 35 MINUTES

INGREDIENTS

| | |
|---|---|
| White radishes | 2 long, sliced into thin rounds and boiled in water until tender |
| Ginger | 1 tsp, minced |
| Garlic | 1 tsp, minced |
| Turmeric powder | ½ tsp |
| Oil | 2 tbsp |
| Onions | 4 small, sliced finely |
| Salt | to taste |
| Red chilli powder (optional) | ¼ tsp |
| Shelled shrimps | 125 grams, more or less according to taste |
| Coriander leaves and green chillies | to garnish |

METHOD

Heat oil in a pan. Sauté onions till transparent.

Add turmeric, ginger, and garlic to onions and sauté till spice mixture is pale gold, and the smell of turmeric is gone.

Add a little water if necessary from time to time to prevent spices from burning.

Add the shrimps to the spices and sauté till lightly browned. Add a few tablespoons of water and simmer till the shrimps are opaque and seem cooked.

Add the boiled radish slices and sauté for a minute or two more. Serve garnished with coriander leaves and green chillies.

# KHOW SUEY

SUNITA KOHLI                                                BURMA

SERVES: 4                              PREPARATION TIME: 30 MINUTES

INGREDIENTS

| | |
|---|---|
| Oil | 1 tbsp |
| Coconut milk | 400 ml |
| French beans | ¼ cup, chopped |
| Carrots | ½ cup, chopped |
| Small broccoli florets | ½ cup |
| Basil leaves | 10, roughly torn |
| Soy sauce | 1–2 tsp |
| Salt | to taste |
| Any noodles | 2½ cups, cooked |

For the paste

| | |
|---|---|
| Onions | ½ cup, roughly chopped |
| Garlic cloves | 7 |
| Ginger | 1 inch |
| Dried Kashmiri red chillies | 4 (stems and seeds removed), soaked in hot water for 10 minutes |
| Coriander powder | 1 tsp |
| Cumin powder | 1 tsp |
| Turmeric powder | 1½–2 tsp |

Suggested garnishes (quantities as desired)

| | |
|---|---|
| Coriander leaves | chopped |
| Chilli flakes | |
| Garlic | sliced and fried |
| Onions | sliced and fried |
| Spring onions | roughly chopped |

| | |
|---|---|
| Shelled peanuts | roasted |
| Lemon | cut into wedges |
| Green chillies | chopped |

METHOD

Blend all the ingredients for the paste together to a smooth consistency using 2–3 tablespoons of water.

Heat oil in a non-stick pan, add the paste and cook it for 5 minutes till the oil starts showing on the sides.

Add the coconut milk along with 1½ cups of water. Stir and let it cook on a low flame for about 5 minutes.

Add the chopped vegetables. Let the vegetables cook on a low flame for about 7–8 minutes. Keep stirring in between so that the coconut milk doesn't curdle.

Once the vegetables are almost cooked, add soy sauce and add salt. Mix well and let it cook for 2 more minutes. Add boiling water at this point, to adjust consistency if the curry is too thick.

Turn off the flame and sprinkle the basil leaves on top. To serve, place noodles in a deep bowl, pour the hot curry over it. Top with garnishes of your choice and enjoy hot!

# SPICY PINEAPPLE CURRY

MOHAN TISSANAYAGAM                    COLOMBO, SRI LANKA

SERVES: 4–6                                    PREPARATION TIME: 40 MINUTES

INGREDIENTS

| | |
|---|---|
| Pineapple | 1 whole, cut into one inch cubes |
| Curry leaves | a sprig |
| Onion | 1 large, chopped |
| Garlic | 2 tbsp, chopped |
| Cardamom pods | 2, slightly crushed |
| Cinnamon | 1 inch piece |
| Turmeric powder | 1½ tsp |
| Chilli powder | 1 tsp |

| | |
|---|---|
| Curry powder | 1 tsp, roasted |
| Mustard seeds | 1 tbsp |
| Sugar | 1 tbsp |
| Thick coconut milk | ½ cup |
| Salt | to taste |

METHOD

Marinate the pineapple in curry powder, chilli powder, turmeric, and salt. Leave aside for 10 minutes.

Heat a pan on low. Add curry leaves and mustard seeds and dry roast until mustard seeds start popping. Add garlic, cinnamon, and chopped onions. Continue frying the ingredients over low heat for a few minutes until onions are soft and transparent.

Add the marinated pineapple and cook over medium heat for 10–15 minutes. After the pineapple juice has reduced add the sugar and let it cook for a couple of minutes. Add the coconut milk. Simmer on low heat until gravy thickens. Serve hot.

# KHADE DAHI KI TIKKI

INDIRA KOHLI                    DEOBAND AND MANSEHRA, PAKISTAN

SERVES: 4                    PREPARATION TIME: 30 MINUTES (PLUS 6 HOURS
                                          TO MAKE HUNG CURD)

INGREDIENTS

| | |
|---|---|
| Yoghurt | 2 kg |
| Black pepper | 1 tsp |
| Oil | 2 tbsp |
| Coriander powder | 1 tsp |
| Garam masala | 1 tbsp |
| Coriander leaves | 1 tbsp, chopped |
| White bread cream | 1 tbsp |
| Ginger and garlic | 1 tbsp, thinly grated |
| All-purpose flour | 1 tbsp |
| Egg without yolk | 1 |

| | |
|---|---|
| Onion | 1 small |
| Salt | to taste |

METHOD

Hang the yoghurt in a cheesecloth for 6 hours.

After 6 hours, remove the hung curd into a large bowl. To it add the white bread cream, flour, grated ginger and garlic, coriander leaf, coriander powder, garam masala, chopped onion, egg white, and salt as per taste. Mix well.

Take equal quantities of the above mixture in your palm and flatten them to make circular kebabs.

Heat oil in a frying pan and fry the kebabs in this until golden on both sides. Serve hot with choice of chutney.

# SHAKARQANDI CHAAT (SWEET POTATO)

NASREEN RAHMAN & NUZHAT ARSHAD, NUSRAT JALAL
(MANTO'S DAUGHTERS) & SUNITA KOHLI          ALEPH IN LAHORE

SERVES: 6                                   PREPARATION TIME: 15 MINUTES

INGREDIENTS

| | |
|---|---|
| Sweet potatoes | 3 medium to large |
| Amchur powder | ½ tsp |
| Cumin seed powder | ½ tsp |
| Lemon juice or lime juice | 1 tsp |
| Starfruit | ½, medium, finely sliced (if in season) |
| Rock salt | to taste |

METHOD

Rinse the sweet potatoes thoroughly under running water. Then boil them in a pan of water. If cooking in a pressure cooker, then pressure cook for about 3 to 4 whistles with water just about covering the sweet potatoes. While still warm peel them lightly and chop them into squares. Arrange these in bowl. Sprinkle ½ tsp amchur powder and ¼ tsp roasted cumin powder. Sprinkle rock salt to taste. Then pour over it the lemon or lime juice.

Mix gently. If available, add the starfruit. Serve.

# NAARANGEE (ORANGE) PILLAU

NUSCIE JAMIL                                           LAHORE

SERVES: 8–10                          PREPARATION TIME: 2 HOURS

INGREDIENTS

| | |
|---|---|
| Mutton | 1½ kg leg of young goat |
| Rice | 3 cups |
| Fresh orange juice | 1 litre |
| Black cardamom | 3 |
| Cinnamon stick | 2 medium |
| White jeera | 1 tsp |
| Bay leaf | 3 medium |
| Aniseed whole | 1 tsp |
| Fresh ginger | 2-inch piece, finely sliced |
| Garlic | 10 cloves of garlic, peeled |
| Ginger garlic paste | 2 tbsp |
| Onion | 2 medium |
| Desi ghee | 4 tbsp |
| Orange peels | 2, cut in slim slivers of 1½ inches and caramelized in jaggery |
| Saffron | 12 strands, soaked in 1 tsp of warm milk/water |

METHOD

In a large pot of fresh orange juice boil leg of mutton with all the whole masalas, including the fresh ginger and garlic till totally tender. Fry the mutton leg in desi ghee or oil with finely chopped and sautéed onions and 2 tablespoons of ginger garlic paste till the mutton is brown in colour.

To prepare the pillau, boil the pre-soaked long grain basmati rice in already cooked and strained orange juice yakhni, removed from the leg of mutton.

Spread rice in a large dish and place the hot mutton leg on top. Sprinkle the fresh caramelized peels of oranges and the saffron strands.

# BHUTANESE EMA DATSHI

KUSUM AND SALMAN HAIDER                                    BHUTAN

SERVES: 4                                    PREPARATION TIME: 10 MINUTES

## INGREDIENTS

| | |
|---|---|
| Red chillies | 10 medium size |
| Grated cheese (a combination of American cheese and Farmer cheese) | 5 tbsp |
| Onion | 1 |
| Tomato | ½ |
| Garlic cloves | 5–6, crushed/sliced |
| Oil | 3 tbsp |
| Salt | to taste |
| Spring onion leaves | 3 |
| Garlic leaves | 3 |

## METHOD

Rinse the chillies, onion, tomato, spring onion leaves, and garlic. Cut the chillies lengthwise and tomato, onion, garlic, and spring onion stalks into thin slices. Put it all together into a skillet.

Add ½ cup water, oil, salt, and cheeses on top. Cover and cook for 3–5 minutes on a high flame. Then turn off the flame and let it sit for 2 minutes.

Finally, give a thorough mix and check the seasoning. Add more salt if desired.

Serve with rice.

# RAW MANGO BHARTA

AGNESE BAROLO AND GOWHER RIZVI          DHAKHA/MURSHIDABAD

SERVES: 4                               PREPARATION TIME: 15 MINUTES

INGREDIENTS

| | |
|---|---|
| Mango | 2, medium |
| Sugar | 2 tsp |
| Salt | to taste |
| Beet salt | ½ tsp |
| Green chillies | 2–3, chopped |
| Kasundi | ⅓ cup |

METHOD

Skin and cut the mangoes lengthwise into small pieces. Coarsely grind.
Then mix in all the ingredients (except kasundi) one by one by hand.
Before serving, pour the kasundi in and gently mix.

**Note:** Kasundi is the Bengali variety of mustard sauce or relish, easily found in
Indian stores.


# SRI LANKAN WATTALAPPAM

## (CUSTARD WITH COCONUT MILK, JAGGERY AND SPICES)

KOHELIKA KOHLI                                      SRI LANKA

SERVES: 6                          PREPARATION TIME: 1 HOUR 30 MINUTES

INGREDIENTS

| | |
|---|---|
| Kithul jaggery (from tail palm) or molasses | 250 gms |
| Eggs | 6 |
| Coconut milk | 1 cup |
| Cashew nuts | 100 gms |
| Vanilla essence | 1 tsp |
| Grated nutmeg | ¼ tsp |
| Cardamom seeds | 8 powdered |

METHOD

Break the jaggery into pieces. In a saucepan put in 2 or 3 tablespoons of water, add the jaggery and heat it, stirring constantly until the it dissolves. Strain this mixture.

Leave it to cool for approximately 15 minutes, or until cool to touch. Then add the coconut milk, vanilla, nutmeg, cardamoms, and cashew nuts. Mix well.

In a separate bowl, beat the six eggs, then add to the mixture and mix well.

Preheat the oven to 175°C. Transfer the mixture to a medium size and not too deep or pan. Cover with foil. Put the bowl in a larger pan with about 2 inches of water.

Bake for 50-60 minutes, or until the custard is just set.

Refrigerate and serve cold.


# DHANIA MURGH

YOUSAF SALAHUDDIN                                        LAHORE

SERVINGS: 6                              PREPARATION TIME: 1 HOUR


INGREDIENTS

| | |
|---|---|
| Chicken | 1 kg, cut into medium size pieces |
| Fresh coriander leaves | ½ kg |
| Onions | 3 medium, sliced |
| Tomatoes | 3 medium, grated |
| Garlic paste | 2 tbsp |
| Ginger paste | 2 tbsp |
| Ginger | 1 inch, finely chopped |
| Garlic cloves | 6, finely chopped |
| Cumin seeds | 1 tsp |
| Green chillies | 3, made into a paste |
| Bay leaves | 2 |
| Black cardamoms | 3 |
| Green cardamoms | 4 |
| Cloves | 4 |
| Black peppercorns | 12 |

| | |
|---|---|
| Turmeric powder | ¼ tsp |
| Garam masala | 1 tsp |
| Coreiander powder | 1 tsp |
| Ghee | 2 tbsp |
| Yoghurt | ½ cup |
| Fresh cream | 100 gms |
| Fresh coriande | 2 tbsp for garnishing |

METHOD

Heat a large pan and add the ghee. Once melted add the chicken, onions, tomatoes, garlic and ginger and green chilli paste, coriander powder, and salt. Once the chicken is browned, add all the coriander leaves with 2 cups of water and finely chopped ginger and garlic. Cook the chicken till tender.

Then stir in 2 tbsp of yoghurt. Once mixed, add the cream, gently stirring the chicken curry. Add 2 tbsp of water, cover and cook on a low flame till the ghee separates from the curry. Then mix in the sliced ginger and garlic and dry coriander powder. Leave for 1 minute. Remove from the flame. Garnish with fresh sprigs of coriander.

Serve hot.

# KADDU DAL

MARINA FAREED                                    LAHORE

SERVES: 4                          PREPARATION TIME: 30 MINUTES

INGREDIENTS

| | |
|---|---|
| Split Bengal gram | 1 cup |
| Pumpkin | 500 gms, cut into small pieces |
| Mustard oil | 4 tbsp |
| Tomatoes | 3 medium, chopped |
| Ginger | 1 tsp |
| Garlic | 1 tsp |
| White jeera | 1 tsp, dry roasted in pan |
| Turmeric powder | 1 tsp |
| Dry chillies | 3 |

| | | |
|---|---|---|
| Vinegar | 3 tbsp | |
| Sugar | 1 tsp | |

METHOD

Brown the onions, add ginger and garlic; fry. Add the masalas then fry. Add tomatoes. Cook until oil surfaces. Finally, add the pumpkin pieces. Cover and cook until oil emerges.

Separately heat 2 tablespoons oil in another pot. Add the dal and fry. Add 3 cups water. Cover and cook on medium heat until water dries. Mix in the pumpkin pieces. Cover and cook on medium heat for 10 minutes.

Uncover and add vinegar and sugar. Cover and cook on low for 5 minutes. Serve hot.

# Acknowledgements

Grateful acknowledgement is made to the following copyright holders for permission to reprint copyrighted material in this volume. While every effort has been made to locate and contact copyright holders and obtain permission, this has not always been possible; any inadvertent omissions brought to our notice will be remedied in future editions.

Aaryaman Mohanvir Singh Bhati: Peanut Roast

Agnese Barolo and Gowher Rizvi: Raw Mango Bharto

Anadya Bhadarya Bhati: Meva ki Barfi

Advaita Kala: Panaucha

Alka Pande: Moong Dal ke Pakore with Tamarind Chutney and Mint Chutney

Aman Nath: Bichhubooti Soup

Amita and Khalid Baig: Hinterland Bouillabaisse

Anita Behl: Mutton Kathi Roll

Anita Ratnam: Alagar Kovil Dosai

Annu Palakunnathu Matthew: Kachiya Moru and Meen Vevichathu

Anu and Iqbal Malhotra: Baked Crabs

Arun Kapur: Mutton Curry

Aruna Sairam: Adai

Bapsi and Fali Nariman: Machchi No Saas, Pakki Keri No Ambakalio

Beatrice and Andre Correa do Lago: Cocado

Birgitta Knudsen Björk: Paella

Bobby Uripok: Nganam

Chanda Choudhury: Roasted Fish Salad

Charu Gupta Abraham: Chicken Kebabs

Chef Hammar: Doh Nei Iong

Chinna and Vinod Dua: Sat Saag

Chitrangada Raje Singh: Til Ande ka Achaar

Christine Wisner: Sweet and Sour Spare Pork Ribs

Cristina and Prem Patnaik: Prawn Curry

David Housego: Fesenjan

Devi Cherian: Dum Aloo

Devieka and Suresh Bhojwani: Sitaphal Ice Cream

Dilip Cherian: Amma's Red Fish Curry

Dilshad Sheikh: Surkh Murg

Doreen and Peter Hassan: Haleem and Khatta Meetha Aam Chutney

Ezra Jah (from Falaknuma Palace): Kachchey Gosht ki Biryani

Farooq and Nasrin Sobhan: Bangladeshi Mooli Curry with Shrimp

Gita Abhyankar: Vangi Bath

Gauri Keeling: Green Mango Chutney

Gursharan Kaur: Pakora Karhi

Gunmala Singh and Darshan Singh: Grilled Lamb Chops

Hammarsing Kharhmar Sawyan: Rawtuai Leh Behlawi Nhah Bai

Indira Baptista Gupta: Petha Kheer

Jane Churchill: Kedgeree

Jean Claude Kugener: Coconut Quinotto

Jimmy Jahangirabad: Ras ki Kheer

Jyotsna Suri: Gucchi aur Safed Mushroom ki Galouti

Kaveri Ponnapa: Kodava Pandi Curry

Kohelika Kohli: Sri Lankan Wattalappam

Komal Sharma: Ambal

Kusum Ansal: Stuffed Paneer

Kusum and Salman Haider: Bhutanese Ema Datshi

Laila Khan: Yakhni

Latha Reddy: Pongal

Madhavi Kuckreja and Askari Naqvi: Sunehre Baingan

Madhu and Harshvardhan Neotia: Chitol Macher Muitha

Mallika and Chirayu Amin: Instant Rava Dhokla

Mallika Sarabhai: Armenian Samosa

Manjari and Lalit Nirula: Fresh Figs Poached in Red Wine

Maria Couto: Prawn Cake

Marina Fareed: Kaddu Dal

Meenakshi Meyappan: Chicken Chettinad Pepper Masala

Meera and Muzaffar Ali: Himalayan Terai Pasanda

Minnal and Shahrayar Khan: Shakarkandi ka Halwa

Minu Bakshi: Okra Ghosht

Mohan Tissanayagam: Spicy Pineapple Curry

Momina Aijazuddin: Aubergine Borani Raita

Monika Correa: Kori Kachpu, Panpole/Neer Dosa

Naazish Ata-Ullah: Gajar ki Bhujia

Naghat Abedi: Dhuan Gosht, Rampuri Machli Anda, Khubani ka Meetha

Najma Currimjee: Lamb Pasindas, Tomato Chutney

Nalini and P. Chidambaram: Crab Masala

Nalini Singh: Garlic-Herb Carrot Slivers

Nasima Faridi Aziz: Pearly Lucknow Firni, Kali Gajar ka Halwa, Chaney ki Dal ka Halwa

Nasreen Rahman, Nuzhat, Nusrat, Sunita Kohli: Shakarqandi Chaat

Navina Najat Haidar and Pia Sarah Haykel: Quinoa and Lentil Salad

Nayana Goradia: Sabudana Khichari

Neelam and Ashok Khanna: Chicken Curry

Nidhi Choudhari: Rabri

Nila Mehta: Khar Fish Curry

Nilofer Afridi Qazi: Doli Roti, Khadda Kebab

Nuscie Jamil: Naarangee Pillau

Nirupama Menon Rao: Tara's Biscuit Roti

Nishat Siddiqui: Baked Egg Halwa

Nita Khanna: Kolhapuri Sukka Mutton, Chironji ki Barfi and Chuhara

O. P. Jain: Hare Chane ki Sabzi

Oreno Lotha: Bastanga Gahori Mangsho

Poonam Muttreja: Vatha Kulambu

Rati and Dhruv Sawhney: Dried Fruit in Orange Sauce with home-made

Renuka and Pavan Varma: Nimona and Jimmikand

Pheroza and Jamshed Godrej: Baked Eggs, Cheese Akuri, Eggs Akuri, Rava Kheer, Sev, and
Copra Pak

Preetha Reddy: Pickled Avakkai Biryani

Princess Rajyashree: Bikaner Mohan Maas

Raghunath Mohapatra: Santula

Rajesh and Nishi Mehra: Saag Ghosht

Rajshree Pathy: Sago and Potato Vada

Ramola Bachchan: Iraqi Date and Walnut Cake with Caramelized Walnut Topping

Raana Shaikh: Fish Cauliflower Rice

Rashid Rana: Gichay

Razi and Saira Ahmed: Chicken Karahi, Bihari Aloo, Lamb Bihari Kebabs

Reba and Himachal Som: Dry Cabbage Curry with Shrimp

Renuka and Rana Talwar: Pardah Pulao

Richard Holkar: Murgi Survedar

Rinke Saran: Bhutta Curry

Rita Lal Mathur: Bhune Pasande

Rohit Khattar: Tabak Maaz, Khubani Chaawal, Nadroo Yakhni, Khattey Seb Baingan

Rome Kohli: Mutton Pickle

Romi Chopra: Chicken Biryani

Rupin Pahwa: Goshtaba with Mooli ki Chutney

Sabene Saigol: Lahore River Fish

Sagari and Ajay Handa: Savji Keema Curry

Sagarika Ghose: Chingri Malaikari

Sameer Seth and Floyd Cardoz: Dahi Gujiya Chaat with Spinach and Date Chutneys

Seran and Ravi Trehan: Semolina Halvah

Shabana Azmi: Hyderabadi Biryani

Shahenshah Mirza: Awadhi Calcutta Biryani with Potatoes

Padma Mukundan: Roasted Coconut Curry, Mango Pulissery

Sharan Apparao: Kanda Pulusu

Sharmila Tagore: Mutton Kebabs

Shashank Singh: Doodh-Pithi Kheer, Rikwach Vegetable with Mustard

Shashi Tharoor: Idlis

Sheeba Iqbal Jairajpuri: Qeema Lal Mirch, Galawat ke Kebab

Latika Dikshit: Arhar Dal

Shiban Ganju: Rishta

Sinawati Mungyak and Suwana Mungyak: Steamed Rice Cake and Paachaw

Shirin and Priya Paul: Sindhi Kadhi, Sai Bhaji

Shobhaa De: Masale Bhaat

Shobita Punja: Spinach Thoren

Shovona Narayan: Dal Pitha

Simran Kanwar: Prawn Curry

Subhalakshmi Khan: Chicken Korma

Sudha and N. Ravi: Akkara Adisil

Sunaina Malhotra: Kalonji ke Baigan

Sundeep Bhutoria: Daab Bhapa Sondesh, Mishti Doi

Sunil Mehra: Methi Chicken

Sunil and Mukta Munjal: Amritsari Aloo Paratha

Sunita Kumar and Preah Narang: Carrot Soufflé, Cheese Soufflé

Surina Narula: Butter Chicken

Suvidha Choudhari: Mutton ki Karhi, Dahi Ghiya

Syed Yawar Ali: Spicy Corn

Syeda Bilgrami Imam: Jumman ka Korma

Syeda Hameed: Rampuri Taar Gosht

Veena Talwar Oldenburg: Dahi Wala Kukkar

Vandana and Yogesh Chandra: Kali Kanji

Vidya Gajapathi Raju: Podi Kura Maamsam

Vijay Thakur and Vishwajit Singh: Qeema Matar

Visalakshi Ramaswamy: Beetroot Poriyal, Kozhi Uppu Kari, Elaneer Payasam

Vishakha Kawetkar: Poha

Wangchuk Densapa: Tibetan Thukpa Soup

William Dalrymple: Tiger Prawns

Yamini and Ashok Jaipuria: Bikaneri paratha

Yousaf Salahuddin: Dhania Murg

Zakia Zaheer: Paye ki Nihari

Zarine and Sanjay Khan: Parsi Style Mutton Curry, Goan Fish Curry
Zohravar Singh Bhati: Dahi Chicken

*The India Cookbook*

# Notes on the Contributors

**Aaryaman, Anadya, and Zohrawar Singh Bhati** are Sunita and Rome's grandchildren. They inherited their love for cooking and experimenting with food from their great-grandmother, grandparents, and Masi. They are all exhibited artists and have put together an art book: *Children's Book on Delhi's Architecture*.

**Agnese Barolo** is a counsellor who comes from the Barolo family from the Piedmont area of Italy that makes the famous red wine. **Dr Gowher Rizvi** is a public intellectual, and reputed scholar. When he was representative of the Ford Foundation, he asked Sunita to travel to several locations across the subcontinent where the foundation had set up projects and to write about their work.

**Advaita Kala** is a screenwriter, author, and columnist. She is the author of two novels, the bestselling *Almost Single* and *Almost There!*, and frequently writes for the *Dhaka Tribune* and *Dainik Jagran*.

**Aleph in Lahore** Nasreen Rahman, author of Manto, published by Aleph, established this as a sorority during the Lahore Lit Festival of 2023. The sorority consists of **Nasreen Rahman, Nuzhat, Nusrat, who are Manto's daughters, and Sunita**, whose *The Lucknow Cookbook* is also published by Aleph. Manto and his daughters lived at Lakshmi Mansions and Sunita is the only one they know who was born there.

**Alka Pande** is a prominent art critic, cultural theorist, educator, curator, and author who has been passionately involved in the world of art for nearly three decades. She was the chairperson of the Chandigarh Lalit Kala Akademi and is a recipient of the prestigious Charles Wallace Award in 1999–2000. In December 2006, she was awarded the Knight of the Order of Arts and Letters by the French government. Presently, she is the consultant arts advisor and curator of the Visual Arts Gallery at the India Habitat Centre in New Delhi.

**Aman Nath** is a historian, painter, poet, graphic designer, copywriter and the author of books on history, art, architecture. He restored thirty of India's unlisted architectural ruins which are now run as the award-winning Neemrama 'non-hotels' which have won awards from UNESCO, and the Indian travel trade industry. He was appointed Chevalier de l'Ordre national de la Legion d'Honneur (Knight in the National Order of the Legion of Honour) by the President of the French Republic.

**Amita Baig** has stewarded conservation projects across the country, including several award-winning ones. She has over three decades of experience managing historic sites in India and Asia. She is the author of *Forts and Palaces of India* and *Taj Mahal: Multiple Narratives* (with Rahul Mehrotra) following an eight-year engagement at the site.

**Anita Behl** and her late husband, Prem, built a very successful business in the Exhibitions India Group where she's still a director. With her keen nose and sharp taste buds, she ensures that her favourite recipes stay on point even if she enters the kitchen sparingly.

**Anita Ratnam** is an Indian classical and contemporary dancer and choreographer. She has received formal training in several dance forms, including Bharatanatyam, Kathakali, and Mohiniattam, alongside T'ai chi and Kalarippayattu, enabling her to create a distinct style she calls 'Neo Bharatam'. For her imaginative and extensive work, she has received several prestigious awards. She is the founder of Arangham Dance Theatre, a performance company, and Narthaki.com, an online community and portal for all aspects related to Indian dance.

**Annu Palakunnathu Matthew** is an artist renowned for her photo-based creations that are an exciting blend of moving and still imagery, videos, sculptures, and sounds. Her solo exhibitions have been hosted at the Royal Ontario Museum, Nuit Blanche Toronto, Newport Art Museum, and the sepiaEYE in New York. She headed the department of photography at Rhode Island School of Design.

**Anu Malhotra** is a photographer, filmmaker and artist who is known for showcasing the cultures of the people of the Northeast. **Iqbal Malhotra** is a producer of films, a practising black belt in karate, and a master of Shinjuku Qi Gong. His other passions include tennis and cooking.

**Arun Kapur** is an educator with more than four decades of experience with leading schools and many government and non-governmental forums in the education sector. He began his career as a teacher at the Doon School and is currently the director of the Royal Academy in Bhutan, a director of the Vasant Valley School in New Delhi, and the chairman of Ritinjali, an NGO focused on community development in marginalized societies. He founded the Pallavan chain of pre-schools, an inclusive institution that caters to diverse learning needs. Apart from his love for teaching, he is passionate about food and is a man of eclectic tastes. He is the author of a definitive book on education and learning.

**Aruna Sairam** is one of the leading exponents of South Indian classical music. A trained Carnatic vocalist and composer, she has performed in prestigious venues across the globe, including the Rashtrapati Bhavan, Royal Albert Hall, and Carnegie Hall. Alongside her husband, she is the founder of the Nadayogam Trust which imparts musical education to underprivileged children. She is the recipient of the Padma Shri and is currently the vice chairperson of the Sangeet Natak Akademi, New Delhi.

**Bapsi Nariman** was a celebrated cookbook author whose renowned works include *A Gourmet's Handbook of Parsi Cuisine, Microwave Cookery for the Indian Palate, Cooking with Yoghurt,* and *Rush Hour Cookbook: Great Dishes in 30 Minutes or Less.* **Fali Nariman** is a reputed jurist and a specialist in constitutional law.

**Beatrice do Lago** is the wife of Andre Aranha Correa do Laho, the Brazilian ambassador to India. Born in Paris, she is of mixed Italian, French, Spanish, and Greek ancestries. Her grandfather was Paul-Louis Weiller, the famous aviator war hero of World War I.

**Birgitta Knudsen Björk** was born in a Sweden and moved to Lisbon, Portugal with her family. She married the late Alvaro de Castilla Bermudez-Cañete and travelled the world. They were posted in Delhi for three years where they made many good friends.

**Chand Sur** was born in 1925 in Bahawalpur, Undivided Punjab, and brought up in Quetta. She was an inventive cook who placed great emphasis on nutritious and healthy meals. Her lunch, dinner, and tea parties were legendary. She has passed on her love of cooking to her children, grandchildren, and great-grandchildren. A voracious reader and an adventurous traveller Chand Sur was deeply interested in other cultures and people.

**Charu Gupta Abraham** is an engineer and also has a marketing degree from Stanford University. She has worked in multinational companies around the world. She is a multifaceted investor and is on a mission to spread financial literacy. She loves to travel, explore, and savour global cuisines and is a movie and music enthusiast.

**Chinna Dua** was a noted radiologist associated with the prestigious Diwan Chand Aggarwal Imaging Center for twenty-four years. Her daughter and stand-up comedian Mallika Dua introduced her to social media, where she garnered a massive following of nearly forty thousand followers and spoke about health, cooking, music, and her love for traditional saris. **Vinod Dua** was a noted journalist known for his work in *Doordashan and NDTV India.* In 1996, he became the first electronic media journalist to receive the prestigious Ramnath Goenka Excellence in Journalism Award. He was known for his political programs, ranging from election analysis to current affairs, as well as food shows like *Zaika India Ka.*

**Chitrangada Raje Singh** is the president of The Delhi Society for the Welfare of Special Children, an NGO established in 1965 by her mother-in-law is a businesswoman and the eldest child of late politician Madhav Rao Scindia, daughter-in-law of Dr Karan Singh and Asha Raje. She is the co-manager of two heritage properties: Karan Mahal in Srinagar and

Taragarh Palace in the Kangra Valley.

**Christine Wisner** is the former wife of former ambassador of the United States of America to India, Frank Wisner. She was one of the founding members of Umang, a Delhi-based charitable society that worked closely with NGOs involved in the upliftment of underprivileged children. Sunita has known them from their Egypt days when Frank was posted there as the US ambassador.

**Cristina and Prem (Guddu) Patnaik** are Delhi-based entrepreneurs.

**David Housego** has lived in Middle East, Europe, Iran, Lebanon, India, and China, and has collected myriad experiences and culinary traditions from all these places. In the 1980s, he learnt cooking in Paris when he was posted as the bureau chief of the *Financial Times*. He co-founded Shades of India.

**Devi Cherian** is an entrepreneur, political journalist, and columnist. She is actively involved with initiatives for the empowerment of disabled children and is a trustee on the board of Action India. **Dilip Cherian** is regarded as India's 'Image Guru'. He has worn many hats, including that of a bureaucrat, editor, columnist, and entrepreneur.

**Devieka Bhojwani** is a singer, artist, and organizer of events for good causes. Her mother, Usha Khanna, ran Café Samovar which was the haunt of poets, artists, and intellectuals. She is vice president of Women's Cancer Initiative—Tata Memorial Hospital of which Sunita has been a patron since its inception. She organized the launch of *The Lucknow Cookbook* in Mumbai. She is married to **Suresh Bhojwani**, a singer and an entrepreneur.

**Dilshad Sheikh** is a fantastic cook and hosts legendary dinners in her home in Srinagar She is the only sister of actors and producers Feroze, Sanjay, and Akbar Khan.

**Doreen Hassan** was one of Delhi's finest hostesses and known for the elegant parties she hosted. She crafted exquisite culinary experiences that celebrated heirloom recipes that had been in her family for generations. Her husband **Peter Hassan** has been an advisor to companies and government and non-governmental organizations.

**Ezra Jah** is credited with the renovation and restoration of Chowmahalla Palace and Falaknuma Palace. Chowmahalla Palace was awarded the UNESCO Asia-Pacific Heritage Merit Award for Culture Heritage Conservation. The recipe included in book the is one of the famous dishes that is served in the Falaknuma Palace.

**Farooq Sobhan** is a former diplomat from Bangladesh. During his career, he has served in numerous important posts such as the ambassador to China, high commissioner to Malaysia and India, and the foreign secretary of Bangladesh. He is the chairman of the board of trusteess at the CSR Centre, an independent Dhaka-based organization focussed on corporate social responsibility. His wife, **Nasrin Sobhan,** is a freelance writer.

**Frenny Billimoria** is an author, artist, and social worker. She studied classical music and the violin and received formal training in the social sector at the All-Bengal Women's Home in Calcutta.

**Gauri Keeling** belongs to the Shriram family who have been great promoters of Indian classical music since Independence as well as educational institutions such as Lady Shri Ram College, which is where Sunita and Gauri first met.

**Gita Abhyankar** is the wife of late Dr Uday Abhyankar, who was a diplomat and UN official.

**Gunmala Singh** taught English in Shimla and Delhi and subsequently followed her true passion inspired by her childhood in the mountains—gardening, painting, and cooking. **Darshan Singh** studied at the Doon School. He is a mountain climber and sailor and has been actively involved in the management of Welham Boys School.

**Gursharan Kaur** is a trained musician with a degree in Hindustani classical music. She enjoys participating in kirtans with a selective audience. She is mother to three illustrious daughters—Upinder, Daman, and Amrit—and wife of the former prime minister of India, Dr Manmohan Singh.

**Indira Baptista Gupta** is a Delhi and Goa-based independent researcher. She has previously held teaching positions at the universities of Delhi and Bombay, before joining the Indian Council of Historical Research as a part of their editorial and publication department.

**Indira Kohli** was the most well-known and well-respected gynaecologist and obstetrician of an era. She studied and worked in the UK and then in India. She was Sunita's doctor and sister-in-law. She had an exceptional moral compass.

**Jane Churchill** is a name synonymous with British interiors. She is known for her traditional sense of style and her take on modern design and her contemporary flair. She is the author of *Entertaining Lives,* a book that documents the lives of her two aunts, Nancy Astor and Nancy Lancaster, their tastes and love of good food.

**Jean Claude Kugener** is a career diplomat who has held diplomatic posts in Luxembourg, the United Kingdom, Russia, and Germany. He is the current Director for Consular Affairs and International Cultural relations at the MFA in Luxembourg and Non Resident Ambassador to the Holy See and was previously Ambassador to India (2018-2021) and non-resident Ambassador to Nepal and Sri Lanka.

**Jimmy Jahangirabad** lives in and operates the oldest living palace in Lucknow—Jahangirabad Palace in Hazratganj. He has donated properties where a university and school have been made with the goal to provide affordable and quality education to students from underprivileged communities.

**Jyotsna Suri** is the driving force behind the Lalit Suri Hospitality Group, one of the largest privately owned hotel chains in India. She has held several important positions, including the chairperson of FICCI Tourism Committee, past president of FICCI, council member of the World Travel and Tourism Council, and a member of the board of governors of the Indian Institute of Corporate Affairs.

**Kaveri Ponnapa** writes on heritage, food, and wine. She is the author of *The Vanishing Kodavas*, an acclaimed cultural study of the Kodava community. She received the Karnataka Kodava Sahitya Academy's Gaurava Puraskara. Her next book is on the cuisine of Kodagu.

**Kohelika Kohli** is a trained architect and carpenter from the Pratt Institute of Design, New York. She interned with Sir Norman Foster and studied architecture for a year in Italy. At present, she is the CEO and creative director of K2 India, a company she started in 2010 with her mother, Sunita Kohli. She is a trustee of the Museum of Women in Arts. Her love for cooking is inherited from her grandmother and she enjoys hosting friends and family in her holiday homes.

**Komal Sharma** is the editor of *Architectural Digest*. She has been managing editor of *Harper's Bazaar* and design and lifestyle editor of *Mint Lounge*.

**Kusum Ansal** is a writer whose oeuvre includes critically acclaimed novels, poems, short stories, and travelogues that have been translated into English, Punjabi, Bengali, Greek, Russian, and French. Her novel, *Ek Aur Panchvati*, was adapted into a film by Basu Bhattacharya.

**Kusum Haider** is a widely acclaimed theatre actor who is also trained in mime and Tai Chi. She has acted in a variety of plays including classic dramas of the west and by India's new dramatists. She has worked with some of the most significant directors of Indian theatre. **Salman Haidar** is a former Indian diplomat who served as the Foreign Secretary of India, high commissioner of India to the United Kingdom, and ambassador to Bhutan.

**Laila Khan** is an artist trained from Slade School of Fine Arts and Central St Martins School of Fine Art. She has held many shows and her artworks are part of many private collections. She is the daughter of actor Feroz Khan and was married to Sunita's cousin. She is the creative head of Furniturewalla, a very well-known furniture and décor brand.

**Latha Reddy** was a diplomat from 1975-2011 and served as the Indian ambassador to Portugal and Thailand, Secretary (MEA), and as Deputy NSA. She now lives in Bangalore, and works on cyber security, as well as with several Indian and international organizations. Her many interests include heritage, travel, literature, theatre, and the performing arts.

**Madhavi Kuckreja** completed her master's in international politics from the New School of Social Research, New York. In 1994, she started Vanangana, an organization aimed at integrating Dalit women into the development of rural areas in Uttar Pradesh and address the caste-based atrocities in the rural belt. **Askari Naqvi** is a lawyer-turned performing artist and entrepreneur. He received his musical training under Pandit Amit Mukherjee. He is an accomplished Dastango and has performed in several national and international creative spaces. He is the co-founder of Sanatkada Festival. He is the founder of Naimat Khana, a Lucknow-based restaurant specializing in home-cooked regional cuisine.

**Madhu Neotia** runs The India Story (TIS), a Neotia Arts Trust initiative. She is on the governing board of the Neotia University. **Harshvardhan Neotia** is the chairman of the Ambuja Neotia Group, a conglomerate headquartered in Kolkata. They run speciality restaurants where they promote Bengali cuisine.

**Mallika Amin** is the chief executive officer, managing and executive director at Alembic Pharmaceuticals. She is also on the board of Sierra Investments, Aavaran Textiles, and Sierra Healthcare. **Chirayu** is a business and cricket administrator. He has held several important positions, including the chairman and managing director of Alembic Pharmaceuticals.

**Mallika Sarabhai** is a classical dancer (an exponent of Bharatanatyam and Kuchipudi), choreographer, actress, writer, and social activist. In 1977 she took over the Ahmadabad-based performing arts academy Darpana, which her mother, Mrinalini, had established decades earlier, and led its dance troupe in festivals around the world. Mallika also writes scripts for film, stage, and television productions and was a columnist for several publications.

**Manjari Nirula** is a wannabe chef with over forty years of experience with revival of crafts, documentation, design development, and marketing of crafts. She is advisor and honorary member of World Crafts Council. She has been President of Delhi Crafts Council. She is married to **Lalit Nirula** of the famous Nirula's restaurants. Lalit is a classmate of Sunita's husband, Rome, from the Doon School, year of 1959

**Maria Couto** was a writer and educator from Goa. A recipient of the Padma Shri in 2010, she has held prestigious teaching positions at Lady Shri Ram College and Dhempi College. She is the author of multiple books including a definitive biography of Graham Greene, and articles on literature, history, environmental issues, and India's multicultural social fabric.

**Marina Fareed** is known as a facilitator, connector, hostess, and spirit of goodwill. She is also the author of a book that celebrates friendship and hospitality, *You are Invited*. The daughter of a high-ranking bureaucrat and wife of an ambassador and United Nations official, Marina's life has been colourful and diverse.

**Meenakshi Mayappan** set up Chettinad's first heritage hotel, The Bangla, in Karaikudi. She is also the author of a cookbook, *The Bangala Table*.

**Meera Ali** is a fashion designer, architect, and cookbook author. She has extensive experience in slum rehabilitation and developing socially conscious housing for the underprivileged. In 1990, she married **Muzaffar Ali**, and they moved to Kotwara, an erstwhile princely state at the foothills of the Himalayas. Meera and Muzaffar then started Kotwara, a design label committed to reviving the region's traditional crafts. Their collections have been showcased across India as well as in New York, London, Paris, Dubai, Singapore, and Kuwait.

**Minnal Shahrayar Khan** is the daughter of Syed Akhtar Hussain, former Foreign Secretary and Ambassador to Italy, Iran, USSR, Algeria, and Austria, and Zakia Hussain, daughter of Nawab Mushtaq Ali Khan of Mankula. **Shahryar Khan** is a former career diplomat. He was ambassador to Jordan and France as well as Head of Permanent Mission to UN in Geneva. He also served as High Commissioner to UK. He was Foreign Secretary of Pakistan. He is the author of many well-regarded books.

**Minu Bakshi** is a poet, social worker, and professor of Spanish. She is a singer trained by Ustad Ghulam Hussain Khan. Her other passions include Urdu poetry and Punjabi folk music. In 2014, she was conferred the Order of Isabella la Catolica, the second highest honour awarded to a foreigner by the king of Spain.

**Mohan Tissanayagam** is one of the foremost art collectors of Sri Lanka and a patron of the arts. He supports classical music, opera, art, and dance. He is the Chairman of the Columbo Chamber Music Society. He holds cultural salons in his various homes. His Columbo home on Queens Road was designed by Sunita and Kohelika. He is a member of Chaîne des Rôtisseurs, the world's most exclusive international gastronomic society.

**Momina Aijazuddin** has over two decades of experience in financial inclusion, microfinance, and investment transactions. She has held important portfolios on multiple boards such as

Blue Orchard MIFA and the Microfinance Enhancement Facility. She currently serves as the global head of microfinance at the International Finance Corporation. She is the daughter of Pakistani historian Syed Aijazuddin and author Shahnaz.

**Monika Correa** is a textile artist renowned for her experimental designs. A self-taught weaver, she has been keen about exploring the potential of textiles as a medium of art. Her creations are a part of famous collections at the Metropolitan Museum of Art, Museum of Modern Art, Minneapolis Institute of Art, and the Tate in London. **Charles Correa** was India's most eminent architect and urban planner. Sunita and Charles worked as honorary consultants on the Rashtrapati Bhavan and Sunita was the interior designer of his British Council Building project.

**N. Ravi** is a journalist and the current Director of Kasturi & Sons Ltd. He served as the Editor-in-Chief of *The Hindu* from 1991 to 2003 and took over the position again in October 2013. **Sudha** is a craft and handloom enthusiast.

**Naazish Ata-Ullah** is a Lahore-based artist, educator, curator, and human rights activist. She is on the boards of several cultural, educational and social development institutions. She retired as principal of National College of Arts and was awarded a knighthood by the Republic of France for Arts and Literature.

**Naghat Abedi** hails from the royal family of Rampur and is the daughter of the last nawab, Murtaza Ali Khan. She is famous in Delhi for her fabled parties where the crowning glory is the Rampur cuisine. She is an avid traveller and appreciates diverse cultures and art. Sunita and Naghat were in college together.

**Najma Currimjee** was from Hyderabad, a vivacious and genuine person. She lived in a stylish home designed by Geoffrey Bawa and entertained in great style. She and Sunita were friends from college. She showed indomitable courage during the last years of her life.

**Nalini Chidambaram** is a senior advocate practising in the Supreme Court of India and in the Madras High Court. **P. Chidambaram** is an eminent politician, public intellectual, and member of parliament. He has been the minister of Finance and Home Affairs. He currently serves as an MP in the Rajya Sabha.

**Nalini Singh** is a television journalist whose areas of specialization include national politics and the politics of injustice. Bihar is her favourite haunt.

**Nasima Faridi Aziz** is the author of the 2019 cookbook, *Lucknow: Wandering in the Lanes of History, 1700s and 1800s*. She has travelled the world with her diplomat husband. She has been friends with Sunita since kindergarten in Loretto Convent, Lucknow.

**Nathalie Trouveroy** is a noted art historian. She is passionate about exploring the architecture of old Delhi, especially Jama Masjid and Chandni Chowk. She and her friend Agnes Montanari created a photo album of William Dalrymple's masterpiece on Delhi, *City of Djinns*. She is married to a Belgian ambassador to India.

**Navina Najat Haidar** is an art historian and curator. She currently leads the Department of Islamic Art at The Metropolitan Museum of Art in New York. **Pia Sarah Haykel** is a student of history and language at Princeton university. Their inspiration in life is Kusum Haidar, actress, tai-chi teacher and grandmother, from whom they have learned their best recipes.

**Nayana Goradia** is a historian and a writer and advises a school. She is the author of *Lord Curzon: The Last of the British Moghals*. She helped Sunita with background research when she was designing the Curzon Room at the Oberoi Maidens Hotel.

**Neelam and Ashok Khanna** run the world-famous wellness retreat Ananda in the Himalayas. They offer a delicious Ayurveda based cuisine at their resort.

**Nidhi Choudhari** is associate partner in K2India. Before joining, she started a social networking group called The Chatterbox Club. She is passionate about cooking and is a very creative cook.

**Nila Mehta** is a self-made textiles and embroidery entrepreneur based in New Delhi's Nizamuddin. Nila is a firm believer that good food tastes better when shared with good company and rarely does anyone decline an invitation from her for a fresh, home-made meal. To ensure that all parts of the Northeast were represented in the book, Nila kindly collated recipes from her friends, Bobby Uripok (Manipur), Chanda Choudhury (Tripura), Chef Hammar (Meghalaya), Hammarsing Kharhmar Sawyan (Mizoram), Sinawati Mungyak and Suwana Mungyak (Arunachal Pradesh), and Oreno Lotha (Nagaland).

**Nilofer Afridi Qazi** is the producer of an online series called 'Pakistan on a Plate', documenting the less explored heritage cuisines of the country. She is the daughter of Ashraf Jehangir Qazi, the former high commissioner of Pakistan to India and Abidah Qazi, an artist, social worker, and horticulturalist.

**Nirupama Menon Rao** is a retired Indian diplomat. In the course of her distinguished career in the Indian Foreign Service, she served as the country's ambassador to the United States of America, China, Peru, Bolivia, and Sri Lanka. She was the second woman to hold the post of India's foreign secretary. She is the recipient of several prestigious awards. She co-founded the South Asian Symphony Orchestra.

**Nishat Siddiqui** ran a fine jewellery business in Connecticut before moving on to several successful medical practices. She retired in 2006 and, since then, has been pursuing her love for travelling, oil painting, and bridge. Sunita and Nishat studied together in Loretto Convent, Lucknow.

**Nita Khanna** has an academic background in English literature and critical theory from the University of Bombay and the University of Oxford. She has had a diverse career trajectory, during which she has managed multiple portfolios in academia, writing, media, and film production. She was born and raised in Sagar, Madhya Pradesh, and remains attached to her roots. In recent years, she has restructured and revamped a traditional labour-intensive family business in her home state.

**Om Prakash Jain** is an Indian art collector, patron, and philanthropist. He is the Founder-President of the Sankriti Foundation which runs the Sanskriti Kendra Museums at Anandagram, Delhi. He was the convenor of the Indian National Trust for Art and Cultural Heritage (INTACH) for fifteen years. He is a recipient of the Padma Shri. Sunita has sourced artefacts from his warehouse starting from the late seventies. She ideated aspects of the foundation with him before its inception.

**Pheroza Godrej** is an author, art historian, and environmentalist. She is actively involved with the CSMVS, National Gallery of Modern Art and other major cultural institutions. In 1971, she founded the reputed Cymroza Art Gallery. **Jamshed Godrej** is the MD of Godrej and Boyce.

**Preetha Reddy** is the vice chairperson of Apollo Hospitals, a trained dancer, and Carnatic music enthusiast.

**Princess Rajyashree** is the daughter of Maharaja Dr Karni Singhji of Bikaner. She is the chairperson of several charitable trusts, a former championship shooter and an author.

**Poonam Muttreja** is is the executive director of the Population Foundation of India. She was the Country Director of the MacArthur Foundation and has made an active contribution to the NGO sector in India. She has also founded organizations working in the area of social justice (SRUTI), craft (DASTKAR), and leadership (Founder Director of the Ashoka Foundation in India), specifically focusing on the field of women's health.

**Raghunath Mohapatra** was a traditional legendary architect and sculptor. He crafted many masterpieces such as the Tara Tarini temple in Odisha, the sandstone Buddha statues at Dhauligir Shanti Stupa, the Konark horses at Barabati Stadium, the Mukteshwar Gate at Surajkund, and the lotus at Rajiv Gandhi's memorial at Vir Bhumi in New Delhi. He is the only sthapathi to have been awarded the Padma Vibhushan. He was a close colleague of Sunita's from the Oberoi Bubhaneshwar days.

**Rati Sawhney** is known for the excellence of her table. She is from Lucknow and is married to **Dhruv Sawhney** a batchmate of Rome's from the Doon School.

**Rajesh Mehra** is the director of the prolific Jaquar group of companies, one of India's leading sanitary ware brands. In 2018, he was honoured at the EY Entrepreneur of the Year Awards by Shri Devendra Fadnavis. He has contributed his sister-in-law **Nishi Mehra**'s famous saag ghosht recipe.

**Rajshree Pathy** is an entrepreneur from Coimbatore. She is the chairperson and managing director of the Rajshree Group of Companies. An art enthusiast, she extensively promotes performing arts and contemporary art. She is the recipient of several honours, including the Padma Shri.

**Ramola Bachchan** is a fashion designer and frequently organizes high-profile exhibitions and events. She runs an haute catering business in Delhi.

**Raana Shaikh** studied English literature at St Hilda's College, Oxford. She has directed several musicals, plays, and series based on folk legends and traditional music, as well as adapted celebrated works by Wilkie Collins, Emily Bronte, and Daphne Du Maurier. As managing director and cultural secretary under Benazir Bhutto, she headed and directed cultural events across fourteen venues during the World Cup. On television, she introduced programmes that focussed on women's empowerment and promoted classical music. She is currently working on a book on culture and identity.

**Rashid Rana** is a prolific artist whose work has been showcased at galleries and museums worldwide. In 2015, his artwork was part of the prestigious Treasures of the World, a landmark exhibition that featured nearly 239 pieces from the British Museum. His 2013 survey exhibition at the Mohatta Palace Museum in Karachi is the largest ever exhibition held in Pakistan by a single artist. He is currently the founding faculty member and dean of the School of Visual Arts and Design, Beaconhouse National University, Lahore.

**Razi Ahmed** is the Chairman of Lahore Arts Council (Alhamra), a public body since 1948, promoting the arts in Lahore. He is also the founder and CEO of the Lahore Literary Festival, founded in 2013, that has earned international acclaim and brings together literary luminaries from South Asia and the rest of the world. Ahmed has served in 2015 on the DSC

Prize Jury for South Asian fiction, and has authored opinion pieces for various publications. His mother, **Saira Ahmed**, whose recipes he has contributed, is a wonderful hostess and an urban farmer.

**Reba Som** served as the regional director of the Rabindranath Tagore Centre, ICCR, Kolkata, from 2008 to 2013. She has authored several publications including *Differences Within Consensus: The Left-Right Divide in the Congress, Subhas Chandra Bose and the Resolution of the Women's Question, Rabindranath Tagore: The Singer and His Song,* and *Margot: Sister Nivedita of Vivekananda.* She is a trained practitioner of Rabindrasangeet and Nazrul Geeti. Sunita was present with Reba for her recording of her Rabindrasangeet by the Vatican in a recording studio in a villa near Palestrina with its brilliant mosaic. Her husband, **Himachal**, was the Indian ambassador to Italy and a great fusion cook. As director general ICCR he facilitated the first International Festival of Indian literature in 2002, which was the precursor to the many subsequent literary festivals that followed. Sunita was on the core committee with him.

**Renuka Talwar** is a golfer and a director on the board of her family's real estate company, DLF India. Sunita first met her when she worked on K. P. Singh's corporate office on Parliament Street. She is exceptionally helpful when a medical need arises. **Rana Talwar** comes from a banking background and is the founding chairman of Sabre Capital.

**Renuka Varma** is an artist. She is married to **Pavan Varma**, diplomat, writer, and politician.

**Richard Holkar** is the princely descendant of Maharani Ahilyabai and son of the last maharaja of Indore. He is responsible for the restoration of the historic Ahilya Fort and for converting it into a luxurious heritage property. He is deeply passionate about the production and preservation of traditional weaves and handloom through the Rewa Society, an organization that plays an important role in empowering local craftsmanship. He, along with his former wife, Sally Holkar, revived Maheshwari saris when they had no money with help from friends like Sunita, who each bought a loom for the endeavour.

**Rinke Saran** is a former actor and the daughter of veteran actors Dimple Kapadia and Rajesh Khanna. She is the daughter-in-law of one of Sunita's closest friends, Adarsh Saran. She has a keen eye for fashion and has worked with *SEVENTEEN* magazine.

**Rita Lal Mathur** grew up in Lucknow, absorbing its culture and cuisine. She cooks with love and instinct but does not strictly follow recipes. Sunita and Rita were in school together. As teenagers, they would play hooky from school and experiment with Rita's father's cigarillos, who was then chief secretary of UP.

**Rohit Khattar** is Founder Chairman of Old World Hospitality Private Limited. While he is is known best for his concept Indian Accent in New Delhi, New York, and Mumbai as well as the newer restaurants Comorin, Hosa, Koloman NYC, his favourite restaurant is still his first one Chor Bizarre, which opened in 1990 in New Delhi. It was the first time that Kashmiri cuisine from the valley came to New Delhi.

**Rome Kohli** is an equity investor who studied at the Doon School, St Stephen's College, and law from Delhi University—Faculty of Law. He broke sixteen-year-old records for long-distance running at the Doon School. They remain unbroken because of the change from the imperial to the metric system. He is deeply interested in carpentry and furniture manufacturing as well as organic farming. He was a sculptor and created the tallest sculpture by a public school boy which is still displayed in the grounds of the Doon school. He is the best cook in the family.

**Romi Chopra** is a man of many interests including architecture and textile. He read philosophy from Cambridge. He and Sunita have worked pro bono on many important memorials in Delhi and Sriperumbudur.

**Rupin Pahwa** is an expert on corporate and commercial law. He is an author and a collector of vintage furniture.

**Sabene Saigol** is the editor of the fashion magazine, *Libas* and has contributed her mother's recipe for this book. Her mother **Sehyr Saigol** is the chairperson of the Pakistan Fashion Design Council. She has extensive experience in fostering ties among Pakistani artisans and the craft and design industry. Her boutique brand, Libas, is known for its experimentation with fabric and colour. She is married to **Naseem**, who is an industrialist.

**Sagari and Ajay Handa** run a hotel in Hubballi. There they serve traditional dishes that are local to the region.

**Sagarika Ghose** is a journalist, columnist, and author who has been associated with leading newspapers and publications, including the *Times of India, Outlook*, and *Indian Express*. She is the author of two novels, *The Gin Drinkers* and *Blind Faith*, and three works of non-fiction, *Indira: India's Most Powerful Prime Minister, Why I AM a Liberal: A Manifesto for Indians Who Believe in Personal Freedom*, and *Atal Bihari Vajypayee: India's Most Loved Prime Minister*. She has shared her mother, Chitra's recipe—who was a great cook and ran a home catering enterprise.

**Sameer Seth** has nearly a decade of experience in the restaurant business during which he has worked with some of the most prominent names in the trade, including Chef Daniel Boulud and Danny Meyer. In 2013, he founded The Bombay Canteen alongside his classmate from Cornell, Yash Bhanage, and award-winning chef, Floyd Cardoz. **Floyd Cardoz** was an Indian American chef celebrated for his characteristic cuisine that melded Indian flavours and Western sensibilities. He was a four-time James Beard Award nominee and worked as a culinary consultant on the feature *The Hundred Foot Journey.* The season three winner of Top Chef Masters, he donated the prize money for cancer research at the Icahn School of Medicine at Mount Sinai.

**Seran Trehan** was born in Cyprus to Turkish parents and settled in the USA. She worked at the World Bank and UNICEF. Seran has continued her family's tradition of having family gatherings with a wonderful table of a huge assortment of dishes by blending the Turkish foods of her heritage with her husband, Sunita's cousin **Ravi Trehan**'s Lucknow food heritage. Seran and Ravi collect Mughal and Ottoman art and are passionate about architecture and landscaping. Ravi and Seran are 'Friends of Islamic Art' at the MET and Seran is on the Board of the Turkish Philanthropy Fund.

**Shabana Azmi** has had an illustrious career in film industries across the world, with more than 150 films to her credit in independent and neorealist parallel cinema. One of India's most acclaimed actresses, she has won a record five National Film Awards for Best Actress in addition to multiple other accolades. Alongside her work in cinema, she has been a passionate social and women's activist for many decades, voicing her concerns regarding issues such as communalism, the ostracization of those with AIDS, and injustices against children. In 2012, she was honoured with the Padma Bhushan.

**Shahenshah Mirza** is the great-great-grandson of King Wajid Ali Shah, the last ruler of Awadh who was exiled to Bengal by the British. A keen heritage and environmental activist, he is actively involved in preserving the rich cultural legacy of his illustrious family.

**Shailaja Jayakrishnan** and Sunita have been friends and neighbours since their school days. Her mother **Padma Mukundan** is an excellent cook and the author of a recipe collection, *Padma's Cookbook for Family and Friends* that was brought out by her grandson **Sumant Jayakrishnan** who is a brilliant scenographer.

**Sharan Apparao** has been associated with the visual arts for over three and a half decades and founded the Apparao Galleries in 1983, to exhibit, promote and encourage contemporary art. She is known for her sense of aesthetics and sharp eye for picking the best artists and giving them a platform. To know Sharan in Chennai is to know the city.

**Sharmila Tagore** is one of the most prominent figures in Indian cinema. In 1959, she began her acting journey in Satyajit Ray's 1959 film *Apur Sansar*, after which she frequently collaborated with the director. Simultaneously, she had an illustrious career in Hindi films, some of her landmark work being *An Evening in Paris, Aradhana, Chupke Chupke*, and *Namkeen*. She has served as the chairperson of the Central Board of Film Certification. She was married to celebrated cricketer Mansoor Ali Khan Pataudi.

**Shashank Singh** owns the wonderful Hotel Ganges View at Assi Ghat in Varanasi. It has hosted some of the world's greatest including Sting, Diana Eck, and others. Along with Sunita he is a director of Satyagyan Foundation which has worked on women's literacy in 400 slums in Varanasi and its environs.

**Shashi Tharoor** is the bestselling author of nineteen books, both fiction and non-fiction, besides being a noted critic and columnist. He has won numerous literary awards. He is a former Under Secretary-General of the United Nations when Sunita first met him. He is a three-time member of the Lok Sabha from Thiruvananthapuram and chairs Parliament's Standing Committee on Information Technology (IT). He has been minister of state for External Affairs.

**Sheeba Iqbal Jairajpuri** is a chef and the founder of Aab-O-Dana, a culinary initiative that organizes customized and curated dining experiences in a 119-year-old haveli in Lucknow. She frequently hosts pop-up dining experiences in leading hotels and has been featured on several shows for her contributions to popularizing authentic Awadhi cuisine.

**Sheila Dikshit** was the longest-serving chief minister of Delhi and the longest-serving female chief minister of any Indian state. Sunita and Sheila Diskshit become friends while working together for a few trusts and foundations as well as samadhi projects. She was the chief guest at the launch of *The Lucknow Cookbook* and Chand Sur's *Continental Cuisine for the Indian Palette*. Her daughter **Latika Dikshit** runs an MCD school in Jasola.

**Shiban Ganju** is a brilliant doctor of Internal Medicine and Gastroenterology and has worked in India and the USA. He conceptualized and founded the NGO Save a Mother that works to reduce maternal and infant mortality in India. He is a generous host and friend.

**Shirin Paul** was the chairperson emeritus of the Apeejay Surendra Group, Kolkata, a conglomerate whose business interests span the hospitality, shipping, retail, and real estate industries. Her daughter **Priya Paul** runs the Park Hotels chain. Her brother Karan and sister Priti handle other aspects of the conglomerate.

**Shobhaa De** is a novelist, journalist, and columnist, best-known for her works of fiction such as *Socialite Evenings, Starry Nights, Sandhya's Secret*, and *Srilaaji: Diary of a Marwari Matriarch*. She is the founder of *Stardust*, one of the leading entertainment magazines in the country.

**Shobita Punja** was the author of over fifteen books including *Museums of India; Divine Ecstasy: The Story of Khajuraho*; and *Daughters of the Ocean: Discovering the Goddess Within*. She was invited to lecture on Indian art at various institutions and universities in India and abroad and has worked with several cultural organizations. When Sunita had cervical fractures, Shobita was with her every day for three months during her treatment.

**Shovona Narayan** is a Kathak exponent and an academic on dance. She was a career officer in the Indian civil service. She is married to **Herbert Traxl** who was an Austrian ambassador to India. Sunita first met Herbert when she made furniture for him which is still being used in their homes.

**Simran Kanwar's** mother Raj Gill is one of Sunita's oldest and dearest friends. She was Miss India in 1971. Simran is her only child. Simran is extremely well-read and is an avid collector of old and rare books. She and has a flair for renovating their homes. She is married to **Neeraj Kanwar**, MD of Apollo Tyres.

**Sunaina Malhotra** worked in advertising and then as an art educator at Vasant Valley School. She launched the jewellery brand Zayn to integrate Mughal design into everyday wear and make it more accessible. She is Sunita's cousin.

**Subhalakshmi Khan** is a Bharatnatyam exponent, trained in Kalakshetra. She has performed all over India and around the world. She is married to sarod maestro **Ustad Amjad Ali Khan**.

**Sundeep Bhutoria** has been at the helm of conceptualizing, curating, and strategizing a plethora of social and cultural initiatives spread across fifty cities in India. A passionate connoisseur of the fine arts, he has worked closely with both aspiring and celebrated practitioners to actively promote their work through multiple international initiatives and organizations. He launched *The Lucknow Cookbook* in Bangalore, Hyderabad, Raipur, and Kolkata.

**Sunil Mehra** is a full-time doggie dad. In his other life he's a journalist, author, tv producer/anchor, actor, and dastango. Cooking is a multi-sensory experience he revels in. So is eating.

**Sunil Munjal** is an intrepid investor and an enlightened entrepreneur who has engaged with policymaking and advocacy for decades. He is passionate about education, healthcare, arts, and India's cultural heritage. Serendipity Arts, their foundation, is working on multiple fronts to ensure the revival and patronage of arts and is amongst the leading multidisciplinary arts festivals. **Mukta** is an accomplished pianist and a multi-faceted writer of travel writing as well as stories for *Target*, a popular children's magazine in the 1990s.

**Sunita Kumar** is a self-taught painter, design consultant, and a close aide of Mother Teresa for thirty-two years until the latter's demise in 1997. In 1998, she authored a book entitled *Mother Teresa of Calcutta*. Her exhibitions have been held in Kolkata, Delhi, Florence, London, and Mumbai. With a natural flair for design, she has been associated with the House of Hermes as a consultant. She and her daughter **Preah Narang** have contributed Anglo-Indian recipes from Calcutta.

**Surina Narula** is deeply passionate about encouraging creative voices from South Asia. She is a co-founder of the prestigious DSC Prize for South Asian Literature and the founder-sponsor and advisor of the Jaipur Literature Festival. She has been actively involved in women's and children's rights for the past twenty-five years, instituting the Consortium for Street Children to advocate for their rights on a global platform. For her admirable work she was honoured with the Asian of the Year Award in 2005.

**Suvidha Choudhari** is the co-founder of The Chatterbox Club, a networking group. She is an event stylist. Her husband **Aseem** is a home baker specializing in sourdough breads and coffee. His hobby is graphic design.

**Syed Yawar Ali** is a Pakistani businessman who has been at the head of various companies. He is currently the chairman of Nestle Pakistan.

**Syeda Bilgrami Imam** is a writer, advertising professional, activist, and former member for the National Commission for Minorities. She has received several prestigious prizes for her literary and social endeavours. Her works have been showcased at prestigious film festivals across the world. **Askari Imam** and Sunita's husband, Rome, are classmates from the Doon School.

**Syeda Hameed** is a noted social and women's rights activist, author, educator, and a former member of the Planning Commission of India. She chaired the Steering Committee of the Commission of Health which evaluated the critical National Health Policy in 2002. She is the founder trustee of the Women's Initiative for Peace in South Asia and a former member of the National Commission for Women. In 2007, she was conferred the Padma Shri. She was Sunita's English Literature teacher at Lady Shri Ram where she directed the first three-act play, *Kitna Hai Khushnaseeb Zafar*, the Urdu adaption of *The Importance of Being Earnest* where Sunita played Lady Bracknell.

**Vandana Narain Chandra** is a school friend of Sunita's. She is married to Yogesh Chandra, with whom Sunita used to act in Raj Bisaria's Theatre Art Workshop.

**Veena Talwar Oldenburg** is the granddaughter of steel tycoon Swaran Baljit Singh. As a young woman, she was deeply inspired by her mother's passion for culinary delights from the Punjab and the North West Frontier Province. With a doctorate in history from the University of Illinois at Urbana-Campaign, she has held prestigious teaching positions. She has authored several critically acclaimed books on Indian history. Sunita's and Veena's parents were great friends and have known each other since Partition.

**Vidya Gajapathi Raju** was born into the princely state of Vijayanagaram in Andhra Pradesh. She is a patron of the Karunnai School for underprivileged children. A passionate sports and fitness enthusiast, she is an avid trekker, cyclist, swimmer, marathon runner. She has been a fitness columnist for the *Economic Times, Madras Plus, Eve's Touch, Chennai Frappe*, and *Apollo Life*. For the past twelve years, she has been running two event management companies specializing in weddings, product launches, and fashion shows.

**Vijay Thakur Singh** joined the Indian Foreign Service in 1985. She has held critical positions in several embassies across the world such as Madrid, Singapore, Ireland, and Kabul, and has been a part the Ministry of External Affairs from 1989 to 1999 during which she handled diplomatic relations with Afghanistan and Pakistan. From 2000 to 2003, she served as the counsellor in the Permanent Mission of India to the United Nations in New York. Since 2018, she was secretary (east) in the Ministry of External Affairs before retiring in September 2020. Her husband, **Vishwajit Singh**, was a politician with the Indian National Congress and the great-grandson of Colonel the Honourable Pratap Singh of Kapurthala. In 1982, he was elected to the Rajya Sabha, representing the state of Maharashtra, and returned for a second term in 1988. His articles on public policy and economic planning have been published in leading newspapers of the country. He shared his enthusiasm for food with Sunita.

**Visalakshi Ramaswamy** is an author, textile expert, and the founder of the M. Rm. Rm. Cultural Foundation. A passionate advocate of the development and preservation of traditional crafts, she has worked extensively to preserve the heritage of Indian textiles, regional art forms, and techniques of handloom weaving. In 2000, the M. Rm. Rm. Foundation was established to document, research, and resurrect the fast-disappearing crafts of South India. She has in-depth knowledge of Kanjeevaram and Chettinad sarees and set up the Textile Museum in Dakshinchitra.

**Vishakha Kawetkar** is qualified as a conservation architect. She is coordinator of the Masters in Architecture (Conservation) program and Center for Cultural Knowledge System at School of Planning and Architecture, Bhopal. Along with her students, she has worked on the Ashapuri archaeological site of twenty-seven fallen temples where they identified every historical rock and 'stitched' together three temples. Sunita met her when she was chairperson of SPA where she organised the first South Asian Conference of Vernacular

Architecture with 400 delegates.

**Wangchuk Densapa** runs a hotel in Gangtok. He studied with Sunita's son in the Doon School.

**William Dalrymple** is a renowned historian, author, critic, and curator. His celebrated works include *In Xanadu, City of Djinns: A Year in Delhi, White Mughals, The Last Mughal: Fall of a Dynasty, Delhi 1957,* and *The Anarchy: The Relentless Rise of the East India Company.* He is one of the co-founders and co-directors of the prestigious Jaipur Literature Festival. In 2018, he was awarded the President's Medal of the British Academy, the academy's highest honour in recognition of exemplary contribution to humanities and social sciences. Sunita has known him since the time he was researching his first book in India, *City of Djinns.*

**Yamini Jaipuria** has been part of the senior leadership of GE. She is Managing Trustee of Cosmo Foundation that works for the education of rural children. **Ashok Jaipuria** is an industrialist. Sunita's daughter Kohelika was the architect, designer, and furniture manufacturer for their home.

**Yousaf Salahuddin** is a philanthropist and cultural icon in Lahore. He is the maternal grandson of the poet and literary scholar Allama Iqbal. Sunita and Rome met him in the early 1990s and they have been friends since.

**Zakia Zaheer** is an Urdu litterateur and a literary, cultural, and social activist. She has written articles and poems for a wide range of publications and has authored a biography of Maulana Azad. She has also translated into Urdu William Dalrymple's *The Last Mughal.* She pioneered a unique form of dramatic presentation involving stage, multimedia techniques, and dastangoi through 'HUM' or Humari Urdu Mohabbat which has presented many performances on cultural and literary themes across India.

**Zarine Khan** is a renowned interior designer and the author of *Family Secrets: The Khan Family Cookbook* which was awarded the Best Book of the Year at the 2016 World Gourmand Awards held in China. She has hosted the popular television cookery show *Spices and Secrets* on Living Foodz. As a designer, she has worked with leading film stars, royal families, corporate houses, and luxury hotels. She is married to **Sanjay Khan**. They have three wonderfully talented daughters, Simone Arora, Farah Khan, and Suzanne Khan.

# Ingredient Index

## Mutton and Lamb

## Onion and Tomato

Made in the USA
Monee, IL
10 May 2026

a8546023-dd4b-4f91-82a5-3d6ad2e5332fR01